BLACKSTONE'S GUIDE TO

The Consumer Credit Act 2

Blackburn
College

Library
01254 292120

Please return this book on or before the last date below

BLACKSTONE'S GUIDE TO

The Consumer Credit Act 2006

Richard Mawrey QC and Tobias Riley-Smith

OXFORD

UNIVERSITY PRESS

OXFORD
UNIVERSITY PRESS

Great Clarendon Street, Oxford OX2 6DP

Oxford University Press is a department of the University of Oxford.
It furthers the University's objective of excellence in research, scholarship,
and education by publishing worldwide in

Oxford New York

Auckland Cape Town Dar es Salaam Hong Kong Karachi
Kuala Lumpur Madrid Melbourne Mexico City Nairobi
New Delhi Shanghai Taipei Toronto

With offices in

Argentina Austria Brazil Chile Czech Republic France Greece
Guatemala Hungary Italy Japan Poland Portugal Singapore
South Korea Switzerland Thailand Turkey Ukraine Vietnam

Oxford is a registered trade mark of Oxford University Press
in the UK and in certain other countries

Published in the United States
by Oxford University Press Inc., New York

British Library Cataloguing in Publication Data

Data available

Library of Congress Cataloging in Publication Data

Data available

Typeset by RefineCatch Limited, Bungay, Suffolk
Printed in Great Britain
on acid-free paper by
Biddles Ltd., King's Lynn

ISBN 0–19–920526–4 978–0–19–920526–4

1 3 5 7 9 10 8 6 4 2

Contents—Summary

Contents

Contents

Table of Cases

Table of Statutes

Table of Statutory Instruments

Table of Abbreviations

1

INTRODUCTION

A. THE CONSUMER CREDIT ACT 1974 AND ITS HISTORY

In this book, we shall refer to the Consumer Credit Act 1974 as the CCA 1974. **1.01**
The Consumer Credit Act 2006 will be referred to as the CCA 2006.

Statutory controls on certain forms of credit agreement have existed since at **1.02**
least the Great War (arguably in the case of 'usury' since the Middle Ages) and
hire-purchase became subject to a complete legal regime in the inter-war period.
No attempt was made to create a universal system for credit and hiring until the
passing of the CCA in 1974. The CCA 1974 was passed largely to implement the
Report of the Committee on Consumer Credit (the Crowther Report) published
in 1971.

The CCA 1974 was designed to regulate all categories of consumer credit and **1.03**
consumer hire contracts. The word 'consumer' in the title was, however, misleading: the Act operated to regulate agreements where the debtor or hirer was not a
consumer and did not regulate other agreements where the debtor or hirer was
undoubtedly a consumer.

The CCA 1974 regulated agreements principally by the amount 'financed' **1.04**
by the agreement (equating hire contracts, somewhat uneasily, with credit contracts for this purpose), and all contracts below the financial ceiling were to a
greater or less extent regulated. Although the Act excluded agreements where
the debtor or hirer was a body corporate (or a group of such bodies), it covered
partnerships and mixed groups of individuals and bodies corporate.

The objective of the CCA 1974 was the protection of debtors and hirers by: **1.05**

(a) licensing all branches of the credit and hire business, including credit-
    brokerage;
(b) controlling advertising and canvassing;

1

(c) requiring full information to be given by creditors;

(d) regulating the form and content of documents;

(e) restricting rights of termination and enforcement;

(f) giving debtors and hirers rights of early termination;

(g) making the creditor liable for faulty goods and services;

(h) giving relief from extortionate bargains.

1.06   The CCA 1974 was passed, however, in troubled times. Except for well-established commercial contracts such as hire-purchase and conditional sale, consumer credit was fairly primitive. In 1974 there was only a handful of credit cards available and 'plastic' was used by relatively few traders or customers. The 1970s were a period of economic depression and high inflation, and governments had rather better things to do than worry about the CCA 1974.

1.07   Consequently it was not until the early 1980s that people began to notice that most of the Act had not been brought into force and virtually no regulations other than the Consumer Credit (Total Charge for Credit) Regulations 1980 had been made. A chance remark by one of the authors of this book to Professor (now Sir) Roy Goode QC led to a magisterial, indeed Jovian, letter to *The Times* newspaper drawing public attention to the fact that the CCA 1974 was, to all intents and purposes, dormant. This galvanized the Department of Trade (now the Department of Trade and Industry (DTI)) into action and the autumn of 1983 saw the making of a large number of regulations and orders, including commencement orders, virtually all of which came into force on 19 May 1985. Thus, just under 11 years from receiving the Royal Assent, the CCA 1974 became fully operative.

1.08   In the two decades that followed full implementation of the CCA 1974, relatively few changes were made to the Act or to the Regulations. Perhaps the most significant changes were the increases of the financial limits for regulation, first from £5,000 to £15,000 (again after 19 May 1985) and then to £25,000 from 1 May 1998. Most of the other changes to the Act were consequential upon other legislation in the field—for example, the reorganization of the Office of Fair Trading (OFT) led to the OFT being substituted for the Director General of Fair Trading who had been established by the original Act as the regulator.

1.09   There was endless tinkering with the Regulations, particularly the Exempt Agreement Orders. It was realized that the provision for quotations contained in s 52 of the 1974 Act and the Consumer Credit (Quotations) Regulations 1989, though appearing a good idea back in 1974, had never caught on and it was quietly abandoned in 1997.

1.10   In general, however, by the early 2000s, the CCA 1974 and its attendant subordinate legislation were very much as they been conceived in the 1970s and implemented in the 1980s. Though there were problems, most of them had been surmounted, largely owing to the pragmatic good sense of the finance industry which realized that credit was a major growth industry capable of generating huge turnover, not only for the credit providers themselves but for the rest of the retail economy.

B. THE MOVE TOWARDS CHANGE

As indicated above, for a long time the CCA 1974 was perceived as working 1.11 reasonably well. True it made credit (and to a lesser extent hire) agreements hugely complicated and their enforcement likewise, but many of the finance providers had cut their teeth on the pre-1974 hire-purchase legislation and could live with hyperactive regulation.

The Act was widely seen as being unnecessarily harsh on minor slips in the 1.12 formulation of agreements and the provisions of s 127(3) to (5), which made certain non-compliant agreements wholly unenforceable in all circumstances, were greatly resented. Indeed, in *Wilson v First County Trust Limited (No 2)*[1] the Court of Appeal off its own bat suggested that this might contravene the Human Rights Act 1998 and, in particular, Part I Article 6 and Part II Article 1 of the European Convention on Human Rights. Having heard argument from the parties and the Secretary of State, the Court duly declared s 127(3) incompatible with the Convention and granted a certificate accordingly. Although this was overturned on an appeal by the Secretary of State to the House of Lords,[2] it was a straw in the wind.

The DTI and the OFT had from time to time invited submissions on particu- 1.13 larly knotty problems arising under the CCA 1974. The provisions for multiple agreements contained in s 18 had always been incomprehensible and much futile ink had been spilled on trying to work out how it was meant to operate. Although consultation took place and views canvassed from the finance indus- try and the lawyers, the DTI and the OFT always fought shy of actually entering this minefield and it is noticeable that s 18 remains untouched by the 2004–06 reforms of consumer credit law.

By the early 2000s, therefore, although it realized that a new look at the CCA 1.14 1974 would be sensible, there was no move towards a root-and-branch reform of the regulatory system for consumer credit such as had been considered necessary in the financial services industry and had led to the Financial Services and Markets Act 2000. Given that the trend for a long period stretching over gov- ernments of different political complexion had been towards more regulation rather than less, there was no prospect that the consumer credit might be deregu- lated, or even less regulated. To be blunt, regulation was employing too many people for deregulation to be a thinkable political solution, and media attitudes, though occasionally condemning over-regulation in other fields (health and

---

[1] [2002] QB 74.
[2] *Wilson v First County Trust Limited (No 2)* [2004] 1 AC 816.

safety for instance), did not run to relaxing the law for what could always be termed 'loan sharks'.

1.15   Consequently, when the DTI and the OFT turned their attention to reform of the consumer credit industry in 2003, their concerns were largely social rather than legal or economic. Government and the economy were faced with the undoubted fact that credit, and in particular consumer credit, had increased in the 30 years since Crowther at a rate that would have been unimaginable in 1971. Payment by credit or debit card had become the norm, not simply for the well-heeled middle classes, but for virtually the whole population. Credit was available to virtually everyone, though for those at the lower end of the economic spectrum, at a price. Citizens were bombarded daily with offers for new, better, cheaper credit cards.

1.16   Easier credit, however, had it social price. Those who, in the past, had had to live within their means or resort, in desperation, to unofficial back-street money-lenders (true 'loan sharks') could now obtain reasonably cheap and very available credit. This credit fuelled a huge consumer boom. The principle of instant gratification induced a general mood of 'buy now, pay later'.

1.17   Consequently, by the early 2000s the national total of credit debt had risen to a level which worried most political and social commentators. Less-well-off families were carrying a vast and unsustainable burden of debt, many of them because they were ill-educated in the operation of credit and the effects of debt and simply let their purchases get out of hand.

1.18   Governments were, if not wiser, at least better informed than their predecessors. In the past, the governmental reaction to excessive credit debt was, as it were, to slam on the brakes (indeed, on some occasions, throw the economy into reverse). Orders were made controlling hire-purchase and hire agreements by requiring minimum deposits or maximum repayment periods. These not only produced unfortunate effects on the retail economy (they were a minor but nonetheless real factor in the problems of the British car industry) but were also counter-productive as they led to widespread fraud and evasion.

1.19   Draconian measures to restrict credit were not, therefore, on the table in 2003. The DTI's approach was to seek to identify particular areas of consumer credit law and practice and to see how these might be improved in order to reduce undesirable and unsustainable debt without making credit so troublesome as to prejudice the retail economy.

1.20   The result was a White Paper *Fair, Clear and Competitive—The Consumer Credit Market in the 21st Century*[3] published in December 2003 (referred to in this book as the White Paper).

1.21   The White Paper started by identifying five 'drivers for reform' and then proposing solutions to those problems. The drivers were as follows.

---

[3] Cm 6040.

(a) 'Informational problems pre-purchase'. The calculation and expression of the APR (annualized percentage rate) had always caused confusion and the terms used in consumer agreements were often incomprehensible to the average customer. Reform was therefore needed to the rules concerning the APR, advertising, and the form and content of agreements.

(b) 'Undue surprises post-purchase'. Early settlement fees and other hidden costs (including compounding of interest) not only prejudiced the debtor but also led to creditors using these costs as an unjustified profit generator.

(c) 'Unfair practices'. Though acknowledged to be rare, these were thought to be sufficient to necessitate a tightening of regulation.

(d) 'Illegal moneylenders'. This was an amalgam of two problems, the first being that there were still too many unlicensed moneylenders (the White Paper itself calls them 'loan sharks'[4]) exploiting vulnerable debtors and the second being that the current licensing regime was letting too many unsuitable moneylenders loose on the market.

(e) 'Over-indebtedness'. This was at the heart of the White Paper. The answer was seen to lie both in tighter control and in better information for consumers.

1.22 The proposals for reform of the domestic consumer credit system (consideration was also given to the EU dimension not relevant here) were grouped under three heads. Reform was to be effected both by amendment of the CCA 1974 itself and by changes to the Regulations.

1.23 Under the head 'Establishing a transparent market',[5] the White Paper made five proposals:

(a) reforming the hugely complicated and bureaucratic rules for credit and hire advertising (see Chapter 10 below);

(b) reforming the even more complicated and bureaucratic rules for the form and content of agreements (see Chapter 6 below);

(c) making adequate provision for online agreements (see Chapter 11 below);

(d) reforming the rules relating to early settlement of loan agreements (see Chapter 8 below);

(e) giving more 'teeth' to the enforcement authorities by introducing civil penalties (see Chapter 3 below).

1.24 Under the head 'Creating a fairer framework'[6] there were four proposals:

(a) reforming the licensing of credit (see Chapter 3 below);

---

[4] Paragraph 1.44 of the White Paper.
[5] Chapter 2 of the White Paper.
[6] Chapter 3 of the White Paper.

(b) reforming and replacing the existing provisions for 'extortionate credit bargains' with the concept of 'unfair relationships' (see Chapter 9 below);

(c) improving consumer redress by bringing consumer credit within the purlieu of the Financial Services Ombudsman scheme (Chapter 4 below);

(d) the abolition of the financial limits for control (see Chapter 2 below).

1.25   Chapter 3 of the White Paper also considered whether the time had come to impose interest rate ceilings but decided against it for the time being.[7]

1.26   The head of 'Minimising over-indebtedness'[8] was more diffuse and some of the ideas proposed have not yet found their way into legislation. It did, however, contain concrete proposals:

(a) better information for debtors and hirers (see Chapter 5 below);

(b) a clamp-down on illegal moneylenders (seen as part of the reform of licensing) (see Chapter 3 below);

(c) a reform of the debt-collection processes by providing more information when default or termination occurs and by building more safeguards into the system (see Chapter 7 below);

(d) changing the legal procedures (particularly the operation of time orders and the repeal of s 127(3) to (5)) (see Chapters 2 and 7 below).

C. THE CONSUMER CREDIT ACT 2006

1.27 After a period of consultation, the DTI decided to implement most of the proposals contained in the White Paper. Changing the Regulations was obviously going to be the easier task and the year 2004 saw the following statutory instruments being made:

- Consumer Credit (Advertisements) Regulations 2004
- Consumer Credit (Disclosure of Information) Regulations 2004
- Consumer Credit (Agreements) (Amendment) Regulations 2004
- Consumer Credit (Early Settlement) Regulations 2004
- Consumer Credit (Enforcement, Default and Termination Notices) (Amendment) Regulations 2004
- Financial Services (Distance Marketing) Regulations 2004
- Consumer Credit Act 1974 (Electronic Communications) Order 2004

1.28   At the same time the DTI introduced the Consumer Credit Bill into Parliament. It was fully debated and passed most of its readings in both Houses. It was

---

[7] Paragraphs 3.49 to 3.55 of the White Paper.
[8] Chapter 5 of the White Paper.

set to become the Consumer Credit Act 2005 when the Prime Minister decided to call a general election and asked for a dissolution of Parliament on 5 April 2005. A number of bills were lost in the process and the Consumer Credit Bill was among them.

The Government having been returned at the general election, the Bill was **1.29** once again introduced. This time it completed its passage successfully and received the Royal Assent on 30 March 2006. As will be seen below, however, the CCA 2006 is due to be brought into force by order and, save for the one section making that provision, has not yet been implemented (see Chapter 2 below). It is to be hoped that implementation takes somewhat less than the 11 years required for the original Act.

2

SCOPE OF THE ACT

A. GENERAL SCOPE OF THE ACT

1. Scope

As will have been seen from the Introduction in Chapter 1, neither in the White **2.01**
Paper *Fair, Clear and Competitive—The Consumer Credit Market in the 21st
Century* (the White Paper) nor in the Consumer Credit Act 2006 (CCA 2006) did
the Government propose or effect a root-and-branch reform of the law on
consumer credit. Substantial changes have undoubtedly been made but the
opportunity was lost to rethink the basic concepts of credit that may have served
well in the financial and social climate of the 1970s when the original Act was
passed but have become less relevant with the credit explosion of the last 30 years.

The result has been a series of piecemeal changes, some of them brought **2.02**
about by the CCA 2006 itself and others by updating the regulations made
under the CCA 1974.

2.03   In this chapter we shall discuss in detail the general changes brought about by the first group of sections and the final two groups, and summarize the other changes which are the subject of individual chapters.

2. Commencement

2.04   Commencement is governed by s 71 of the CCA 2006. With the necessary exception of s 71 itself, none of the Act comes into force on receipt of the Royal Assent. Instead the Act is to be brought into force by statutory instruments made by the Secretary of State. There is a power to appoint different days for particular provisions to be brought into force.

2.05   At the time of going to press, the Department of Trade and Industry (DTI) had just announced its working timetable for the implementation of the CCA 2006. It is intended that the various provisions of the Act will come into force between June 2006 and October 2008. The DTI's timetable is reproduced at Appendix 9.

2.06   This timetable reflects the DTI's intention that:

(a) the Act should be implemented as soon as is practicable: some provisions will be commenced earlier than others, depending on lead times for preparation and interdependencies between clauses;

(b) relevant guidance will be published at least three months before the dates on which measures come into force, so as to give those affected time to prepare for compliance; and

(c) in relation to those areas affecting business, the DTI will where appropriate adhere to its prescribed 'Common Commencement Dates for Regulation'. Under this policy, legislation that requires compliance by businesses will be brought into force on one of two dates in the year, namely 6 April or 1 October.

2.07   At the date of goint to press, only one commencement order has been made—the Consumer Credit Act 2006 (Commencement Order No 1) 2006, SI 2006/1508.

2.08   In general the new Consumer Credit Regulations have come into force, although, as will be seen, in some cases (early settlement is a good example) some of their provisions have a very long lead-in time. Commencement dates in relation to the regulations discussed will be set out in the relevant chapters.

B. DEFINITION OF 'INDIVIDUAL'

2.09   The first five sections of the CCA 2006 address the fundamental problem inherent in the CCA 1974 from the outset. Although proudly labelled 'the

Consumer Credit Act 1974' and largely launching the concept of 'consumer credit' on the public, the CCA 1974 was not drafted in such a way as to restrict its application to 'consumers' properly so called.

There is no doubt that, even in the early 1970s, the concept of the 'consumer' **2.10** was recognized. It was enshrined in legislation, of which the Unfair Contract Terms Act 1977 is perhaps the best-known example, though even that Act is very muddled about who is and is not a consumer.[1] In general terms it is now accepted that a consumer is an individual who is acting in a private capacity and not in the course of a business. The Unfair Terms in Consumer Contracts Regulations 1999,[2] for example, define a 'consumer' as 'any natural person who . . . is acting for purposes which are outside his trade, business or profession'.[3]

The CCA 1974, on the other hand, while excluding corporate bodies from the **2.11** protection afforded by the Act, chose to regulate credit and hire agreements by reference to financial limits and not by reference to the purpose for which the agreement was made. Thus a firm of solicitors (even a major City firm) that, say, hired a piece of equipment under an agreement which was within the financial limits of the CCA 1974 was entitled to the same protection as a teenage mother on a housing estate hiring a television or a washing machine. On the other hand a person who entered into a hire-purchase agreement for a car for his personal use (thus a 'consumer' for the purposes of the Unfair Contract Terms Act or the 1999 Regulations) would be excluded from protection if the credit exceeded the limits.

The CCA 2006 attempts to address these anomalies. It first redefines the **2.12** concept of 'individual' for the purposes of regulation and then removes the financial limits of regulation completely. At the same time it mitigates what would otherwise be the startling consequences of removing the financial limits (all loans to individuals of any amount and for any purpose would be regulated) by exempting agreements by reference to both the financial worth of the debtor or hirer and the purpose for which the agreement has been made. The last three of these changes will be discussed in the following sections of this chapter.

In redefining 'individual', the framers of the CCA 2006 have not been willing **2.13** to take the opportunity to harmonize the law relating to consumer protection. They remain wedded to the idea that a group of individuals may qualify for protection. The thinking behind this is unclear, given the desire to limit the use of the CCA 1974 to protect business debtors and hirers. Many people believe that the sensible course would have been to go the whole hog and to define 'individual' in the same way as is done by modern consumer statutes as being a

---

[1] For example, alone of consumer protection statutes, the 1977 Act is wide enough to encompass the concept of a body corporate being a 'consumer'—see *Feldaroll Foundry plc v Hermes Leasing (London) Ltd* [2004] EWCA Civ 474, [2004] AER(D) 138.747.

[2] Implementing EU Directives and thus reflecting Europe-wide consumer policy.

[3] Regulation 3(1) of the 1999 Regulations.

single natural person. What is left is an unhappy middle course which will probably cause more problems than it solves.

2.14 In the CCA 1974[4] 'individual' is not defined as such. What is said is that the term 'individual includes—a partnership or other unincorporated body of persons not consisting entirely of bodies corporate'. In other words unless the contracting party is a single body corporate or a body made up wholly of other corporate bodies, that party is protected by the Act. Why a corporate body consisting of one natural person and, say, 20 limited companies, should be deemed worthy of protection was somewhat of a mystery in 1974 and the mystery has not become any less mysterious with the passage of the years.

2.15 The new definition, which is to apply from late 2006,[5] is only slightly more limited:

'individual' includes—
(a) a partnership consisting of two or three persons not all of whom are bodies corporate; and
(b) an unincorporated body of persons which does not consist entirely of bodies corporate and is not a partnership.

2.16 Thus there are limits on the size of partnerships entitled to the protection of the Act: the big City firm of solicitors would now be excluded under the definition of 'individual' whereas the small, high-street firm would not. There are no limits, however, on the size of the unincorporated bodies who are protected nor does it apparently matter what the ratio of natural persons to bodies corporate may be in such unincorporated bodies. Thus an informal 'group' consisting of limited companies and natural persons will be 'individuals' even if there is only one human being to a dozen companies. One can, of course, see the desire to protect, say, members clubs which might be inhibited by restrictions on numbers but the problems faced by such clubs needing to contract could be solved otherwise than by this wide definition of 'individual'.

2.17 The obvious infelicities of the new definition of 'individual' will, it is hoped, be mitigated by the provisions relating to exemptions.

C. REMOVAL OF FINANCIAL LIMITS AND NEW EXEMPTIONS FROM REGULATION

1. Removal of Financial Limits

2.18 Perhaps the most dramatic change wrought by the CCA 2006 is the abandonment of the financial limits for regulation which have been at the core of the CCA 1974 since it was enacted. The implications of this, however, are not perhaps as wide as might at first blush appear. The wide range of exemptions

---

[4] CCA 1974 s 189(1).
[5] Introduced by CCA 2006 s 1.

contained in the existing s 16 of the CCA 1974 will rule out most land mortgages from regulation even when the limits are removed but certain higher value loans, hire-purchase, and hiring agreements will now be caught.

The mechanism for achieving this is referential. The original s 9(1) of the CCA 1974 read: **2.19**

A personal credit agreement is an agreement between an individual ('the debtor') and any other person ('the creditor') by which the creditor provides the debtor with credit of any amount.

This has been altered by s 2(1)(a) of the CCA 2006 to commence 'A *consumer* **2.20** credit agreement is an agreement . . .' This change may fairly be regarded as cosmetic.

The original s 9(2) provided: **2.21**

A consumer credit agreement is a personal credit agreement by which the creditor provides the debtor with credit not exceeding £5,000.

The figure of £5,000 was increased over the years to reach £25,000 but the **2.22** limit remained. Section 2(1)(b) of the CCA 2006 simply removes that subsection in its entirety. This change is expected to affect all agreements made after 6 April 2008.

Under s 15(1) of the CCA 1974 a consumer hire agreement was defined by **2.23** three criteria, the third being that it 'does not require the hirer to make payments exceeding £5,000'. This sum was increased commensurately with the credit limit and now stands at £25,000. The relevant paragraph establishing this criterion— s 15(1)(c)—is again deleted from the CCA 1974.

Advertisements are covered by Part IV of the CCA 1974. Section 43 defines **2.24** the advertisements which are subject to control and s 43(3) exempted credit advertisements where (*inter alia*) the advertisement stated that the credit must exceed the financial limit and that no security was required or that any security would not be on land. This provision—s 43(3)(a)—is deleted and the only category of advertisements excluded by s 43(3) is that for advertisements for credit only available to a body corporate.

2. Exemption Relating to High Net Worth Debtors and Hirers

Section 3 of the CCA 2006 adds a new s 16A to the CCA 1974. It is by any **2.25** standards a bizarre provision, the effect of which will be to deprive individuals of the protections afforded by the CCA 1974 if they are of 'high net worth'. The cry of the public bar grumbler since time immemorial has been 'there's one law for the rich and another for the poor': s 16A may be the first time that this has been quite deliberately enacted into law by Parliament.

This provision was not really signalled by the White Paper but arose in the **2.26** responses to it, particularly from the finance industry. The industry's particular complaint is that well-heeled and, more importantly, well-advised people were entering into hire-purchase agreements for expensive motor cars and using the provisions of s 99 to terminate those agreements when changing vehicles. Properly managed, s 99 can be a great deal more financially advantageous than selling the old car to the dealer by part exchange and paying off the former agreement from the proceeds. Thus, it was said, provisions designed to protect the vulnerable were helping the rich to avoid the usual contractual corollary of such a decision.

2.27   Be that as it may, this modest nut has called forth the full might of the legislative steamroller to crack it.

2.28   The scheme of s 16A, which is expected to come into force in April 2008, is that high net worth debtors or hirers would (at this stage apparently voluntarily) agree to forgo the protections and remedies of the CCA 1974 when entering into what would otherwise be a regulated agreement.

2.29   Under s 16A(1), the Secretary of State is empowered to make an order providing that the CCA 1974 shall not regulate a consumer credit or consumer hire agreement when four conditions are met:

(a) the debtor or hirer is a natural person (thus, presumably, excluding the partnership or other unincorporated body);

(b) the agreement contains a declaration by the debtor or hirer that he agrees to forgo CCA 1974 protection;

(c) a 'statement of high net worth' has been made in relation to him;

(d) that statement is still current and a copy was supplied to the creditor or owner.

2.30   What is a statement of high net worth? Under s 16A(2) such a statement is a statement that, in the opinion of the person making it, the subject of the statement received during the financial year[6] income of a specified description totalling an amount of not less than the specified amount, or had 'throughout that year' assets of a specified description with a total value of not less than a specified value. The descriptions and amounts are to be decided by the Secretary of State and enshrined in an order made under s 16A(4). As this has not been fully discussed either in the White Paper or elsewhere, we must wait to see what the Secretary of State considers to be relevant limits and assets with such patience as we may muster.

2.31   Who can make the statement of high net worth? Clearly not the person concerned—this is excluded by s 16A(3)(a). It will in fact be made by a person of a 'specified description'[7] (again to be decided by the Secretary of State).

2.32   A statement will be 'current' in relation to an agreement if it is made in the period of one year immediately preceding the date of the agreement.[8]

---

[6] Defined as a period of one year ending on 31 March—CCA 1974 as inserted by CCA 2006 s 16A(7).

[7] CCA 1974 as inserted by CCA 2006 s 16A(3)(b).

[8] Ibid s 16A(3)(c).

Where there are two or more debtors or hirers concerned the exemption will **2.33** only apply if all of them meet the high net worth criteria of s 16A.[9]

How this provision will work out in practice is not easy to predict in advance **2.34** of the relevant subordinate legislation. Presumably it is believed that a person who obtains a statement of high net worth and agrees to forgo his CCA 1974 rights and remedies will expect to obtain credit or hire at more favourable rates than otherwise. If he does not, then there could be no possible incentive to go through the elaborate procedures of s 16A. The suspicious may have had the unworthy thought that s 16A could easily be used as a springboard for *compulsory* exemption of the better off from the benefits of the CCA 1974 but time will tell.

Parliament is not, however, entirely heartless towards the undeservedly **2.35** affluent. The provisions governing unfair relationships contained in the new ss 140A to 140C will apply notwithstanding the exemptions contained in s 16A.[10]

3. Exemption Relating to Businesses

Having taken away the £25,000 limit with one hand, Parliament has restored it **2.36** with the other for businesses which enter into consumer credit or consumer hire agreements.

Section 4 of the CCA 2006 adds a new s 16B to the CCA 1974. Section 16B(1) **2.37** provides that the Act shall not regulate consumer credit agreements or consumer hire agreements exceeding the £25,000 limit if the agreement 'is entered into by the debtor or hirer wholly or predominantly for the purpose of a business carried on, or intended to be carried on, by him'.

Under s 16B(2) where an agreement includes a declaration by the debtor or **2.38** hirer that it is made wholly or predominantly for such purpose, the agreement shall be 'presumed' to have been entered into for such purpose. The form of this declaration is to be fixed by a statutory instrument made by the Secretary of State.[11]

Parliament is not, however, entirely naïve. It is recognized that the wily trader **2.39** may include such a declaration in his agreements in order to entrap the guileless debtor or hirer acting in a private capacity. Section 16B(3), therefore, disapplies the presumption if, when the agreement is entered into, the creditor or owner or anyone acting on his behalf knows or has reasonable cause to suspect that the agreement is not being entered into wholly or predominantly for business purposes. If there are two or more creditors or owners, it is sufficient if any of them knows or has cause to suspect under s 16B(3).[12]

---

[9] Ibid s 16A(5).
[10] Ibid s 16A(8). See Chap 9 below.
[11] Ibid s 16B(4).
[12] Ibid s 16B(5).

2.40   Business debtors or hirers, like those of high net worth, are protected against the consequences of unfair relationships, and ss 140A to 140C apply to agreements otherwise exempted by s 16B.[13] These changes are expected to come into force from April 2008.

D. CHANGES TO THE TERMINOLOGY OF THE CONSUMER CREDIT ACT 1974

2.41 The changes brought about by ss 1 to 4 of the CCA 2006 have necessitated a number of alterations to the terminology of the CCA 1974. The change to the definition of 'individual' has been discussed in paragraphs 2.09 to 2.17 above.

2.42   Section 5 of the CCA 2006 sets out a series of consequential amendments to the CCA 1974. Most are entirely mechanical and arise from the repeal of s 8(2) of the CCA 1974 or from the addition of the new ss 16A and 16B.

2.43   Section 10 of the CCA 1974 is amended by substituting 'consumer' for 'personal', thus harmonizing the provisions of the CCA 1974.[14] The concept of a personal agreement has been abandoned and all regulated agreements are now referred to as 'consumer' agreements.

2.44   The category of ancillary credit businesses has been widened somewhat by s 5(4) of the CCA 2006. Section 145(2) defines credit brokerage as including the effecting of introductions '(b) of individuals desiring to obtain goods on hire to persons carrying on businesses to which this paragraph applies'. Section 145(4) defines those businesses as consumer hire businesses or ones which would be consumer hire businesses but for the fact that the proper law of the agreements they make is non-UK law. Section 5(4) adds a new category of businesses which comprise or relate to consumer hire agreements which are exempt agreements, unless the exemption is under s 16(6).[15]

2.45   Section 158 of the CCA 1974 is intended to be tidied up by s 5(5) and (6) of the CCA 2006 but there are problems with this section. Under s 158(1) a credit reference agency must give a copy of his file to any individual making a written request, the individual being then defined as 'the consumer'. The new s 158 simplifies this to say that the copy file must be provided upon 'a request in writing to that effect from a consumer' but it then defines a 'consumer' by saying it 'means' a partnership consisting of two or three persons not all of whom are bodies corporate and unincorporated bodies of persons not entirely consisting of bodies corporate. The difficulty arises because by an oversight, the draughtsman has put 'means' when clearly, in line with the amendment to s 189(1) noted above, he means 'includes'. This will require either amendment or sensible judicial interpretation.

---

[13] CCA 2006 s 16B(6).
[14] Ibid s 5(2)(a).
[15] Essentially hire contracts made by utilities.

E. REFORM OF THE LICENSING SYSTEM

A major feature of the White Paper was the proposal to carry out a fundamental 2.46
reform of the licensing system. There is no doubt that, under the CCA 1974,
licences were far too easily obtainable, and effective control and monitoring of
licensed traders too cumbersome for the Office of Fair Trading (OFT).

The new rules for licensing are fully discussed in Chapter 3 below. 2.47

F. CIVIL PENALTIES AND REFORM OF THE
APPEALS PROCEDURES

It was felt by both the DTI and the OFT that the OFT lacked real 'teeth' when 2.48
dealing with rogue traders. Consequently ss 52 to 54 of the CCA 2006 added
new ss 39A to 39C to the CCA 1974 empowering the OFT to impose civil
penalties on those who fail to comply with requirements imposed under the new
licensing regime.

The provisions for civil penalties are discussed under Chapter 3 below. 2.49

The opportunity was also taken by the CCA 2006[16] to revamp the appeals 2.50
procedures by the creation of a Consumer Credit Appeals Tribunal. This also is
discussed in detail in Chapter 3.

G. CREATION OF THE OMBUDSMAN SCHEME

An innovation suggested by the White Paper and implemented by the CCA 2006 2.51
is the bringing of consumer credit within the ambit of the Financial Services
Ombudsman scheme under the Financial Services and Markets Act 2000.

The new ombudsman scheme is discussed in detail in Chapter 4 below. 2.52

H. STATEMENTS

The existing provisions concerning the giving of statements to debtors and 2.53
hirers contained in ss 77 to 79 of the CCA 1974 are strengthened and augmented
by new rules under ss 6 and 7 of the CCA 2006. These changes are set out in
Chapter 5 below.

---

[16] CCA 2006 ss 55 to 58 adding new ss 40A and 41A to CCA 1974.

I. NEW PROVISIONS FOR DEFAULT AND TERMINATION

2.54 Default and termination have been made a great deal more difficult. There is obviously both governmental and public concern at the level of consumer credit debt and the level of default by debtors. While strengthening the default provisions to make it tougher for creditors and owners, therefore, Parliament has imposed a duty to inform defaulters not only of general matters relating to default but also, to a greater extent than currently, of the courses open to debtors in default.

2.55 Creditors and owners do get some measure of relief. The hated provisions of s 127(3) to (5) which made some improperly executed agreements incapable of being rescued by an enforcement order and which, for a brief period, were declared by the courts to be incompatible with the Human Rights Act 1998, have finally been repealed.

2.56 Important changes have also been made to the provisions for time orders.

2.57 All the changes to default and termination are set out in Chapter 7 below.

J. UNFAIR RELATIONSHIPS

2.58 The intention of the CCA 1974 was to confer wide powers on courts to intervene in cases of grossly unfair dealings between creditor and debtor. Sections 137 to 140 created the concept of the 'extortionate credit bargain' and empowered the court to reopen an agreement which was held to amount to such a bargain. These provisions were very general. They applied to all credit agreements involving an 'individual' (as defined by the Act) whether regulated or not and were, in theory at least, fully retrospective. At the time of the CCA 1974 it was considered that these provisions would be widely invoked and applied.

2.59 In practice, however, ss 137 to 140 were greatly underused. Judicial conservatism, coupled with memories of the operation of the provisions of the Moneylenders Acts 1900 and 1927 concerning harsh and unconscionable transactions by moneylenders, meant that there were very few cases where a court felt it could properly intervene and rewrite the credit agreement before it. Even those cases tended to be very extreme, for example involving rates of interest which, expressed as an APR, exceeded 100 per cent.

2.60 Parliament has therefore determined to try again and has added new provisions to deal with what are now called 'unfair relationships'. Sections 19 to 22 of the CCA 2006 add new ss 140A to 140D to the CCA 1974 eventually to replace ss 137 to 140 which are repealed.

2.61 Unfair relationships are discussed in Chapter 9 below.

K. MISCELLANEOUS CHANGES

Finally the CCA 2006 makes a number of small miscellaneous changes. **2.62**

Section 62 gives the OFT an express power which, in reality, it has been **2.63** exercising from the outset of the CCA 1974. Section 1(1) of the CCA 1974 adds to the functions of the OFT the power 'to monitor, as it sees fit, the businesses being carried on under licences'.

Section 101 of the CCA 1974 gave a hirer under a regulated consumer hire **2.64** agreement the right to terminate the agreement by giving notice to the owner. Section 101(8) entitled a person carrying on a consumer hire business to apply to the OFT for exemption from this provision and, if the OFT considered it was in the interests of hirers to do so, it could by notice provide that s 101 should not apply to agreements made by the applicant. Under s 63(3) of the CCA 2006 this provision has been slightly tidied up but a new provision is added by s 63(1) which adds a new subsection (8A) to s 101.

The new s 101(8A) gives the OFT the power, if it considers it in the interests of **2.65** hirers to do so, to direct by general notice that, subject to any conditions it considers appropriate, the section shall not apply to any consumer hire agreements within specified descriptions. In other words, the OFT can grant a blanket exemption to defined categories of consumer hire agreements.

Largely cosmetic changes are made to the powers of the OFT to vary or **2.66** revoke determinations on non-licensing matters contained in s 183 of the CCA 1974 and to the financial provisions contained in s 190.

L. CHANGES IN CONSUMER CREDIT REGULATIONS

Many of the changes in the application of the CCA 1974 have been brought **2.67** about by changes to the regulations and subsequent chapters will discuss the changes to the Agreements Regulations (Chapter 6) and the Early Settlement Regulations (Chapter 8) together with provisions concerning electronic contracting (Chapter 10).

3

LICENSING OF CREDIT BUSINESSES

A. THE EXISTING SYSTEM OF LICENSING UNDER THE CONSUMER CREDIT ACT 1974

Licensing of consumer credit businesses was at the heart of the Consumer **3.01** Credit Act 1974 (CCA 1974). Some credit providers had been required by statute to obtain licences since the introduction of the first of the Moneylenders Acts in 1900 but the old system was cumbersome and ineffective. The CCA 1974 introduced a comprehensive scheme of registration to include not only credit providers but also ancillary businesses such as credit brokers. Licences were formerly issued by the Director General of Fair Trading and from 1 April 2003 have been issued by the Office of Fair Trading (OFT).

The existing scheme is contained in Part III and Part X of the CCA 1974. **3.02** Under s 21 a licence is required to carry on a consumer credit business or consumer hire business. A consumer credit business is defined[1] as 'any business so far as it comprises or relates to the provision of credit under regulated con-

---

[1] CCA 1974 s 189(1).

sumer credit agreements' and a consumer hire business[2] as 'any business so far as it comprises or relates to the bailment . . . of goods under regulated consumer hire agreements'. Under s 145 a licence is required for an ancillary credit business, defined under five categories: credit brokerage, debt adjusting, debt counselling, debt collection, and the operation of a credit reference agency.

3.03   Under the original CCA 1974 there are six categories of licence (covering seven types of activity—debt adjusting and debt counselling being covered by the same licence): consumer credit, consumer hire, credit brokerage, debt adjusting and debt counselling, debt collection, and credit reference agencies. A person may hold a licence covering more than one category. Licences are issued for five years and are either standard licences or group licences.[3] Licences are unassignable by the holder[4] and the trader must use only the trading name or names specified in the licence itself.[5]

3.04   To be granted a licence, an applicant must satisfy the OFT that he is a 'fit person to engage in activities covered by the licence' and that his trading name is neither misleading nor otherwise undesirable (s 25). There are provisions to avoid overlap with licences granted under the Financial Services and Markets Act 2000. Unsurprisingly, in determining fitness, the OFT can have regard to criminal convictions, past contraventions of the CCA 1974 or any European Economic Area (EEA) equivalent, unlawful discrimination, and other deceitful, oppressive, unfair, or improper practices.

3.05   The CCA 1974 legislates for the issue,[6] renewal,[7] variation,[8] suspension, and revocation of licences,[9] and provides for appeals from decisions of the OFT to the Secretary of State for Trade and Industry.[10]

3.06   Where a regulated agreement is made by an unlicensed trader,[11] it is enforceable against the other party only when the OFT has made an order to that effect, although the OFT has the power retrospectively to validate such agreements. The same regime applies to regulated agreements introduced by an unlicensed credit-broker.[12]

3.07   A person engaging in activities for which a licence is required when not being licensed or, if licensed, carries on business under an unlicensed name, commits a criminal offence.[13]

---

[2]   CCA 1974 s 189(1).
[3]   Ibid s 22.
[4]   Ibid s 22.
[5]   Ibid s 24.
[6]   Ibid ss 27 and 28
[7]   Ibid ss 29.
[8]   Ibid ss 30 and 31
[9]   Ibid ss 32 and 33.
[10]   Ibid ss 41 and 150.
[11]   Ibid s 40 (credit and hire businesses) and s 148 (ancillary credit businesses).
[12]   Ibid s 149.
[13]   Ibid s 39.

B. SCOPE OF BUSINESSES COVERED BY THE CONSUMER CREDIT ACT 2006

1. Redefinition of Terms: 'Credit Business' and 'Hire Business'

The definitions contained in s 189(1) have been expanded.[14]   3.08

'Consumer credit business' means any business being carried on by a person so far as it comprises or relates to—
(a) the provision of credit by him, or
(b) otherwise his being a creditor
under regulated consumer credit agreements.

'Consumer hire business' means any business being carried on by a person so far as it comprises or relates to—
(a) the bailment . . . of goods by him, or
(b) otherwise his being an owner
under regulated consumer hire agreements.

What these changes really add to the definitions is obscure. The explanatory   3.09
notes on the Bill merely said that they were intended to 'clarify' the definitions. The old definitions had caused little trouble in the past and were wide enough to catch any business activity involving consumer credit or consumer hire agreements whether or not it was the principal activity of the business. The CCA 2006 leaves untouched the provision in s 189(2) that 'a person is not to be treated as carrying on a particular type of business merely because occasionally he enters into transactions belonging to a business of that type'. It is thus wise to assume that the new definitions will in practice add nothing to the existing law.

That said, the abolition of the financial limits will bring a large number of   3.10
businesses within the categories of business requiring a licence.

2. Ancillary Credit Businesses

The four existing categories of ancillary credit business remain. Two further   3.11
categories are added by ss 24 and 25 of the CCA 2006, which are expected to come into force in April 2008.

Section 24 adds the category of 'debt administration' which is defined as: 3.12

the taking of steps—
(a) to perform duties under a consumer credit agreement, or a consumer hire agreement on behalf of the creditor or owner, or
(b) to exercise or to enforce rights under such an agreement, on behalf of the creditor or owner,
so far as the taking of such steps is not debt-collecting.

---

[14] CCA 2006 s 23.

3.13   New subsections and paragraphs are added to s 146 of the CCA 1974 to avoid overlap between categories.

3.14   Debt administration would include negotiation on behalf of the creditor or owner with the debtor or hirer on terms for the discharge of a debt (ie the 'mirror image' of debt adjusting which is negotiating on behalf of the debtor or hirer). It would also cover some activities related to repossession of goods which were only dubiously within the category of 'debt collecting'. This is really a tidying-up provision rather than any major extension of the law.

3.15   Section 25 is more complex and concerns what are termed 'credit information services'. This section inserts three subsections—(7B), (7C), and (7D)—into s 145 of the CCA 1974. Section 145(7B) states that a person provides credit information services if he takes any of the steps in subsection (7C) on behalf of an individual or gives advice to an individual in relation to taking those steps.

3.16   The 'steps' in subsection (7C) cover four categories of activity:

(a) ascertaining whether a credit information agency holds information relevant to the financial standing of an individual;

(b) ascertaining the contents of information held by an agency;

(c) securing correction, omission, or modification of information;

(d) securing that the agency stops holding information or does not supply it to another.

3.17   A credit information agency comprises persons carrying on any of the original seven categories of business or the new category of debt administration and persons carrying on what would be a consumer credit business but for the fact that the business relates to certain types of exempt agreement.

3. Nine Categories of Business

3.18   There are now thus nine categories of business:

(a) consumer credit;

(b) consumer hire;

(c) credit brokerage;

(d) debt adjusting;

(e) debt counselling;

(f) debt collecting;

(g) debt administration;

(h) provision of credit information services;

(i) operation of a credit reference agency.

C. CONSEQUENCES OF TRADING WITHOUT A LICENCE

Section 26 of the CCA 2006 replaces subsection (1) of s 40 of the CCA 1974 **3.19** with two subsections:

(1) A regulated agreement is not enforceable against the debtor or hirer by a person acting in the course of a consumer credit business or a consumer hire business (as the case may be) if that person is not licensed to carry on a consumer credit business or a consumer hire business (as the case may be) of a description which covers the enforcement of the agreement.
(1A) Unless the OFT has made an order under subsection (2) which applies to the agreement, a regulated agreement is not enforceable against the debtor or hirer if—
    (a) it was made by the creditor or owner in the course of a consumer credit business or a consumer hire business (as the case may be); and
    (b) at the time the agreement was made he was not licensed to carry on a consumer credit business or a consumer hire business (as the case may be) of a description which covered the making of the agreement.

The new provisions, which are expected to come into force in April 2008, **3.20** made a distinction not made by the original s 40 between being licensed to *enforce* an agreement of the relevant category and being licensed to *make* an agreement of the relevant category. In the latter instance, the OFT has the power to make an order under subsection (2), but in the former it has not. If, therefore, the trader does not hold a licence which entitles him to enforce the agreement, it cannot be saved.

The new s 40(2) reads: **3.21**

Where—
(a) during any period a person (the 'trader') has made regulated agreements in the course of a consumer credit business or a consumer hire business (as the case may be), and
(b) during that period he was not licensed to carry on consumer credit business or a consumer hire business (as the case may be) of a description which covered the making of those agreements,
he or his successor in title may apply to the OFT for an order that the agreements are to be treated for the purposes of subsection (1A) as if he had been licensed as required.

The procedures for obtaining an OFT order contained in the remaining sub- **3.22** sections of s 40 of the CCA 1974 are maintained. Other provisions preserve the exemptions of local authorities and other statutory bodies under s 21(2) and (3) and consumer credit EEA firms under s 40(6).

D. APPLYING FOR A LICENCE: THE 'FITNESS TEST'

1. Standard Licences

The CCA 2006 embodies the decision to put more of the mechanism of **3.23** applying for licences into the body of the statute. It also creates two new concepts:

the 'type' of business and the 'description' of business. The 'types' of business are the nine categories set out in paragraph 3.18 above.[15] 'Description' is much more amorphous. ' "Description of business" means, in relation to a type of business, a description of business specified in a general notice [to be issued by the OFT]'.[16] At the time of going to press, no such notice has been issued.

3.24   The mechanism is achieved by inserting a new s 24A into the CCA 1974.[17] This requires an applicant to state, in relation to each type of business covered by the application, whether he is (a) applying for a licence to carry on that type of business without limitation or (b) for a licence to carry on that type of business only to the extent that it falls within one or more descriptions of business. In case (b) the application must set out the relevant descriptions of the business.

3.25   The OFT is given power to issue general notices specifying the descriptions of business that can be set out in an application and may also decree that applications in case (b) cannot be made at all in relation to one or more of the types of business other than consumer credit and consumer hire. No such notice has yet been issued.

3.26   Section 29 of the CCA 2006 modifies s 25(1) of the CCA 1974 by substituting five subsections—(1), (1AA), (1AB), (1AC), and (1AD)—to deal with case (a) and case (b) applications. If a case (a) applicant satisfies the OFT that he is a fit person to carry on the type of business applied for without limitation, he is entitled to a licence to do so. Similarly, if a case (b) applicant satisfies the OFT that he is a fit person to carry on that type of business in accordance with the description given in the application, he is entitled to the appropriate licence.

3.27   In either case, however, an applicant may fail to satisfy the OFT that he is a proper person to be issued with the licence he has applied for but, nevertheless, the OFT may still issue him with a standard licence to carry on business of a stated type within a stated description if satisfied that the applicant would be a fit person to do so (provided the original application was wide enough to comprise this business).

3.28   The requirement to satisfy the OFT that the business name is not misleading or otherwise undesirable is preserved by the new s 40(1AD).

3.29   Note also that s 22 of the CCA 1974 will be amended by the addition of a new subsection (5A) providing that 'a group licence to carry on a business may limit the activities it covers in any way the OFT thinks fit'.[18]

---

[15] New s 24A(4) of the CCA 1974 inserted by CCA 2006 s 28.
[16] New s 25(1AC) inserted into the CCA 1974 by CCA 2006 s 29.
[17] By s 28 of the CCA 2006.
[18] CCA 2006 s 33(2).

2. Consumer Credit EEA Firms

The CCA 2006 inserts a new s 27A into the CCA 1974 to legislate for consumer **3.30** credit EEA firms. Firms from other EEA States who carry on business in the United Kingdom have been able to obtain permission for activities which include consumer credit activities under the Financial Services and Markets Act 2000.[19] The DTI wishes to avoid confusion by consumer credit EEA firms having also to apply for standard licences under the consumer credit legislation to carry on the same activities.

Thus, where such a firm applies for a standard licence and all the activities **3.31** covered by the application are or would be permitted under the 2000 Act, the licence must be refused. Hence, if the firm could have applied for permission under the 2000 Act but has failed to do so, it still cannot obtain a standard licence under the CCA 1974.

If, however, such a firm applies for a standard licence and some of the **3.32** activities covered by the application are or would be permitted under the 2000 Act and some are not, the firm can be issued with a standard licence. In relation to activities covered by the 2000 Act, the firm does not have to satisfy the OFT of its fitness but, by the same token, the standard licence does not confer any authority to carry on those activities. If the firm does not already have 2000 Act permission for those activities, it must do so. A standard licence will not assist. Insofar as the activities are outwith the 2000 Act, the firm must satisfy the OFT as to its fitness in the normal way and the licence will authorize those activities.

3. The Fitness Test

The fitness test has been expanded and made more stringent. These new pro- **3.33** visions are at the heart of the new Act and are designed to meet the criticism of the old system that almost anybody, however inexperienced or unsuitable, could obtain a licence provided he could show a clean record. The DTI has undertaken to be much more selective in the issuing of licences and we can expect a retreat from the wholesale distribution of licences that marked the CCA 1974.

Section 29(2) of the CCA 2006 replaces s 25(2) with two subsections. The new **3.34** s 25(2) provides:

In determining whether an applicant for a licence is a fit person for the purposes of this section the OFT shall have regard to any matters appearing to it to be relevant including (amongst other things)
(a) the applicant's skills, knowledge and experience in relation to consumer credit businesses, consumer hire businesses or ancillary credit businesses;
(b) such skills, knowledge and experience of other persons who the applicant proposes will participate in any business that would be carried on by him under the licence;

---

[19] Schedule 3 para 15.

(c) practices and procedures that the applicant proposes to implement in connection with any such business;

(d) evidence of the kind mentioned in subsection (2A).

3.35 The new s 25(2A) slightly expands the negative considerations. As before, the OFT must have regard to 'evidence tending to show' that the applicant, his employees, agents, or associates have been guilty of named misconduct. The new list of misconduct contains the old categories: offences involving fraud, dishonesty or violence, unlawful discrimination, and deceitful, oppressive, unfair, or improper business practices. It adds contravention of Part 16 of the Financial Services and Markets Act 2000 to the existing categories of contravention of (a) the provisions of the Act itself and (b) 'any other enactment regulating the provision of credit to individuals or other transactions with individuals'. Contravention of similar provisions in any other EEA jurisdiction is also to be taken into account.

3.36 The main difference between the CCA 2006 and the CCA 1974 is that the emphasis is now on the applicant establishing the positive aspects of his business—his skills and experience and his business practices—and not just the absence of the negative considerations. The questions asked of applicants will thus be much more searching. The DTI is determined to root out what it habitually calls 'loan sharks' and the new application procedure will spearhead this effort.

3.37 The OFT intends to back this up by issuing guidance, after due consultation, and the guidance will be updated from time to time.[20]

E. VARIATION OF LICENCES

3.38 The new s 24A has, as we have seen, considerably tightened up the licence process. This has been mirrored by a major redrafting of the variation provisions, which are expected to come into force in April 2008.

1. Variation by Request

3.39 This was very general under the CCA 1974. Section 30(1) simply provided that on application by a licensee 'the OFT may if it thinks fit by notice to the licensee vary a standard licence in accordance with the application'. This subsection will be considerably expanded by the substitution of three new subsections (1), (1A), and (1B).[21]

3.40 The new s 30(1) lists the categories of variation that the OFT is empowered to make but provides that the OFT may vary a licence under subsection (1) 'only in

---

[20] The power to achieve this is contained in a new s 25A inserted into the CCA 1974 by CCA 2006 s 30.

[21] Substituted by CCA 2006 s 31(1).

accordance with an application made by the licensee'. This would appear to mean that, faced with an application, the OFT can grant or refuse it but cannot, *under s 30*, vary the licence in a way the applicant does not want. The OFT retains its power of compulsory variation, but under s 31 (see below).

The types of variation permitted under s 30 are: 3.41

(a) in the case of a licence which covers the carrying on of a type of business only so far as it falls within one or more descriptions of business, vary the licence by
    (i) removing that limitation;
    (ii) adding a description of business to that limitation; or
    (iii) removing a description of business from that limitation;
(b) in the case of a licence which covers the carrying on of a type of business with no limitation, vary the licence so that it covers the carrying on of that type of business only so far as it falls within one or more descriptions of business;
(c) vary the licence so that it no longer covers the carrying on of a type of business at all;
(d) vary the licence so that a type of business the carrying on of which is not covered at all by the licence is covered either
    (i) with no limitation; or
    (ii) only so far as it falls within one or more descriptions of business; or
(e) vary the licence in any other way except for the purpose of varying the descriptions of activities covered by the licence.

2. Compulsory Variation

The OFT's powers of compulsory variation under s 31 of the CCA 1974 were 3.42 always very wide. Essentially the mechanism is that if, at any time during the currency of a licence, the OFT is of the opinion that, if the licence had expired, it would only be reissued on different terms and thus that the licence should be varied, the OFT will give notice to the licence holder to that effect. There is a procedure for the licence holder to make representations and an appeal procedure but, at the end of the day, if these are unsuccessful, the OFT will impose a variation on the licence.

Amendments to the existing s 31(1) and the addition of a new s 31(1A)[22] and 3.43 s 31(1B),[23] define and restrict the types of compulsory variation possible under s 31. In the case of a standard licence, the variations are those set out in paragraphs (a)(ii) and (iii), (b), (c), and (e) of the list in s 30(1) set out in paragraph 3.41 above. The general power of variation for group licences is retained.

Clearly, there will be cases where a person holds a standard licence who would 3.44 not be entitled to apply for a new licence if the new rules relating to description of business were in force. In other words, once s 24A and the OFT general notices are in place, some licence holders will find it difficult or impossible to

---

[22] By CCA 2006 s 31(2) and (3).
[23] By CCA 2006 s 34(5): for its effect see below.

comply with the new conditions. Elaborate provisions are thus put in place[24] to ensure that such licence holders are not prejudiced by the 'deemed expiry' provisions of s 31(1) before their licences actually do expire.

3.45　　A similar provision has been inserted into s 32 of the CCA 1974.[25] The OFT has no power to revoke or suspend a standard licence 'simply because, by virtue of a provision made in a general notice under s 24A(5), a person cannot apply for the renewal of such a licence on terms which are the same as the licence in question'.

F. 'INDEFINITE' LICENCES

3.46　　This is a real departure from the original Act which had a rigid five-year period for standard licences (although group licences could be indefinite). A much greater degree of flexibility has been introduced by ss 34 to 37 of the CCA 2006, which are expected to come into force in April 2008.

3.47　　The changes are effected by introducing new subsections (1A) to (1E) to s 22 of the CCA 1974. These may be summarized as follows. The OFT may issue a licence for an indefinite period or for a stated limited period. Any application for a standard licence will be taken to be for an indefinite period unless the application states otherwise or the OFT considers the licence should be limited. The OFT will prescribe a maximum period for limited licences beyond which a limited licence cannot be issued.

3.48　　The OFT is given the power to limit the period of an indefinite licence either by voluntary variation under s 30 or compulsorily under s 31.

3.49　　Obviously, the provisions of s 31 for compulsory variation, and s 32 for suspension or revocation, both of which require the OFT to assume an expiry and re-application as the starting point for assessing whether the licence should be varied, suspended, or revoked, would be inapplicable to an indefinite licence unless provision were made for this. Consequently s 34 of the CCA 2006 amends ss 31(1) and 32(1) to enable the OFT to treat an indefinite licence as a limited licence for this purpose.

3.50　　Sections 25 to 37 of the CCA 2006 insert new ss 28A to 28C into the CCA 1974 to make detailed provision for the charges to be made for indefinite licences, for extending the period for payment of the charge, and for penalties for failing to pay the charge. It is clearly the intention of the OFT to increase charges both as a method of raising revenue towards the (not inconsiderable) costs of operating consumer credit legislation and as a method of discouraging marginal operators from applying.

---

[24] By CCA 2006 s 31(4) of the which inserts new subsections (8) and (9) to s 31 of the CCA 1974.
[25] By CCA 2006 s 31(5).

G. POWERS OF THE OFFICE OF FAIR TRADING

1. Imposing Requirements

In conformity with the OFT's stated objective of cleaning up the consumer   **3.51**
credit world, the CCA 2006 has conferred additional powers on the OFT, which
are expected to come into force in April 2008. Five new sections, 33A to 33E, are
inserted into the CCA 1974.[26]

The kernel of the new powers is contained in s 33A(1) and (2):   **3.52**

(1) This section applies where the OFT is dissatisfied with any matter in connection
with—
  (a) a business being carried on, or which has been carried on, by a licensee or by an
  associate or a former associate of a licensee;
  (b) a proposal to carry on a business which has been made by a licensee or by
  an associate or a former associate of a licensee; or
  (c) any conduct not covered by paragraph (a) or (b) of a licensee or of an associate
  or a former associate of a licensee.
(2) The OFT may by notice to the licensee require him to do or not to do (or to cease
doing) anything specified in the notice for purposes connected with—
  (a) addressing the matter with which the OFT is dissatisfied; or
  (b) securing that matters of the same or a similar kind do not arise.

It is immaterial whether the matter giving rise to dissatisfaction on the part   **3.53**
of the OFT arose before or after the licensee became a licensee.[27]

Where a person applies for a licence and the OFT forms an adverse opinion   **3.54**
during the licence process, the OFT can take steps to impose the requirement on
the licence once issued.[28]

Similar wide powers are granted to the OFT to impose requirements on the   **3.55**
bodies supervising group licences under s 33B.

The OFT's powers are not wholly unlimited nor is their use entirely arbitrary.   **3.56**
Any requirement dies with the licence to which it is attached[29] and the OFT
cannot use these powers to require anyone to pay compensation.[30]

The requirement may be varied or revoked by the OFT under s 33C(4) and   **3.57**
may do so at the request of a person on whom a requirement is imposed and
on certain other classes of persons affected. Under s 33C(7), if a requirement
is imposed on a licensee not to employ a named person or to control the activities of a named person, that person may himself apply to the OFT for the
requirement to be varied or revoked.

Section 33D lays down a procedure for the OFT to give advance notice of   **3.58**
its intention to impose the requirement and for the persons affected to make

---

[26] By CCA 2006 ss 38 to 42.
[27] CCA 1974 as inserted by CCA 2006 s 33A(5).
[28] Ibid s 33A(6).
[29] Ibid s 33C(2).   [30] Ibid s 33C(3).

representations. Section 33E empowers the OFT to issue and publish guidance documents on how it exercises or proposes to exercise its powers.

2. Winding up Businesses

3.59   Section 32 inserts a new s 34A into the CCA 1974 to grant wide powers to the OFT in the event of a licensee's business being transferred or wound up. It may authorize the carrying on of certain activities which otherwise the licensee would be prohibited from carrying on by the OFT's decision to refuse to renew a licence or to impose variation, suspension, or revocation of the licence.

3. Provision of Information

3.60   The increased powers of the OFT to require information are dealt with in paragraphs 3.61 to 3.72 below.

H. INFORMATION

3.61   The requirements for applicants to provide information to the OFT were wide but poorly defined by the CCA 1974, in particular by s 6. These requirements have been considerably beefed up by a major rewriting of s 6 and the addition of six new sections 34A to 34F, which are expected to come into force in April 2008.

3.62   The new provisions may be summarized as follows. As before, the OFT will issue general notices but these will now specify the 'information and documents' (formerly the 'particulars') necessary to support an application. When an application is received, the OFT may require the applicant by notice to provide further information or documents.

3.63   New subsections (5) to (9) inserted into s 6 of the CCA 1974 impose new obligations on the applicant. If between application and issue of a licence a new general notice comes into effect, the applicant must provide the OFT with any additional information or documents required by this notice (even if it was not in force when the application was made). The applicant must within 28 days notify the OFT if any information or document has been superseded or otherwise affected by a change in circumstances or if he becomes aware of any error or omission.

3.64   Section 36 of the CCA 1974 required a licensee to notify changes in any particulars entered in the register. This will remain but will be strengthened by the new s 36A. If the OFT issues a general notice, then existing holders of standard or group licences will be obliged to supply the OFT with the information or documents required by the new general notice unless, in effect, that information or documentation has already been supplied as part of the licence application. Further, in relation to matters specified in a general notice as being relevant to fitness of applicants or the public suitability of group licences, there are wide obligations to notify the OFT of changes of circumstances affecting the information or documents already supplied.

To all of this are added by s 36B sweeping powers for the OFT to require information generally. The OFT may serve a notice on any person (licensee or not) requiring him to provide information or produce documents. The notice must give reasons and should specify the period for production and the place to which production should be made. **3.65**

If the recipient of the notice is a licensee, the information and documents must be related to the questions properly to be asked of an applicant. If he is anyone else, the notice can only be given if there are actual or suspected 'acts or omissions', defined as acts or omissions which cast doubt on the fitness of a standard licence holder, affect the public interest of a group licence, give rise to 'dissatisfaction' under ss 33A or 33B, or relate to failure to comply with an earlier notice. **3.66**

A new s 36C confers on the OFT power to serve a notice requiring access to the premises of a licensee to be afforded to an officer of an enforcement authority in order to observe the carrying on of the business or to inspect documents specified in the notice. The notice must state reasons and cannot apply to domestic premises. This power can only be exercised if there has been an 'act or omission' of the kind listed in s 36B. **3.67**

In the event that the OFT has reasonable grounds for believing that there are documents or information on the premises of a licensee which it could require to be furnished under s 36B but that if a requirement were issued the material would be refused or would be 'tampered with', the OFT can apply for a warrant from a justice of the peace to authorize an officer of an enforcement authority to enter and search the premises and to preserve or seize the material, using such force as may be reasonably necessary. **3.68**

If there is a failure by a person to do something required by s 36B or s 36C, the OFT can apply to the county court under s 36E for an order compelling the person (the defaulter) to comply. **3.69**

Under the new s 36F, officers of enforcement authorities may only exercise the powers under s 36C or s 36D if there are prior arrangements between the OFT and the relevant enforcement authority but, if these arrangements are in place, the officer is treated as being an officer of the OFT itself when exercising those powers. **3.70**

A new s 174A is inserted into the CCA 1974 controlling the powers to require information or documents. The power includes the right to demand that information is put into a legible form (eg from electronic sources), to take copies or extracts from documents, and to require the person required to produce the material to say where it is, to explain it, to verify it, or to secure it. **3.71**

Section 174A(3) and (4) preserves the right of a person from whom information or documents are demanded to assert legal professional privilege. **3.72**

I. PENALTIES

3.73 The CCA 1974 made contravention of a wide range of provisions into criminal offences, subject to prosecution in the criminal courts. The CCA 2006 adds a new range of civil penalties capable of being imposed by the OFT itself, which are expected to come into force in April 2008.

3.74 Sections 52 to 54 of the CCA 2006 add three new sections to the CCA 1974, ss 39A, 39B, and 39C. These are pretty draconian. Where the OFT is satisfied that a person (the defaulter) has failed to comply with a requirement to produce information or documents made under s 33A, 33B, or 36A, it may by notice impose on him a penalty of 'such amount as it thinks fit', subject to an upper limit of £50,000.[31]

3.75 The defaulter has a right of appeal under s 41. If the penalty is not successfully appealed it is recoverable as a civil debt and carries interest at the judgment rate.[32]

3.76 The penalty procedure is the standard procedure for notices under the CCA 1974.[33] The OFT must inform the defaulter in advance of its intention to impose a penalty, informing him of the proposed amount and the reasons both for the penalty itself and for the amount, and inviting him to make representations. In imposing a penalty, the OFT must have regard to any penalty or fine imposed on the defaulter by any other body (eg the Financial Services Authority (FSA)) and any other steps the OFT has taken or might take to deal with the default.

3.77 Again following the scheme of the new Act, the OFT is to publish a statement of policy on the exercise of its powers to impose civil penalties, to be approved by the Secretary of State.[34]

J. THE CONSUMER CREDIT APPEALS TRIBUNAL

1. Establishment of the Consumer Credit Appeals Tribunal

3.78 Section 41 of the CCA 1974 gave a right of appeal to the Secretary of State to persons listed in the section against specified determinations by the OFT. This appeals mechanism has been rationalized by the creation of a Consumer Credit Appeals Tribunal.

3.79 The Tribunal is constituted by a new s 40A of the CCA 1974,[35] and its constitution and powers are set out in a new Schedule A1 to be added to the CCA 1974.[36] The Tribunal will be controlled by the Lord Chancellor who will appoint

---

[31] CCA 2006 s 39A(1) and (3).
[32] Ibid s 29A(5).
[33] Ibid s 39B.
[34] Ibid s 39C.
[35] Inserted by CCA 2006 s 55(1).
[36] By Sch 1 to the CCA 2006.

its President and Deputy President, a panel of legally qualified chairmen, and a lay panel.

The Tribunal will resemble other such tribunals (eg in the employment field), **3.80** sitting with a chairman and, normally, two lay members, and having the right to appoint experts to assist. There will be rules of procedure and the Tribunal will have the power to confirm, quash, vary, or remit the OFT's decision and to give the OFT directions. In cases involving civil penalties, it can reduce but not increase the penalty imposed by the OFT. There is a provision for majority decision and for the imposition of costs.

The appeal is by way of rehearing.[37] **3.81**

New subsections (1A) to (1D) are added to the existing s 41 to replace the old **3.82** subsections (2) to (5), which are repealed.[38] These subsections provide for the mechanics of an appeal and there will eventually be a prescribed form of notice of appeal.

2. Appeals from the Consumer Credit Appeals Tribunal

A new section 41A is inserted by s 57 of the CCA 2006. This provides a right of **3.83** appeal on a point of law from the Tribunal to the Court of Appeal.[39] Leave to appeal is required from the Tribunal or the appellate court and an application for leave may only be made to the appellate court if it has been applied for and refused by the Tribunal. The appellate court may quash or vary the decision of the Tribunal, substitute a decision of its own, or remit to the Tribunal for rehearing. Appeal to the House of Lords requires the usual leave of the appellate court concerned or the House itself.

---

[37] Section 41(1C) added by s 56 of the CCA 2006.
[38] CCA 2006 s 56.
[39] In Scotland, to the Court of Session and in Northern Ireland to the Northern Ireland Court of Appeal.

4

FINANCIAL OMBUDSMAN

A. INTRODUCTION

In the course of the Government's consultation on the White Paper, it became **4.01** apparent that consumers and businesses found court action costly, complex, and lengthy. There was widespread support for the introduction of some kind of alternative dispute resolution (ADR) system in order to make the resolution of disputes quicker, fairer, and less expensive.

To meet this perceived need, the Consumer Credit Act 2006 (CCA 2006) **4.02** extends the jurisdiction of the Financial Ombudsman Service (FOS), a service that was established under Part 16 of the Financial Services and Markets Act (FSMA) 2000, to cover complaints involving licensed persons under the Consumer Credit Act 1974 (CCA 1974). From the date of implementation, the FOS will be responsible for handling disputes relating to consumer credit alongside its other jurisdictions.

Although the detailed arrangements are yet to be finalized, it is likely that this **4.03** new consumer credit jurisdiction will be broadly consistent with existing FOS rules. It is expected that these provisions will come into force in April 2008.

B. THE FINANCIAL OMBUDSMAN SERVICE

4.04 The FOS is an independent organization that was created by the FSMA. It replaced a number of the former complaints-handling schemes, including the Banking Ombudsman, Building Society's Ombudsman, Insurance Ombudsman, Investment Ombudsman, and the Securities and Futures Authority (SFA) Complaints Bureau.

4.05 The FOS deals with complaints by consumers about a variety of financial products and services provided in the United Kingdom. It is not a regulator, nor a trade body, nor a consumer champion. It helps, without taking sides, to resolve certain types of disputes involving certain types of activities[1] between certain types of consumers[2] and certain types of financial firms[3] within certain time limits.[4]

4.06 On receiving a relevant complaint from a consumer, the FOS considers the complaint on paper, undertakes any necessary investigation, and then determines the complaint in a manner that is fair and reasonable, taking into account relevant law, codes of practice, regulatory rules, and guidance. The approach often involves mediation or conciliation.

4.07 If the adjudicator cannot find an informal solution that satisfies both sides, a written decision will be prepared. If the complainant accepts the decision, the FOS's rules require the respondent to comply with any award. If the complainant does not accept the decision, he/she may pursue the matter in court. Most complaints are resolved within six months.

C. THE NEW CONSUMER CREDIT JURISDICTION AND RULES

4.08 Section 59 of the CCA 2006 inserts a new s 226A into the FSMA, which expands the scope of the FOS to include a special consumer credit jurisdiction.

4.09 Much of the detail of the new scheme will be contained in Consumer Credit Rules. These Rules will be made by the FOS with the approval of the Financial

---

[1] In broad terms, activities that are regulated by the FSA are the subject of the FOS's compulsory jurisdiction; certain other activities fall under the voluntary jurisdiction.

[2] The FOS may only consider complaints made by certain complainants: private individuals; businesses with an annual turnover of under £1 million; charities with an annual income of under £1 million; or trusts with net assets of under £1 million.

[3] In general, those financial firms that are regulated by the Financial Services Authority (FSA) and those that have agreed voluntarily to be subject to the FOS's procedures.

[4] Within six months of the date on which the licensee firm responded to the complainant's initial complaint; or within six years of the event; or, in any event, within three years of the complainant first becoming aware of the problem. There is, however, discretion to waive these limits in exceptional circumstances.

Services Authority (FSA) for the specific purposes of administering this consumer credit jurisdiction.[5]

4.10 Schedule 2 of the CCA 2006, which adds a new Part 3A to Schedule 17 to the FSMA, provides an indication of the intended scope and extent of the Consumer Credit Rules that will govern this scheme:

16B(1) Consumer Credit Rules—
(a) must provide that a complaint is not to be entertained unless the complainant has referred it under the Ombudsman Scheme before the applicable time limit (determined in accordance with the rules) has expired;
(b) may provide that an Ombudsman may extend that time limit in specific circumstances;
(c) may provide that a complaint is not to be entertained (except in specified circumstances) if the complainant has not previously communicated its substance to the respondent and given him a reasonable opportunity to deal with it;
(d) may make provision about the procedure for the reference of complaints and for their investigation, consideration and determination by an Ombudsman.

4.11 As yet, no such consumer credit rules have been published, and much of the detail of the new scheme remains unclear. The amendments to the FSMA do, however, provide some of the fundamentals of the scheme—including the sorts of cases that fall under its aegis once these amendments come into force.

4.12 Thus, as amended, s 226A(1) provides that the FOS has jurisdiction to consider any complaint if it is made:

(a) by an eligible complainant;[6]

(b) about a particular activity;[7]

(c) involving a particular type of respondent;[8]

(d) carrying out a particular type of business;[9] and

(e) if the complaint cannot be dealt with under the FOS's compulsory jurisdiction.[10]

1. Eligible Complainant

4.13 A complainant is eligible if he is an individual, or a surety to a security provided to the respondent in connection with a debt adjusting business, and he falls within the class of persons that are to be specified in the Consumer Credit Rules.[11]

---

[5] FSMA s 226A(7).
[6] Ibid s 226A(2)(a).
[7] Ibid s 226A(2)(b).
[8] Ibid s 226A(2)(c).
[9] Ibid s 226A(2)(d) and (e).
[10] Ibid s 226A(2)(f).
[11] Ibid s 226A(4).

2. Type of Activity

4.14 As to the type of activities covered by the scheme, these will be described in the Consumer Credit Rules. It is anticipated that FOS could consider, among other things, acts or omissions relating to advice on credit, the making of agreements, or the administration of accounts.[12]

3. Type of Respondent

4.15 The FOS will only consider complaints under the consumer credit jurisdiction if made against the holders of standard licences under the CCA 1974, or persons authorized to wind up licensable businesses under new s 34A of the CCA 1974.[13]

4. Type of Business

4.16 The FOS will only consider complaints about certain types of business. These are listed in s 226A(3), and are: a consumer credit business; a consumer hire business; a business so far as it comprises or relates to credit brokerage, debt adjusting, debt counselling, debt collecting, debt administration, credit information services, or the operation of a credit reference agency.[14] The Secretary of State may bring within the consumer credit jurisdiction any other specific types of business for which a licence is required under the CCA 1974.[15]

5. Not Dealt with Elsewhere

4.17 If the complaint can be dealt with under the FOS's existing compulsory jurisdiction, it will not be dealt with under the consumer credit jurisdiction. For example, a complaint involving an FSA authorized firm engaging in consumer credit activities will be covered by the FSA's rules under s 226 of the FSMA, rather than FOS's rules under s 226A.[16]

D. PRACTICE AND PROCEDURE OF A COMPLAINT TO THE FINANCIAL OMBUDSMAN SERVICE

4.18 In the absence of any Consumer Credit Rules, a summary of the relevant practice and procedure cannot be given. By looking at the procedures in other FOS jurisdictions, and on the basis of the statutory scheme of the FSMA, it is

---

[12] See the explanatory notes published with the Bill.
[13] FSMA s 226A(2)(c).
[14] Ibid s 226A(3).
[15] Ibid s 226A(2)(e).
[16] Ibid s 226A(2)(f).

possible to make some predictions as to the likely manner in which the consumer credit jurisdiction will operate.

1. The Initial Complaint to the Licensee

It is likely that the FOS will not consider a complaint until the potential **4.19** respondent licensee has had a chance to deal with the substance of the complaint itself. The licensee will be given reasonable time to investigate the complaint and decide how to respond to it.[17]

The FSA's rules, which may form the pattern for the Consumer Credit Rules, **4.20** set out various time limits within which the licensee is expected to deal with such initial complaints—including a requirement to send a customer a final response no more than eight weeks from the date the complaint was received.

2. Complaint to the Financial Ombudsman Service

If the consumer is unhappy with the licensee's response, it may then refer the **4.21** matter to the FOS. The time limit for such a complaint will be set by the Consumer Credit Rules. In other jurisdictions, the FOS has set a time limit of six months from the date of the licensee's response, with a longstop of three years from the date of the event or from the date on which the complainant became aware of the problem. The Rules will probably contain a discretion to extend time in exceptional circumstances.

Any complaint will probably have to be made on a particular complaint form, **4.22** which will require the complainant to provide personal details and information about the complaint, including what the consumer would ask the firm to do to put matters right again.

3. Informal Mediation/Conciliation

Once such a form has been received, the case will probably be considered on **4.23** paper by an adjudicator or Ombudsman at the FOS. It is likely that the adjudicator will initially seek to resolve the dispute through mediation and/or conciliation. There will be contact between the FOS and the complainant, and the case generally solved simply on a basis of the papers rather than in face-to-face meetings.

4. Investigation

An Ombudsman may, by notice in writing given to a party to a complaint, **4.24** require that party to provide specified information or to produce specified

---

[17] See para 16B(1)(c) of Part 3A of Sch 17 to the FSMA, as amended by Sch 2 to the CCA 2006.

documents.[18] This information, or these documents, must be provided or produced before the end of a reasonable period specified in the request, and, in the case of information, in such manner or form that may be specified.[19]

4.25 If any person fails to comply with such a requirement, the Ombudsman may certify that fact in writing to the court and the court may enquire into the case.[20] If the High Court is satisfied that a default failed, without reasonable excuse, to comply with such a requirement, it may deal with the defaulter as he were in contempt.[21]

5. Determination

4.26 A complaint to the FOS is to be determined by reference to what is, in the opinion of the adjudicator, fair and reasonable in all the circumstances of the case.[22] It is likely that the adjudicator will take into account relevant law, codes of practice, regulatory rules, and guidance.

4.27 When the adjudicator has determined a complaint, he must give a written statement of his determination to both the respondent and to the complainant.[23] The statement must give the reasons for his determination, be signed by him, and require the complainant to notify him in writing, before a date specified in the statement, whether a determination is accepted or rejected.[24] In most cases, both sides accept the adjudicator's findings and the complaint is then settled. But if either the consumer or the firm does not understand any part of the procedure – or does not agree with the findings of the adjudicator – they are entitled to contact the adjudicator in the first instance. If matters remain unresolved, either the firm or the consumer may ask for a review and final decision by an Ombudsman. This only happens in about one in ten cases. There is no appeal from the review and decision of the Ombudsman.

4.28 If a complaint is determined in favour of the complainant, the determination may include either an award against the respondent of such amount as the Ombudsman considers fair compensation for loss and damage,[25] and/or a direction that the respondent takes such steps as the Ombudsman considers just and appropriate—whether or not a court might order such steps to be taken.[26]

4.29 If the consumer accepts the FOS's decision, it is likely that the Consumer Credit Rules will require the firm to comply promptly with any money award or direction the Ombudsman makes (see below).

---

[18] FSMA s 231(1).
[19] Ibid s 231(2).
[20] Ibid s 232(1).
[21] Ibid s 232(2).
[22] Ibid s 228(2).
[23] Ibid s 228(3).
[24] Ibid s 228(4).
[25] Ibid s 229(2)(A).
[26] Ibid s 229(2)(B).

While respondents have to accept the FOS decision, consumers do not. At **4.30** any stage they are free to go to the court instead. On the other hand, the FOS will not usually handle a case which has already been considered by a court, or where court proceedings are pending—except in very particular circumstances where the outcome of the scheme determination will not affect the court case. For example, where a possession order is due for arrears of £5,000, but there is a dispute between the lender and the borrower over a £50 charge wrongly levied on the account, then the former can be dealt with by the court, and the latter by the FOS, at the same time.

6. Awards

The Ombudsman does not punish firms or fine them—as its job is to settle **4.31** disputes between consumers and firms. It is not a regulator.

However, the FOS may make a money award to compensate for financial loss **4.32** or any other loss or any damage of a specified kind.[27]

The level of compensation awarded by the FOS aims to try to put a consumer **4.33** back in the position they would have been in had the event that they had complained about not happened. In other of its jurisdictions, the FOS usually awards an amount of money to the customer to cover the financial loss they have suffered, along with an amount to reflect damage to reputation or distress and inconvenience. There is no reason to think that different principles will apply to the consumer credit jurisdiction.

The FOS may specify the maximum amount which is regarded as fair **4.34** compensation of a particular kind of loss and damage,[28] and a money award may not exceed that monetary limit. No such specification has yet been made. Such a money award may provide for interest.[29] However, if the Ombudsman considers that fair compensation requires payment of a larger amount, he may recommend that the respondent pay the complainant the balance.[30]

7. Costs

In other of its jurisdictions, by powers conferred by s 230 of the FSMA, the **4.35** FOS's relevant rules include the power to award costs in certain circumstances. There is no reason to think that different principles will apply to the consumer credit jurisdiction. On this basis:

(a) it is likely that any respondent will be asked to make a contribution towards the costs of the FOS on a case by case basis;

---

[27] Ibid s 229(3).
[28] Ibid s 229(4), as amended by CCA 2006 s 61(5).
[29] Ibid s 229(8).
[30] Ibid s 229(5).

(b) the rules are unlikely to provide for making an award against a complainant in relation to a respondent's costs;

(c) however, the FOS will probably make an award against a complainant in favour of the scheme operator itself, for the purpose of providing a contribution to resources deployed in dealing with the complaint, if in the opinion of the Ombudsman, the complaint's conduct was improper or unreasonable, or the complainant was responsible for unreasonable delay.[31]

8. Appeal

4.36 Given that the FSA Rules allow the decision of an adjudicator to be reviewed by the Ombudsman himself, it is likely that the rules will contain a limited right of review. Other than that, it is unlikely that there will be any further right of appeal. Until the Consumer Credit Rules have been published, it is unclear whether, and if so where, the right of appeal from a decision of the FOS would lie.

9. Enforcement

4.37 If the complainant notifies the Ombudsman that he accepts the determination, it is binding on the respondent and the complainant, and is final.[32]

4.38 If by the date specified in the statement, the complainant has not notified the Ombudsman of his acceptance or rejection of the determination, then he is treated as having rejected it.[33] The Ombudsman must notify the respondent of the outcome.[34]

4.39 If the respondent does not comply, the complainant can, if necessary, seek to enforce the award or direction in court.

(a) A money award, including interest, which has been registered in accordance with the Consumer Credit Rules may, if a county court so orders in England and Wales, be recovered by execution issued from the county court (or otherwise) as if it were payable under an order of that court.

(b) Similarly, in Northern Ireland a money judgment may be enforced under the Judgments Enforcement (Northern Ireland) Order 1981.

(c) In Scotland, it may be enforced as if it were a decree of the Sheriff, whether or not the Sheriff could himself have granted such a decree.[35]

4.40 Failure of a licensee to abide by the decision of the FOS would not automatically result in the loss of their consumer credit licence. However, this failure

---

[31] FSMA s 230(4).
[32] Ibid s 228(5).
[33] Ibid s 228(6).
[34] Ibid s 228(7).
[35] Ibid para 16D, Part 3A, inserted by Sch 2 to the CCA 2006.

will be made known to the Office of Fair Trading (OFT) and will be taken into account when assessing the fitness of that trader to hold a licence.

E. FUNDING OF THE OMBUDSMAN SCHEME

4.41 Section 60 of the CCA 2006 prescribes the funding arrangements for the new Ombudsman scheme.

4.42 Section 60 makes it clear that the scheme will be free to consumers. It provides, however, for FOS to levy fees on licensees to meet both the costs of establishing the consumer credit jurisdiction of the Ombudsman Scheme, and to meet the costs of running that consumer credit jurisdiction.

4.43 The licensees to whom this section applies are licensees under standard licences which cover, to any extent, the carrying on of a type of business that is specified by order of the Secretary of State under s 226A(2)(e).

4.44 The FOS will consult on the fees it charges to industry—and in practice this is likely to mean that licensees will pay a small annual levy, and a standard case fee if the case is in excess of a certain number per year. For the vast majority of consumer credit firms, this would mean never having to pay a fee to access the scheme, and simply contributing a small levy for the benefits of an industry-wide dispute resolution mechanism.

4.45 Again, the rules governing funding, and the fees required by way of levy and case fee, will probably be contained in the Consumer Credit Rules.[36]

F. VARIOUS CONSEQUENTIAL AMENDMENTS RELATING TO THE OMBUDSMAN SCHEME

4.46 Section 353 of the FSMA, which relates to powers to allow the disclosure of information, is amended to allow the Ombudsman to disclose information about cases and decisions to the OFT to assist or enable the OFT to discharge its licensing functions under the CCA 1974.

G. THE IMPLICATIONS OF THE CONSUMER CREDIT SCHEME

4.47 The Government's intention, in introducing the consumer credit scheme into the FOS's jurisdiction, was to 'make it easier to resolve disputes in a speedy, fair and inexpensive manner. This would benefit both firms and consumers'.[37]

---

[36] Ibid para 16C(1) of new Part 3A of Sch 17, inserted by Sch 2 to the CCA 2006.
[37] Paragraph 3.44 of the White Paper *Fair, Clear and Competitive—The Consumer Credit Market in the 21st Century*.

4.48   A complaint to the FOS will usually be a precursor to litigation by a consumer. The scheme may resolve many low value disputes initiated by the consumer, and it may therefore have an impact on the number of such claims that are commenced in the county courts. On the other hand, the scheme may encourage people to pursue their legal rights and may, perversely, have the opposite effect. Time will tell.

4.49   The scheme is unlikely to have any discernible impact on the number of actions brought by licensees.

4.50   Once a claim has been issued, it is likely that the courts will be able to stay an action and refer it to the ADR at the judge's discretion. Similarly, the FOS will, of course, be able to refer a complainant to the court if he feels unable to deal with the dispute. It is tolerably clear, however, that most cases will not be able to be dealt with in both the court and the FOS simultaneously, except in very particular circumstances where the outcome of the scheme determination will not affect the civil claim.

5

STATEMENTS

A. INTRODUCTION

One way in which the Consumer Credit Act 1974 (CCA 1974) provides protec- **5.01** tion for the consumer is by requiring the creditor to provide the debtor with information about his statutory rights, and about the state of his account, at various stages in their relationship. Thus:

(a) Before the agreement is made, a creditor is only required to provide a prospective debtor with pre-contractual information in two particular circumstances: where any prospective regulated agreement is to be secured on land;[1] and in cases of distance selling.[2]

(b) On execution of a regulated agreement, of course, the debtor or hirer is provided with copies of the agreements containing all of the information prescribed by the Act and the Agreements Regulations 1983.[3]

(c) After such an agreement has been executed, the debtor or hirer is entitled,[4] on written request and payment of a fee, to be provided with copies of the executed agreement and of each document referred to in that agreement,[5] a

---

[1] Save for purchase money mortgages and bridging loans: CCA 1974 s 58(2). Generally, see s 58(1).

[2] Governed by the Distance Marketing of Consumer Financial Services Directive 2002/65/EC.

[3] See Chap 6.

[4] CCA 1974 ss 77–79.

[5] Within 12 working days of the receipt of the request: Consumer Credit (Prescribed Periods for Giving Information) Regulations 1983. No request made less than one month after a previous such request need be answered: CCA 1974 ss 77(3), 78(3), 79(3).

signed statement setting out the sums paid, sums due, and sums ultimately payable under the agreement. In addition, some debtors (ie those under regulated agreements for running-account credit) are entitled to automatic statements at periodic intervals.[6]

5.02   The White Paper *Fair, Clear and Competitive—The Consumer Credit Market in the 21st Century* (the White Paper) signalled the Government's desire to increase the amount of information given to consumers. It suggested that:

(a) pre-contractual information should hereafter be provided in relation to all prospective regulated credit agreements, so as to allow all consumers to reflect upon the prospective agreement before making a final decision, and to 'shop around' for the best deals available;

(b) post-contractual information should be provided, regularly and without request, in every case, so that all consumers were kept aware of the outstanding amounts owed under any agreement, and such information would enable them to keep abreast of the competitiveness of their arrangement.

5.03   Recent legislation has enacted some of these changes:

(a) the Consumer Credit (Disclosure of Information) Regulations 2004 (the Information Regulations 2004) have extended the requirement to provide pre-contractual information;

(b) the Consumer Credit (Agreements) (Amendments) Regulations 2004 reformed the form and content of regulated agreements. This reform is considered extensively in Chapter 6;

(c) sections 6 and 7 of the Consumer Credit Act 2006 (CCA 2006) have broadened the obligation to provide post-contractual information in relation to consumer credit agreements.

5.04   The new measures in (a) and (c) are considered below.

B. PRE-CONTRACTUAL INFORMATION

5.05   The Information Regulations 2004, which were made under the power in s 55 of the CCA 1974, came into force on 31 May 2005.[7]

5.06   In summary, the Regulations require any prospective creditor or owner to disclose to the debtor or hirer, in a separate document, the information required

---

[6] CCA 1974 s 78(4).

[7] If a consumer returned a signed agreement on the old style form in the three-month transitional period allowed for in Regulation 18 of the Consumer Credit (Agreements) (Amendment) Regulations 2004, he/she should have been provided with pre-contract information. However, provided the relevant terms have not changed, this would be the pre-contract information created for the new style of Agreement that would by then be necessary.

by the Consumer Credit (Agreements) Regulations 1983 (the Agreements Regulations 1983) if the proposed transaction were eventually executed.

Regulation 2 of the Information Regulations 2004 provides that such obliga- **5.07** tions do not apply to agreements to which s 58 of the Act applies (ie agreements secured on land) and to distance contracts (ie a regulated agreement made under an organized distance sales or service-provision scheme).[8] This is because, as explained above, similar obligations already apply in such cases.

Regulation 3 of the Information Regulations 2004 specifies the types of **5.08** information, and the statements of protection and remedies, which must be disclosed to the debtor or hirer before the regulated agreement is made. It provides that:

(a) in the case of any proposed regulated consumer credit agreement, the disclosure must include all of the information and statements prescribed by Regulation 2 of the Agreements Regulations 1983, which includes all of the information relevant to the particular type of contract that is included in Schedule 1 to those regulations;

(b) in the case of a proposed regulated consumer hire agreement, this information must include all the information and statements prescribed by Regulation 3 of the Agreements Regulations 1983, and by Schedule 3;

(c) in the case of a proposed modifying agreement which is, or is treated as, a regulated consumer credit agreement, this information must include all the information and statements prescribed by Regulations 2(3) and 7(2) of the Agreements Regulations 1983, and by Schedule 8;

(d) in the case of a modifying agreement which is or is treated as a regulated consumer hire agreement, the information must include the information and statements prescribed by Regulations 3(3) and 7(9) of the Agreements Regulations 1983, and by Schedule 8.

If the creditor or owner does not know the information at the time of this **5.09** disclosure, he must disclose estimated information based on such assumptions as he may reasonably make in all the circumstances of the case.[9]

Regulation 4 of the Information Regulations 2004 prescribes the manner in **5.10** which that information must be disclosed. It provides that the information and the statements of protection must be:

(a) easily legible and, where applicable, of a colour which is readily distinguishable from the background medium upon which they are displayed;

(b) not interspersed with any information or wording apart from sub-totals, total amounts and cross references to the terms of the agreement;

(c) of equal prominence except that headings may be afforded more prominence whether by capital letters, underlining, large or bold print or otherwise; and

---

[8] See the definition in Regulation 1.
[9] Information Regulations 2004 Reg 3(2).

(d) contained in a document which:
    (i) is separate from the document embodying the relevant agreement (within the meaning of Regulation 3) and any other document referred to in the document embodying that agreement;
    (ii) is headed with the words 'pre-contract information';
    (iii) does not contain any other information or wording apart from the heading referred to in sub-paragraph (ii);
    (iv) is on paper or on another durable medium which is available and accessible to the debtor or hirer; and
    (v) is of a nature that enables the debtor or hirer to remove it from the place where it is disclosed to him.

5.11 This information will mimic that found at the start of the new-form regulated consumer credit or hire agreement. However, the creditor or owner may decide upon the order in which he displays the information.

5.12 Failure to comply with these regulations means that the regulated agreement is not properly executed[10] and is thus enforceable only on an order of the court.[11]

C. POST-CONTRACTUAL INFORMATION

5.13 Under the old scheme, regular periodic statements of account were only obligatory under regulated agreements for running-account credit. The new Act provides that most debtors will be entitled to regular and unprompted statements of account. No such provisions have been introduced in relation to consumer hire agreements, and s 79 is therefore untouched by these reforms.

5.14 This chapter therefore considers the current schemes for the provision of post-contractual information, and discusses the new regimes that will soon apply to credit agreements in context. As fixed-sum credit agreements (such as loan, credit sale, hire-purchase and conditional sale agreements) and running-account credit agreements (such as a bank overdraft or credit card facility) are treated slightly differently, this chapter will deal with each in turn.

1. Fixed-sum Credit Agreements

(a) *The Old Scheme under Section 77: Information on Request*

5.15 Under the old scheme, the creditor under a fixed-sum credit agreement is only obliged to provide a debtor with information about the agreement, and the state of his account, on written request and after payment of a nominal fee.

---

[10] CCA 1974 ss 55(2) and 127.
[11] See Chap 7.

Section 77 of the CCA 1974 requires the creditor under an agreement for **5.16** fixed-sum credit to provide the debtor with a copy of the executed agreement and a statement of account on request. It provides that:

(1) The creditor under a regulated agreement of fixed-sum credit, within the prescribed period after receiving a request in writing to that effect from the debtor and in payment of a fee of £1, shall give the debtor a copy of the executed agreement (if any) and of any document referred to in it, together with a statement signed by or on behalf of the creditor showing, according to the information to which it is practicable for him to refer:
  (a) The total sum paid under the agreement by the debtor;
  (b) The total sum which has become payable under the agreement by the debtor but remains unpaid, and the various amounts comprised in that total sum, with the date when each became due; and
  (c) The total sum which is to become payable under the agreement by the debtor, and the various amounts comprised in that total sum, with the date or mode determining the date, when each becomes due.
(2) If the creditor possess insufficient information to enable him to ascertain the amounts and dates mentioned in subsection (1)(c), he should be taken to comply with that paragraph if his statement under subsection (1) gives the basis on which, under the regulated agreement, they would fall to be ascertained.

Such information must be provided within 12 working days of receipt.[12]   **5.17**
These rights do not apply to: **5.18**

(a) an agreement under which no sum is, or will, or may become, payable by the debtor;[13] or

(b) a request made less than one month after a previous request under that subsection relating to the same agreement was complied with;[14] or

(c) a non-commercial agreement.[15]

A statement given to a debtor under this section is binding upon the creditor, **5.19** subject to the power of the court to grant any necessary relief.[16]

The penalties for failing to comply with a request within the prescribed time **5.20** are set out in subsection (4), which reads:

(4) If the creditor under an agreement fails to comply with subsection (1):
  (a) he is not entitled, while the default continues, to enforce the agreement; and
  (b) if the default continues for one month he commits an offence.

These are serious consequences because: **5.21**

(a) the creditor may not enforce the agreement at all. This operates as a

---

[12] Consumer Credit (Prescribed Periods for Giving Information) Regulations 1983: and see *Goldsmith's Company v West Metropolitan Railway Company* [1904] 1 KB 1.
[13] CCA 1974 s 77(3)(a).
[14] Ibid s 77(3)(b).
[15] Ibid s 77(5). See definition in CCA 1974 s 189(1).
[16] Ibid s 172(3).

complete bar to enforcement—and there is no power in the court to order otherwise;[17]

(b) non-compliance is likely to be a relevant consideration in the exercise of the Office of Fair Trading's (OFT) licensing powers.[18] Indeed, any conviction has to be notified to the OFT.[19]

(b) *The New Provisions Introduced by the Consumer Credit Act 2006: Annual Statements*

5.22 The creditor's duty to react to a request is now supplemented by a duty to provide statements on an annual basis that reflect the current obligations imposed by s 78 in relation to running-account credit.

5.23 Section 6 of the CCA 2006, which is expected to come into force in April 2008, inserts s 77A into the CCA 1974, which requires a creditor under a regulated agreement for fixed-sum credit to:

... within the period of one year beginning with the day after the day on which the agreement is made, give the debtor a statement under this section; and after the giving of that statement, shall give the debtor further statements under this section at intervals of not more than one year.[20]

5.24 There are certain exceptions. Such information need not be given:

(a) where there is no sum payable under the agreement by the debtor,[21] and there is no sum which will or may become so payable.

(b) in relation to non-commercial agreements and small agreements.[22]

5.25 The new s 77A contains no guidance as to the form and content of statements under this section. Regulations made under this section may, however, make such provision.[23]

5.26 Section 7(3) of the CCA 2006 amends s 185(2) of the CCA 1974 to allow a debtor, where credit is extended to two or more debtors jointly, to provide a dispensing notice to the creditor so as to relieve the creditor of the obligation to provide periodic statements to that debtor. Section 185(2) now provides:

(2) Notwithstanding subsection (1)(a), where credit is provided under an agreement to two or more debtors jointly, in performing his duties—
  (a) in the case of fixed-sum credit, under section 77A, or
  (b) in the case of running-account credit, under section 78(4),

---

[17] As enforcement includes the service of the default notice under s 87(1), it appears that a default notice served during the period of such non-compliance is invalid.

[18] See CCA 1974 s 25.

[19] CCA 1974 s 166.

[20] CCA 2006 s 77A(1).

[21] CCA 1974 as inserted by CCA 2006 s 77A(4)(a).

[22] Ibid s 77A(8).

[23] Ibid s 77A(2). See also, for regulations governing such matters in relation to running-account agreements, the Consumer Credit (Running-Account Credit Information) Regulations 1983.

The creditor need not give statements to any debtor who has signed and given to him a notice (a 'dispensing notice') authorising him not to comply in the debtor's case with section 77A or (as the case may be) 78(4).

(2A) A dispensing notice given by a debtor is operative from when it is given to the creditor until it is revoked by a further notice given to the creditor by the debtor.

(2B) But subsection (2) does not apply if (apart from this subsection) dispensing notices would be operative in relation to all of the debtors to whom the credit is provided.

(2C) Any dispensing notices operative in relation to an agreement shall cease to have effect if any of the debtors dies.

(2D) A dispensing notice which is operative in relation to an agreement shall be operative also in relation to any subsequent agreement which, in relation to the earlier agreement, is a modifying agreement.

Section 77A(6) contains the sanctions for non-compliance. They are more **5.27** draconian than under s 77:

(6) Where this subsection applies in relation to a failure to give a statement under this section to the debtor—
  (a) the creditor shall not be entitled to enforce the agreement during the period of non-compliance;
  (b) the debtor shall have no liability to pay any sum of interest to the extent calculated by reference to the period of non-compliance or to any part of it; and
  (c) the debtor shall have no liability to pay any default sum which (apart from this paragraph)—
    (i) would have become payable during the period of non-compliance; or
    (ii) would become payable after the end of that period in connection with a breach of the agreement which occurs during that period (whether or not the breach continues after the end of that period).

2. Running-account Credit Agreements

(a) *The Current Scheme under Section 78*

Running-account credit agreements (such as loan, credit sale, hire-purchase and **5.28** conditional sale agreements) are currently subject to two regimes: information provided on request, and information provided automatically.

(b) *Information on Request: Section 78(1)–(3)*

Creditors under running-account credit agreements are obliged to provide **5.29** copies of the agreement, and financial information to debtors, on request.[24] The provisions of s 78(1)–(3) are in similar form to those in s 77 imposing mirror duties in relation to fixed-sum credit, and are not reproduced here.

As with fixed-sum credit agreements, these rules do not apply to any agree- **5.30** ment under which no sum is, or will or may become, payable, or in a situation in

---

[24] CCA 2006 s 78(1)–(3).

which a request made less than one month after a previous request has been complied with[25] or to non-commercial agreements.[26]

5.31   The same penalties prescribed by s 77 apply for default of these provisions—namely an inability to enforce the agreement in the period of non-compliance, and the commission of offence if the default continues for one month.

(c) *Statements Provided Automatically*

5.32   In addition to the scheme for information on request shared with fixed-sum credit agreements, s 78(4)–(5) provides for automatic statements to be sent at periodic intervals in regulated running-account credit agreements.[27]

5.33   Section 78(4) provides:

> (4) Where running-account credit is provided under a regulated agreement, the creditor shall give the debtor statements in prescribed form, and with the prescribed contents:
>   (a) showing according to the information to which it is practicable for him to refer the state of the account at regular intervals or not more than 12 months, and
>   (b) where the agreement provides, in relation to specified periods, for the making of payments by the debtor, or the charging against him of interest of any other sum or any other sum, showing according to the information to which it is practicable for him to refer the state of the account at the end of those periods during which there is any movement in the account.

5.34   Section 78(5) provides that such statements must be given within a prescribed period,[28] namely:

(a) One month from the end of the period to which the statement relates, if it includes a demand for payment; or

(b) 12 months from the end of the period to which it relates if there is no credit or debit balance at the end of that period; or

(c) where there has been no credit or debit balance on the account at any time in the period in which the statement relates, 12 months from the date of the next credit or debit balance of the account; and

(d) in any other case six months from the end of the period to which the statement relates.[29]

5.35   The form and content of any such periodic statement is prescribed by the Consumer Credit (Running-Account Credit Information) Regulations 1983. They include:

(a) any opening balance standing on the account at the beginning of the period to which the statement relates and the balance at the end of that period;

---

[25] See s (3).
[26] Subsection (7).
[27] Save small agreements.
[28] See the Consumer Credit (Prescribed Periods for Giving Information) Regulations 1983.
[29] See Reg 3 of the Consumer Credit (Running-Account Credit Information) Regulations 1983.

(b) the date of any movement in the account shown on the statement during the period to which the statement relates and the date of the end of that period;

(c) the amount of any payments made into the account by, or to the credit of, the debtor during the period to which the statement relates;

(d) the amount of any drawing on the account by the debtor during the period to which the statement relates, with sufficient information to enable the debtor to identify the drawing;

(e) the amount of any interest or other charges payable by the debtor, and applied to the account during the period to which the statement relates, whether or not the interest or other charges relate only to that period;

(f) where the statement shows that interest has been applied to the account during the period to which the statement relates:
  (i) sufficient information to enable the debtor to check the calculation of the interest so applied; or
  (ii) the rate of interest which has been used to calculate the amount of the interest so applied or, if the rate has varied, each rate of interest which has been so used and the time during which each rate applied; or
  (iii) a statement that the rate, or each rate, of interest which has been used to calculate the amount of interest so applied will be provided by the creditor on request, together with a clear explanation of the manner in which the amount of the interest so applied has been calculated.

Unlike statements provided on request, such periodic statements are not binding on the creditor.[30] Nor does a breach of this requirement for a periodic statement carry any particular sanction for non-compliance—unlike in the case of periodic statements provided in respect of fixed-sum agreements. Repeated non-compliance with the requirements of the subsection would, however, probably be treated as a serious matter by the OFT in the exercise of its functions relating to licensing.[31]   **5.36**

(d) *The New Provisions Introduced by the Consumer Credit Act 2006*
Section 78 has been amended by s 7 of the CCA 2006, which is expected to come into force in April 2008, in two ways: **5.37**

(a) the prescribed information contained in a periodic statement may in future contain information about the consequences of failing to make repayments or making minimum repayments. Section 7(1) inserts a new s 78(4A):

(4A) Regulations may require a statement under subsection (4) to contain also information in the prescribed terms about the consequences of the debtor—
(a) failing to make payments as required by the agreement; or
(b) only making payments of a prescribed description in prescribed circumstances.

---

[30] See CCA 1974 s 172(1); an estoppel may be raised.
[31] See CCA 1974 s 25.

(b) as explained above in relation to statements concerning fixed-sum credit, s 185 of the CCA 1974 is amended to provide that where an agreement is made with more than one debtor, then any one of those debtors may sign a dispensing notice authorizing the creditor not to comply in the debtor's case with ss 77A or 78(4).

D. CONCLUSION

5.38 The CCA 2006 provides that, at regular intervals, consumers should be made aware of the outstanding amounts that they owe under regulated consumer credit agreements—whether fixed-sum credit agreements or running-account credit agreements—and informed if they fall into arrears or have incurred additional charges upon which interest will be charged. Practitioners should be aware that slightly different rules apply depending on whether the agreement is a fixed-sum credit agreement or running-account credit agreement.[32] No such changes are to be introduced in relation to the provision of information about consumer hire agreements.

---

[32] CCA 1974 ss 77, 78, and 79, respectively.

6

AGREEMENTS

A. INTRODUCTION

The form and content of regulated agreements, whether consumer credit agree- **6.01** ments, consumer hire agreements, or modified agreements, are prescribed by various regulations, namely: the Consumer Credit Act 1974 (CCA 1974), the Consumer Credit (Agreements) Regulations 1983[1] (the Agreements Regulations 1983) and the Consumer Credit (Cancellation Notices and Copies of Documents) Regulations 1983[2] (the CCN Regulations 1983).

From 31 May 2005, the Agreements Regulations 1983 were substantially **6.02** amended by the Consumer Credit (Agreements) (Amendment) Regulations 2004 (the Amendment Regulations 2004). Given the importance of these changes, we thought it important to discuss these changes in this work alongside those wrought by the new Act.

B. THE STRUCTURE OF REGULATION

The main statutory provisions governing the formalities required of regulated **6.03** agreements are those in ss 60 to 64 of the CCA 1974. Compliance with these

---

[1] As amended by SI 1984/1600, SI 1985/666, SI 1988/2047, SI 1999/3177, and SI 2004/1482.
[2] As amended by SI 1984/1108, SI 1985/666, SI 1988/2047, and SI 1989/591.

various requirements is vital because a regulated agreement that is not properly executed cannot be enforced except by order of the Court.[3]

6.04 In summary, any regulated agreement must, if it is to qualify as a properly executed agreement, satisfy the following broad requirements:

(a) in all cases, the terms must be embodied in a signed and legible document that complies with s 61 of the CCA 1974;

(b) in most cases, the debtor or hirer must be supplied with copies of the contract document which conform with the requirements of the CCN Regulations 1983;

(c) if the agreement is a cancellable agreement, the agreement must contain a prescribed notice of cancellation rights or, in cases where the agreement is executed on the signature of the debtor or hirer, a separate notice of cancellation rights must be provided.

6.05 This chapter concerns itself only with changes made to the first of these requirements—namely the form and contents of agreements prescribed under s 61 of the CCA 1974. This section provides that a regulated agreement is not properly executed unless a legible document containing all of the prescribed terms and conforming to Regulations made under s 60(1) of the CCA 1974 is signed in the prescribed manner, both by the debtor or hirer, and by, or on behalf of, the creditor or owner.[4]

6.06 The Regulations that prescribe the strict form and content of such agreements are the Agreements Regulations 1983. Its requirements are intended to ensure that any debtor or hirer is made aware of:[5]

(a) the rights and duties conferred or imposed upon him by the agreement;

(b) the amount and rate of the total charge for credit made under any consumer credit agreement;

(c) the protection and remedies available to the consumer under the CCA 1974; and

(d) any other matters which, in the opinion of the Secretary of State, it is desirable to include in the agreement for such purposes.

6.07 The Agreements Regulations 1983, and their Schedules, therefore set out in exhaustive detail the prescribed information to be contained in any documents embodying regulated agreements. Different requirements apply to different types of agreement, depending on whether the agreement is a consumer credit agreement, a consumer hire agreement, or a modifying agreement. Within each of these broad categories, different provisions apply to different situations (such

---

[3] CCA 1974 s 65(1). See also CCA 1974 ss 127–128.
[4] Ibid s 61(1).
[5] Ibid s 60(1).

as running-account or fixed-sum credit, debtor–creditor–supplier or debtor–creditor etc).

These strict requirements have now been revised by the Amendment Regulations 2004. **6.08**

This chapter will consider these amendments to the Agreements Regulations 1983 as they affect, first, consumer credit agreements; second, consumer hire agreements; and, third, modifying agreements. **6.09**

C. AMENDED FORM AND CONTENT OF CONSUMER CREDIT AGREEMENTS

1. Definition of Consumer Credit Agreement

A regulated consumer credit agreement is an agreement made between two parties, one of whom (the debtor) is an individual, and the other (the creditor) is 'any other person', and does not fall into any of the categories of statutory exemption.[6] Until the financial limits are removed by s 2 of the CCA 2006,[7] there is the additional requirement that the credit does not exceed £25,000.[8] **6.10**

The form and content of regulated consumer credit agreements are prescribed by Regulations 2, 5, and 6 of, and Schedules 1, 2, 4, 5(i), 6, and 7 to, the Agreement Regulations 1983 as amended by the Amendment Regulations 2004. These changes came into force on 31 May 2005.[9] **6.11**

2. Amended Regulation 2(1) and Schedule 1 to the Agreements Regulations: Revised Form and Content

Regulation 2(1) of the Agreements Regulations 1983 provides that documents embodying regulated consumer credit agreements (other than modifying agreements) shall contain the information that is set out in column 2 of Schedule 1 to the Agreements Regulations 1983, insofar as it relates to the type of agreements set out in column 1. **6.12**

Schedule 1 has been revised by Regulation 10 of the Amendment Regulations 2004. These revisions require additional information to be included in such consumer credit agreements. **6.13**

The following amendments have been made to the information prescribed by different paragraphs in Schedule 1: **6.14**

(a) Paragraph 1 requires a statement of the type of agreement in prescribed wording (eg 'Hire-Purchase Agreement regulated by the Consumer Credit

---

[6] Ibid s 16.
[7] See Chap 2.
[8] CCA 1974 s 8.
[9] There is a three-month transitional period allowed in Reg 18 of the Amendment Regulations 2004.

Act 1974'). The recent amendments have increased the number of prescribed statements to include 'Fixed-Sum Loan Agreement regulated by the Consumer Credit Act 1974' and 'Credit Card Agreement regulated by the Consumer Credit Act 1974'.[10]

(b) New paragraph 8A requires a statement of the duration—or minimum duration—of the agreement.[11]

(c) Paragraphs 9 and 10 require a statement of the total charge for credit, with a list of its constituent parts, and the rate of interest on the credit to be provided. It is now an additional requirement that the agreement explains how and when interest charges have been calculated and applied, in particular identifying the particular assumptions used in calculating the APR and the total charge for credit in running-account credit agreements.[12]

(d) New paragraph 14A requires a statement of the order, or proportions in which, any amount paid by the debtor, which is not sufficient to discharge the total debt then due under the agreement, will be applied or appropriated by the creditor towards the discharge of those sums should be stated.[13]

(e) Paragraph 22, which prescribes the charges, now includes a list of all and any of the charges payable under the agreement to the creditor—not just those payable on default as before.[14]

(f) New paragraph 23 requires that, in non-cancellable agreements, there should be included an additional statement that the debtor has no right to cancel the agreement under the CCA 1974 or otherwise.[15]

(g) New paragraph 24 requires that, in agreements for fixed-sum credit for a term of more than one month, the agreement should now provide examples showing the amount that would be payable if the debtor exercised its right to discharge its indebtedness under s 94 of the Act, and other information.[16]

3. Amended Regulation 2(4): the Order of the Prescribed Contents

6.15 Regulation 2(4) had previously provided that

the information about financial and related particulars set out in paragraphs 3 to 19 of Schedule 1 to these Regulations, and also the statements of the protection and remedies available to debtors under the Act specified in Forms 5, 7 and 9 of Part I of Schedule 2, shall be shown together as a whole.

---

[10] Amendment Regulations 2004 Reg 10(2).
[11] Ibid Reg 10(3).
[12] Ibid Reg 10(4)–(6). See also Schedule 7 to the Agreements Regulations 1983.
[13] Amendment Regulations 2004 Reg 10(6).
[14] Ibid Reg 10(7).
[15] Ibid Reg 10(8).
[16] Ibid Reg 10(7).

Amended Regulation 2(4) now provides that this information and these state- **6.16** ments shall not be preceded by any information apart from trade names, logos, or the reference number of the agreement, or interspersed with any other information or wording apart from subtotals of total amounts and cross references to the terms of the agreement.[17]

It also provides that this information must be given in a particular order. **6.17** Every such agreement must contain the following information, set out in the order given below under, where applicable, the headings specified below:

(a) the nature of the agreement in the wording set out in paragraph 1 of Schedule 1 to the Agreements Regulations 1983;

(b) the parties to the agreement, under which is provided the information required by paragraph 2 of Schedule 1;

(c) the heading 'key financial information', under which is grouped the financial and related particulars required by paragraphs 6–8B, 11–14, and 15–17 of Schedule 1;

(d) the heading 'other financial information', under which is stated the financial and related particulars required by paragraphs 3–5, 9, 10, 14A, and 18–19A of Schedule 1;

(e) the heading 'key information', including the information set out in paragraphs 20–24 of Schedule 1, the statements of protection and remedies set out in Schedule 2;

(f) the signature box in which is inserted the prescribed form of words and, where applicable, any separate box now required for cancellable agreements or pawn-receipt agreements.

4. Amended Regulation 2(7): Additional Form of Consent for Insurance Products

Regulation 2(7) is amended so as to require, in circumstances where the debtor is **6.18** purchasing certain insurance products on credit, a prescribed form of consent to be signed by a debtor[18] in addition to the usual signature in its prescribed box and any existing requirement for a consent in cases of land mortgages, cancellable agreements, or pawn.[19] The wording of the consent reads:

I understand that I am purchasing the product(s) ticked above on credit provided by you and that the terms relating to the credit for the products can be found in this agreement.[20]

---

[17] Agreements Regulations 1983 Reg 2(4).
[18] Amendment Regulations 2004 Reg 4.
[19] Agreements Regulations 1983 Reg 2(7)(b).
[20] Part III, Sch 5 to the Amendments Regulations 2004, amending Part II, Sch 5 to the Agreements Regulations 1983.

5. Amended Regulations 2(8) and 2(9): Contracts of Shortfall Insurance now Subsidiary Agreements

6.19 New Regulations 2(8) and 2(9) are substituted for old Regulation 2(7A). As before, documents embodying certain consumer credit agreements (the principal agreements) and embodying, or containing the option of, certain agreements (the subsidiary agreements) relating to contracts of insurance (against accident, sickness, unemployment, or death), or any contract related to a guarantee of goods, need only contain the prescribed information, statements, and signature boxes relating to the principal agreement.

6.20 The amendment extends the meaning of subsidiary agreements to cover contracts of shortfall interest.[21] 'Shortfall interest' is defined as anything in writing which contains some promise or assurance that, if the sum payable under a contract of insurance against loss or damage to goods is less than the amount necessary, then a sum up to but not exceeding that shortfall will be paid.[22]

6. Amended Regulation 5: Statutory Forms

6.21 Regulation 5 requires that the wording of any relevant form specified in Schedule 2 is to be reproduced in any such regulated agreement. The wording used in the forms in Schedule 2 has been simplified by Regulation 11 of the Amendment Regulations.

7. Amended Regulation 6: Signing of the Agreement

6.22 Regulation 6(2) still provides that the terms of any such consumer credit agreement 'be easily legible and of a colour which is readily distinguishable from the colour of the paper'.

6.23 The amended regulation requires all lettering, apart from handwriting, to be of equal prominence, except that headings, trade names, and names of parties to the agreement may be afforded more prominence whether by capital letters, underlining, larger or bold print, or otherwise.[23]

8. Amended Schedule 7—Provisions Relating to Disclosure of the APR

6.24 Schedule 7 to the Agreements Regulations 1983 has been amended[24] by providing for the use of particular assumptions in calculating the APR and the Total Charge for Credit that are to be stated in running-account credit agreements.

---

[21] See Reg 2(8)(b).
[22] See definition in Reg 1(2).
[23] See Reg 6(2), as amended by the Amendment Regulations 2004.
[24] Regulation 15 of the Amendments Regulations 2004.

D. AMENDED FORM AND CONTENT OF CONSUMER HIRE AGREEMENTS

1. Definition of Consumer Hire Agreement

A regulated consumer hire agreement is an agreement for the bailment or hire of **6.25** goods between two parties, one of whom (the hirer) is an individual, and the other (the owner) is 'a person', being an agreement that:

(a) is not a hire-purchase agreement;

(b) is capable of subsisting for more than three months;

(c) until the financial limits are removed by s 2 of the CCA 2006,[25] does not require the hirer to make payments exceeding £25,000;[26] and

(d) does not fall into one of the categories of exemption.[27]

The form and content of regulated consumer hire agreements are prescribed **6.26** by Regulations 3, 5, and 6 of, and Schedules 2, 3, 5(ii), 6, and 7 to, the Agreement Regulations 1983 as substantially amended by the Amendment Regulations 2004.[28]

2. Amended Regulation 3(1) and Schedule 3 to the Agreements Regulations: Revised Form and Content

Regulation 3(1) of the Agreements Regulations 1983 provides that documents **6.27** embodying regulated consumer hire agreements (other than modifying agreements) shall contain the information that is set out in column 2 of Schedule 3 to the Agreements Regulations 1983, insofar as it relates to the type of agreements set out in column 1.

Schedule 3 has been revised by Regulation 12 of the Amendment Regulations **6.28** 2004. These revisions require additional information to be included in such consumer hire agreements.

The following amendments have been made to the information prescribed by **6.29** the paragraphs of Schedule 3:

(a) Paragraph 1 requires a statement of the type of agreement in prescribed wording (eg 'Hire Agreement regulated by the Consumer Credit Act 1974'). The recent amendments require, where appropriate, the inclusion of the words 'secured on' and the address of the relevant land at the end of the heading.[29]

---

[25] See Chap 2.
[26] CCA 1974 s 15(1)(c).
[27] Ibid s 16.
[28] For transitional provisions, see Reg 18.
[29] Amendment Regulations 2004 Reg 12(2).

(b) Paragraph 10, which prescribes the charges, is now to include a list of any charges payable under the agreement to the owner upon default by the hirer or his relative. It should also contain a statement indicating any term of the agreement which provides for charges—insofar as such charges are not already shown.[30]

(c) Paragraph 11 is inserted, which now provides that any non-cancellable agreement should contain a statement to that effect.[31]

3. Amended Regulation 3(4): the Order of the Prescribed Contents

6.30 Regulation 3(4) had previously provided that:

the information about financial and related particulars set out in paragraphs 3 to 8 of Schedule 3 to these Regulations shall be shown together as a whole in documents embodying regulated consumer hire agreements and not interspersed with other information apart from subtotals of total amounts and cross-references to terms of the agreement.

6.31 Mirroring the changes introduced into consumer credit agreements, amended Regulation 3(4) provides that, in addition, this information shall not be 'preceded by any information apart from trade names, logos or the reference number of the agreement or interspersed with any other information or wording apart from subtotals of total amounts and cross references to the terms of the agreement'.[32]

6.32 As with credit agreements, this information must henceforth be given in a particular order. Every such agreement must contain the following information, set out in the order given below under, where applicable, the headings specified below:

(a) the nature of the agreement as prescribed in paragraph 1 of Schedule 3 to the Agreement Regulations 1983;

(b) the parties to the agreement as set out in paragraph 2 of Schedule 3;

(c) the heading 'key financial information', under which is grouped the financial and related particulars required by paragraphs 3 to 8 of Schedule 3;

(d) the heading 'key information', including the information set out in paragraphs 9 to 11 of Schedule 3, and the statements of protection and remedies set out in Schedule 4; and

(e) the signature box in which is inserted the prescribed form of words and, where applicable, any separate box now required for cancellable agreements or pawn-receipt agreements.

---

[30] Amendment Regulations 2004 Reg 12(3).
[31] Ibid Reg 12(4).
[32] Agreement Regulations 1983 Reg 3(4).

4. Amended Regulation 5: Statutory Forms

Insofar as it relates to consumer hire agreements, Regulation 5 requires that the **6.33** wording of any relevant form specified in Schedule 4 is to be reproduced in documents embodying any such regulated agreement. The wording used in the forms in Schedule 4 has been simplified by Regulation 13 of the Amendment Regulations.

5. Amended Regulation 6: Signing of the Agreement

Regulation 6(2) still provides that the terms of any such consumer hire agree- **6.34** ment 'be easily legible and of a colour which is readily distinguishable from the colour of the paper'.

As with credit agreements, the amended regulation requires all lettering, apart **6.35** from handwriting, to be of equal prominence, except that headings, trade names, and names of parties to the agreement may be afforded more prominence whether by capital letters, underlining, larger or bold print, or otherwise.[33]

E. AMENDED FORM AND CONTENT OF MODIFYING AGREEMENTS

1. Definition of Modifying Agreement

The provisions of the Agreements Regulations 1983 also apply to modifying **6.36** agreements, namely those agreements which vary or supplement earlier credit agreements or earlier hire agreements, and which are, or are treated under s 82(3) of the Act as, regulated agreements.

The form and content of modifying agreements are prescribed by Regulations **6.37** 5, 6, and 7 of, and Schedules 6 and 8 to, the Agreements Regulations 1983 as amended by the Amendment Regulations 2004.

These amendments follow the same form as the amendments discussed above. **6.38**

2. Amended Regulation 7(1) and Schedule 8 to the Agreements Regulations: Revised Form and Content

Regulation 7(1) of the Agreements Regulations 1983 provides that documents **6.39** embodying modifying agreements (other than modifying agreements) shall contain the information that is set out in column 2 of Schedule 8 to the Agreements Regulations 1983, insofar as it relates to the type of agreements set out in column 1.

---

[33] See Reg 6(2), as amended by the Amendments Regulations 2004.

6.40 Schedule 8 has been revised by Regulation 17 of the Amendment Regulations 2004. As above, these revisions require additional information to be included in such modifying agreements.

6.41 The following amendments have been made to the information prescribed by the Schedule:

(a) Paragraph 1 requires a statement of the type of agreement in prescribed wording (eg 'Agreement modifying a Hire Agreement regulated by the Consumer Credit Act 1974'). The recent amendments require, where appropriate, the inclusion of the words 'secured on' and the address of the relevant land at the end of the heading.[34]

(b) Paragraph 11 is inserted, which now provides that any non-cancellable agreement should contain a statement to that effect.[35]

3. Amended Regulations 7(4) and 7(11): the Order of the Prescribed Contents

6.42 The changes to Regulation 7(4) mirror those to Regulation 2(4), and those to Regulation 7(11) reflect those to Regulation 3(4). Each has been amended in the same way as its counterpart (see above). Modifying agreements must therefore be arranged in the same order, and under the same headings, as the consumer credit agreements or the consumer hire agreements that they modify.[36]

4. Amended Regulation 6: Signing of the Agreement

6.43 Regulation 6(2) still provides that the terms of any regulated agreement 'be easily legible and of a colour which is readily distinguishable from the colour of the paper'.

6.44 As above, the amended regulation requires all lettering, apart from handwriting, to be of equal prominence, except that headings, trade names, and names of parties to the agreement may be afforded more prominence whether by capital letters, underlining, larger or bold print, or otherwise.[37]

---

[34] Amendments Regulations 2004 Reg 17(2).
[35] Ibid Reg 17(4).
[36] Agreement Regulations 1983 Reg 7(4).
[37] See Reg 6(2), as amended by the Amendment Regulations 2004.

7

DEFAULT AND ENFORCEMENT

A. THE EXISTING DEFAULT AND ENFORCEMENT PROVISIONS

1. Default and Termination

The scheme of the Consumer Credit Act 1974 (CCA 1974) has always been that **7.01** the debtor or hirer[1] should be given a detailed notice of any event which might trigger termination or the operation of any other right of the creditor or owner[2] against the debtor or, in the case of credit involving the supply of goods, against the goods themselves.

---

[1] Hereafter in this section the term 'debtor' will be used to connote both debtors and hirers unless the context otherwise demands.

[2] Hereafter in this section the term 'creditor' will be used to connote both creditors and owners unless the context otherwise demands.

7.02   The CCA 1974 has also tried, as far as practicable to ensure that the debtor has an opportunity to remedy his default before termination or any other sanction applies.

7.03   The principal provisions requiring notice to be given to the debtor in a non-default situation are contained in Part VI of the CCA 1974. Section 76 applies to agreements for a fixed period where the creditor can enforce certain rights before the end of the period. The rights are:

(a) demanding earlier payment of any sum, or
(b) recovering possession of any goods or land, or
(c) treating any right conferred on the debtor or hirer by the agreement as terminated, restricted or deferred.[3]

7.04   Section 76(1) obliges the creditor to give not less than seven days' notice before exercising any of those rights and the notice must be in the prescribed form.[4] This does not apply to a right for the creditor to restrict or defer the debtor's ability to draw on any credit, and the section does not apply to non-commercial agreements.

7.05   The principal provisions of the CCA 1974 concerning default are to be found in Part VII. Section 87 provides for the service of a default notice before the creditor can be entitled by reason of the debtor's breach of the agreement:

(a) to terminate the agreement, or
(b) to demand earlier payment of any sum, or
(c) to recover possession of any goods or land, or
(d) to treat any right conferred on the debtor or hirer by the agreement as terminated, restricted or deferred, or
(e) to enforce any security.[5]

7.06   Section 88 prescribes the contents and effect of a default notice. The notice must be in the prescribed form and specify:

(a) the nature of the alleged breach;
(b) if the breach is capable of remedy, what action is required to remedy it and the date before which that action is to be taken;
(c) if the breach is not capable of remedy, the sum (if any) required to be paid as compensation for the breach and the date before which it is to be paid.[6]

7.07   The date specified in the notice must be at least seven days after the date of service of the default notice and the creditor is precluded from taking action before the period has elapsed.[7] If the debtor remedies the breach or pays the sum required to be paid as compensation for breach within the time specified, the breach is to be treated as not having occurred.[8]

---

[3] CCA 1974 s 76(1).
[4] See below for forms.
[5] CCA 1974 s 87(1).
[6] Ibid s 88(1).
[7] Ibid s 88(2).   [8] Ibid s 89.

Under s 90 the creditor is prevented from retaking possession of goods let on **7.08** hire-purchase or sold on conditional sale if the debtor has paid one-third or more of the total price of the goods and the property in the goods remains in the creditor. The penalty for disregarding this is severe. Under s 91, if the goods are repossessed in contravention of s 90, the agreement is automatically terminated and the debtor is not only released from all future liability but can recover from the creditor all sums already paid under the agreement.

Section 93 prohibits charging a debtor who is in default interest on unpaid **7.09** sums at a rate higher than the rate of interest charged on the original credit.

The termination equivalent of s 76 (agreements for a fixed period where the **7.10** creditor can terminate other than for default before the end of the period) is s 98 which provides that a creditor is not entitled to terminate a regulated agreement except on giving not less than seven days' notice in the prescribed form.

The right of the debtor or hirer to terminate hire-purchase, conditional sale, **7.11** or hire agreements[9] is unaffected by the Consumer Credit Act 2006 (CCA 2006) and need not be discussed here.

As may be expected in the light of the rules relating to the form and content **7.12** of agreements, default, termination, and similar notices are the subject of strict regulations, in this instance the Consumer Credit (Enforcement, Default and Termination Notices) Regulations 1983 (the Termination Regulations).

As it has not yet been thought necessary to update the Termination Regula- **7.13** tions and they remain unaffected by the CCA 2006, it is sufficient to say at this stage that they contain detailed rules about content and legibility. Schedules 1 and 3 specify the content of notices served under s 76 and s 98 respectively, and Schedule 2 the content of notices served under s 87. The forms are replete with statements of the debtor's rights and advice as to what to do (obligatorily to be expressed in block capitals) and default notices must contain the necessary statements of remedial action or monetary payment required to deal with the breach.

Finally under this head, it should be noted that s 111 imposes a duty to serve a **7.14** copy of any notice under s 76, 87, or 98 not only on the debtor but also on any surety.

Save for failure to serve notice on the surety, which can be cured by an **7.15** enforcement order under s 127, failure to serve the requisite notice under s 76, 87, or 98 in the requisite form is generally fatal to any enforcement by the court.

2. Enforcement

Enforcement by the court is, of course, the norm. Apart from the restricted right **7.16** of the creditor under a hire-purchase or conditional sale agreement to retake

---

[9] Ibid ss 99–101.

possession of the goods,[10] enforcement, even if it is only an action for arrears of instalments, must be by legal process.

7.17   The CCA 1974 uses enforcement as a sanction to bolster the other provisions of the Act. An application for an enforcement order must be made in the case of:

(a) section 65(1) (improperly executed agreements), or
(b) section 105(7)(a) or (b) (improperly executed security instruments), or
(c) section 111(2) (failure to serve copy of notice on surety), or
(d) section 124(1) or (2) (taking of negotiable instrument in contravention of section 123).[11]

7.18   Where an application for an enforcement order is made by the creditor, the court must dismiss the application if, but only if, it considers it just to do so having regard to the prejudice caused to any person by the contravention and the degree of culpability for it and its own powers to make orders under ss 135 and 136 to impose conditions and vary agreements. A court making an enforcement order can reduce the amount payable by the debtor to compensate him for any prejudice suffered as a result of the contravention.

7.19   The real teeth of s 127 lay in subsections (3) to (5). Subsections (3) and (4) prevented a court from making any enforcement order at all. Under (3), the court could not make an enforcement order where s 61(1)(a) was not complied with unless a document, whether or not in the prescribed form and complying with the Consumer Credit (Agreements) Regulations 1983 (the Agreements Regulations), contained all the 'prescribed terms' and was signed by the debtor. The 'prescribed terms' were laid down by Regulation 6(1) of the Agreements Regulations 1983[12] and their omission was completely fatal to the enforcement of any agreement however much it otherwise complied with the regulations. Even when subsection (3) did permit enforcement, the court could direct that the agreement was to take effect 'as if it did not include a term omitted from the document signed by the debtor or hirer'.

7.20   Subsection (4) forbade enforcement in the case of a cancellable agreement if a provision of s 62[13] or s 63[14] was not complied with and the creditor did not give a copy of the executed agreement and any other document referred to in it to the debtor before the enforcement proceedings were started. It also forbade enforcement where s 64(1) was not complied with. In practice, breach of s 64(1), which obliges the creditor to give notices of cancellation rights in the prescribed form, proved the most common situation in which enforcement was barred. The provisions of s 64 and the Consumer Credit (Cancellation Notices and Copies of Documents) Regulations 1983 were of such complexity that even experienced lawyers and finance houses occasionally slipped up.

---

[10] Paragraph 7.08 above.
[11] CCA 1974 s 127(1).
[12] See Chap 6 above.
[13] Duty to supply copy of unexecuted agreement.
[14] Duty to supply copy of executed agreement.

Subsections (3) and (4) were always considered to be harsh in their applica- **7.21** tion. In the early 2000s, while hearing an appeal concerning a regulated pawn agreement which was held to be unenforceable under s 127(3), the Court of Appeal conceived the bright idea that this might contravene the Human Rights Act 1998 and, in particular, Part I of Article 6 and Part II of Article 1 of the European Convention on Human Rights. Having heard argument from the parties and the Secretary of State, the Court duly declared s 127(3) incompatible with the Convention and granted a certificate accordingly.[15]

The Department of Trade and Industry made it quite clear that it did not **7.22** propose to act on the certificate of incompatibility and appealed to the House of Lords. Although basing itself partly on the absence of retrospective effect of the 1998 Act, the House none the less decided that s 127(3) was not incompatible with the Convention. If Parliament in its wisdom had decided that minor clerical errors in a regulated agreement should deliver a windfall to an undeserving defaulter, then so be it: it was not for the courts to interfere.[16]

3. Time Orders

Under s 129 the court is empowered to make a time order: **7.23**

(a) on an application for an enforcement order; or
(b) on an application made by a debtor or hirer ... after service on him of [a notice under s 76, s 87, or s 98]
(c) in an action brought by a creditor or owner to enforce a regulated agreement or any security or recover possession of any goods or land to which a regulated agreement relates.[17]

A time order can order payment by the debtor or any surety of any sum owing **7.24** to be made by instalments fixed by the court in the light of the means of the debtor or surety.[18] It can also order the remedy by the debtor of any breach of a regulated agreement other than failure to pay money within a time specified by the court.[19]

Ancillary provisions about time orders are contained in s 130 including **7.25** a power in the court when dealing with hire-purchase and conditional sale agreements to legislate for future payments as well as outstanding arrears.

Section 129 does not, however, give a court *carte blanche* to postpone **7.26** repayment indefinitely and the court should normally only grant a time order where the debtor is in temporary financial difficulties and does have some prospect of ultimately paying off his indebtedness.[20]

---

[15] *Wilson v First County Trust Limited (No 2)* [2002] QB 74.
[16] *Wilson v First County Trust Limited (No 2)* [2004] 1 AC 816.
[17] CCA 1974 s 129(1).
[18] Ibid s 129(2)(a).
[19] Ibid s 129(2)(b).
[20] *Southern and District Finance plc v Barnes* [1995] CCLR 62.

B. DEFAULT NOTICES

7.27 A seemingly innocuous but major change to the existing default notice provisions is made by s 14 of the CCA 2006, which comes into force on 1 October 2006. In subsections (2) and (3) to s 88 of the CCA 1974 the date specified in the default notice for the debtor to remedy the breach or pay compensation has been doubled from seven days from service of the notice to fourteen days.[21] This will require all professional lenders to reorganize all their procedures and their paperwork, quite independently of all the other changes to the default and enforcement provisions.

7.28 Consequential changes are also made by s 14 of the CCA 2006. Section 88(4), which provides that a default notice must contain information 'in the prescribed terms about the consequences of failure to comply with it',[22] now provides that the notice must also contain 'any other prescribed matters relating to the agreement', thus legislating for the additional provisions relating to default which are discussed below.

7.29 A new s 88(4A) is added requiring a copy of the 'current default information sheet'[23] to be served with the default notice.

7.30 The provisions of s 14 of the CCA 2006 when brought into effect will be fully retrospective and will apply whenever the breach of the agreement occurred and whenever the agreement was made.[24]

C. 'DEFAULT SUMS'

7.31 The series of changes to the default and enforcement provisions brought about by the CCA 2006 involve the creation of a new concept, the 'default sum'. This is defined by adding a new s 187A to the CCA 1974[25] as follows:

(1) In this Act 'default sum' means, in relation to the debtor or hirer under a regulated agreement, a sum (other than a sum of interest) which is payable by him under the agreement in connection with a breach of the agreement by him.

(2) But a sum is not a default sum in relation to the debtor or hirer simply because, as a consequence of his breach of the agreement, he is required to pay it earlier than he would otherwise have had to.

7.32 Default sum is thus quite tightly defined. It does not include, for example, accrued arrears under an agreement: they are catered for elsewhere. By subsection (2), it does not include provisions for accelerated payment which are

---

[21] CCA 2006 s 14(1).
[22] In essence, those set out in the Termination Regulations.
[23] See paras 7.63–7.66 below.
[24] CCA 2006 Sch 3 para 10.
[25] Inserted by s 18 of the CCA 2006. There is a consequential amendment of the definition section—s 189(1).

triggered by default. It would, however, include liquidated damages (if the clause was otherwise valid under the law relating to penalties) and sums payable to the creditor by way of administration costs, repossession charges, and the like.

As will be seen below, the concept has been created to ensure that the debtor is properly informed of the sums payable by him on default and also to ensure that the debtor is not cleared of indebtedness until all sums due on default have been paid.   **7.33**

D. NOTICE OF DEFAULT SUMS

Provisions for default sums are contained in s 12 of the CCA 2006, which will be discussed here, and in s 13, which will be discussed in the next section.   **7.34**

Section 12 of the CCA 2006 inserts a new s 86E[26] into the CCA 1974 and is part of a range of new provisions concerning notices of sums due which are to be given to the debtor. Section 86E is to apply whenever a default sum becomes payable by the debtor but does not apply to a non-commercial agreement or a 'small agreement'.[27]   **7.35**

It is envisaged that, some time before April 2008, when the section comes into force, regulations will be made under s 86E(7) which will exempt the need for a notice where the default sum is below a stated amount and will provide for the form and content of notices somewhat along the lines of the Termination Regulations. The regulations will also prescribe a period following the date on which the default sum becomes payable within which a notice shall be given.[28] No regulations have been published at the date of going to press.   **7.36**

A notice requiring payment of a default sum may be incorporated into a notice given under some other provision of the CCA 1974.[29] Interest may not be charged on default sums for the first 28 days after service of the notice[30] and the debtor may not be charged any sum in respect of the cost of preparing and serving the notice.[31]   **7.37**

If the creditor fails to serve the default sum notice within the prescribed period, he cannot enforce the agreement at all until such notice is given.   **7.38**

When s 12 comes into effect, it will be retrospective in that s 86E of the CCA 1974 will apply to agreements whenever made but only as regards default sums which become payable after the commencement of s 12.[32]   **7.39**

---

[26] For the new ss 86A to 86D see below.

[27] CCA 1974 as inserted by CCA 2006 s17: in effect agreements for £50 or less and thus not now a significant category of agreement.

[28] CCA 1974 as inserted by CCA 2006 s 86E(2).

[29] Ibid s 86E(3).

[30] Ibid s 86E(4).

[31] Ibid s 86E(6).

[32] CCA 2006 Sch 3 para 8.

E. INTEREST ON DEFAULT SUMS

7.40 Section 13 of the CCA 2006 inserts a new s 86F into the CCA 1974. This provides that, if interest is to be charged on default sums payable under a regulated agreement, it can only be charged as simple interest. Note that this ties up with the provision in the new s 86E which provides that interest is not chargeable on the first 28 days after service of a default sum notice.

7.41 Section 13 will be retrospective in that it applies to agreements whenever made but only to default sums becoming payable after the commencement of s 13. If the new s 86F applies to an agreement made before commencement of s 13 of the CCA 2006, any provision for compound interest on default sums will be retrospectively converted into a provision for simple interest on that date.[33] It is currently expected that this section will come into force in April 2008.

F. NOTICE OF SUMS IN ARREARS: FIXED-SUM CREDIT AGREEMENTS

7.42 The CCA 2006 has made the notification of arrears to the debtor much more onerous for the creditor than under the CCA 1974. Like a number of provisions in the CCA 2006, this is the product of general concern both in Government and in the public about the level of outstanding consumer credit debt and the problems of debtors with unmanageable arrears. The scheme is to ensure that debtors are given early warning of the problem in the hope that it can be contained.

7.43 Section 9 adds a new s 86B into the CCA 1974. The new section applies to regulated agreements for fixed-sum credit or regulated consumer hire agreements but excludes non-commercial and small agreements.[34]

7.44 The conditions of the application of s 86B are complex. It applies:

where at any time the following conditions are satisfied—
(a) that the debtor or hirer under an applicable agreement is required to have made at least two payments under the agreement before that time;
(b) that the total sum paid under the agreement by him is less than the total sum which he is required to have paid before that time;
(c) that the amount of the shortfall is no less than the sum of the last two payments which he is required to have made before that time;
(d) that the creditor or owner is not already under a duty to give him notices under this section in relation to the agreement; and
(e) if a judgment has been given in relation to the agreement before that time, that there is no sum still to be paid under the judgment by the debtor or hirer.[35]

---

[33] CCA 2006 Sch 3 para 9.
[34] CCA 1974 as inserted by CCA 2006 s 86B(12).
[35] Ibid s 86B(1).

Note that, if the agreement provides for payments at intervals of one week or less, the requirements of (a) and (c) are met when four payments are due and not two.[36] If such an agreement was made before the beginning of the 'relevant period' only sums due but unpaid during that period are to count towards the shortfall,[37] the relevant period being 20 weeks ending with the day when the most recent payment fell due under the agreement.[38]   **7.45**

In practice this means that once the debtor is two payments in arrears then, unless the creditor has already given such a notice or has an unsatisfied judgment, the creditor is going to be bound by the section to give a notice.   **7.46**

Once the debtor reaches the point specified in s 86B(1), the creditor must, within 14 days of the debtor reaching that point, serve a notice under the section and, what is more, must go on giving further notices at intervals of not more than six months.[39]   **7.47**

The duty of the creditor to give the notice and go on giving the notice will only cease when s 86B(4) applies but, if s 86B(4) only applies after the original situation triggering the notice has occurred, the creditor has still got to serve the notice to relieve himself of the duty to go on giving notices.[40]   **7.48**

Section 86B(4) applies in either of two cases. The first is where the debtor ceases to be in arrears. This is elaborately defined in s 86B(5) as arising only when there is no sum still owing by way of sums due under the agreement, default sums, interest on default sums, or other interest payments. In short, only when the debtor is bang up to date with all payments will he cease to be 'in arrears'. The second situation is where the creditor obtains a money judgment against the debtor.   **7.49**

As with default sum notices (above) the creditor cannot charge the cost of preparing and serving the s 86B notice on the debtor[41] and the notice must be served with a 'current arrears information sheet'.[42]   **7.50**

It is envisaged that, some time before April 2008 when the section comes into force, regulations will be made under s 86B(8) to provide for the form and content of notices, again somewhat along the lines of the Termination Regulations. No regulations have been published at the date of going to press.   **7.51**

Section 9 of the CCA 2006 is retrospective in that the new s 86B will apply to agreements whenever made. With agreements made before the commencement date of s 9, however, the third condition (that the amount of the shortfall is no less than the sum of the last two payments which he is required to have made   **7.52**

---

[36] Ibid s 86B(9).
[37] Ibid s 86B(10).
[38] Ibid s 86B(11).
[39] Ibid s 86B(2).
[40] Ibid s 86B(3).
[41] Ibid s 86B(7).
[42] See paras 7.59–7.62 below.

before the time of the notice) will only be fulfilled if those two payments fell due after commencement.[43]

G. NOTICE OF SUMS IN ARREARS: RUNNING-ACCOUNT CREDIT AGREEMENTS

7.53 Similar but less onerous provisions to those described in detail in paragraphs 7.43 to 7.52 above are made for running-account agreements. Section 10 of the CCA 2006 adds a new s 86C to the CCA 1974. As in that case, non-commercial and small agreements are excluded.[44]

7.54 The conditions for application are slightly different:

(a) that the debtor under an applicable agreement is required to have made at least two payments under the agreement before that time;

(b) that the last two payments which he is required to have paid before that time have not been made;

(c) that the creditor has not already been required to give a notice under this section in relation to either of those payments; and

(d) if a judgment has been given in relation to the agreement before that time, that there is no sum still to be paid under the judgment by the debtor.[45]

7.55 Here the duty to give a notice is related to the period within which the creditor is required to give a statement under s 78(4) of the CCA 1974: notice must be given no later than the date the next statement is due.[46]

7.56 Again, the cost of preparing and serving the notice may not be passed on to the debtor[47] and it must be sent with a 'current arrears information sheet'.[48] Regulations will be made prescribing the form and content of notices.[49]

7.57 The principal difference with s 86B is that, because this is running-account credit, there does not need to be the provision for notices to cease once the debtor ceases to be in arrears or is subject to a judgment.

7.58 Section 10 of the CCA 2006 is retrospective in that the new s 86B will apply to agreements whenever made. With agreements made before the commencement date of s 10, however, the condition that two payments must be in arrears will only be fulfilled if those two payments fell due after commencement.[50] It is currently expected that this section will come into force in April 2008.

---

[43] CCA 2006 Sch 3 para 6.
[44] CCA 1974 as inserted by CCA 2006 s 86C(7)(b).
[45] Ibid s 86C(1).
[46] Ibid s 86C(2).
[47] Ibid s 86C(4).
[48] Ibid s 86C(3).
[49] Ibid s 86C(6).
[50] CCA 2006 Sch 3 para 7.

H. FAILURE TO GIVE NOTICE OF SUMS IN ARREARS

The requirement to give notices to defaulting debtors is enforced by the pro- **7.59** visions of s 86D of the CCA 1974 which is added by s 11 of the CCA 2006. Section 86D applies where the creditor has failed to give either the original or any of the repeat notices required by s 86B[51] or has failed to give the notice required by s 86C.[52]

Once the creditor has failed to give the notice, he enters into the 'period of **7.60** non-compliance' which begins immediately after the end of the period during which notice ought to have been given, and ends, in the case of a notice under s 86B, on the day notice is given or on the day the debtor ceases to be in arrears and, in the case of a notice under s 86C, on the day notice is given.[53]

During the period of non-compliance the creditor is not entitled to enforce **7.61** the agreement.[54] Furthermore the debtor has no liability to pay any interest relating to the period of non-compliance or any default sum which becomes payable during the period of non-compliance or becomes payable after the period but in relation to breaches occurring during the period.[55]

The combined effect of the new ss 86B, 86C, and 86D will be greatly to **7.62** increase the paperwork demanded of creditors and greatly to increase the opportunity of well-informed defaulters to keep enforcement at bay. Whether it will have any effect in diminishing the overall total of consumer credit arrears is entirely another question.

I. INFORMATION SHEETS

In a well-meaning attempt to induce improvident debtors to see the error of **7.63** their ways and to turn to the paths of righteousness, the Office of Fair Trading (OFT) has come up with the notion of information sheets. Section 8 of the CCA 2006 inserts a new s 86A into Part 7 of the CCA 1974.

The OFT is tasked with preparing and giving general notice of an 'arrears **7.64** information sheet' and a 'default information sheet'.[56] The arrears information sheet is to contain information to 'help debtors and hirers who receive notices under section 86B or 86C' and the default information sheet is to include information to 'help debtors and hirers who receive default notices'.[57]

---

[51] CCA 1974 as inserted by CCA 2006 s 86D(1).
[52] Ibid s 86D(2).
[53] Ibid s 86D(5) and (6).
[54] Ibid s 86D(3).
[55] Ibid s 86D(4).
[56] Ibid s 86A(1).
[57] Ibid s 86A(2) and (3).

7.65   There will be regulations to prescribe the contents of the information sheets[58] and the sheets (whether the original sheets or revised sheets) will take effect at the end of three months from the date of the general notice concerning them.[59]

7.66   The obligation of the OFT under s 86A will be to prepare and give general notice of the arrears information sheet and the default information sheet as soon as practicable after the commencement of s 8 of the CCA 2006.[60]

J. ENFORCEABILITY OF REGULATED AGREEMENTS

7.67   Section 15 of the CCA 2006 contains a surprising U-turn on the part of the Government. Having flatly refused to take any account of the certificate of incompatibility with the European Convention on Human Rights issued by the Court of Appeal in *Wilson*[61] and having expensively (albeit successfully) appealed that decision to the House of Lords, Parliament has now repealed subsections (3) to (5) of s 127 of the CCA 1974.

7.68   Thus when s 15 comes into force, probably on 6 April 2008, there will no longer be any category of improperly executed agreements which will be totally incapable of being enforced and it will be open to the court to make enforcement orders in any appropriate case.

7.69   The repeal of subsections (3) to (5) of s 127 will only affect agreements made after s 15 of the CCA 2006 comes into force.[62]

K. TIME ORDERS

7.70   Provision is made by s 16 of the CCA 2006 for the debtor to be able to apply for a time order if served with a notice of arrears under s 86BH or s 86C. A new paragraph (ba) is added to s 129(1) of the CCA 1974 empowering the court to make a time order:

(ba) on an application made by a debtor or hirer under this paragraph after he has been given a notice under section 86B or 86C.

7.71   A new s 129A is inserted to regulate applications made under the new s 129(1)(ba). If a debtor is served with a s 86B or s 86C notice he must serve a notice on the creditor and cannot apply for a time order until 14 days after that notice is served.[63] The debtor's notice must state that the debtor intends to apply

---

[58] CCA 1974 as inserted by CCA 2006 s 86A(4).
[59] Ibid s 86A(5) to (7).
[60] Ibid Sch 3 para 5.
[61] See paras 7.21 and 7.22 above.
[62] CCA 2006 Sch 3 para 11.
[63] CCA 1974 as inserted by CCA 2006 s 129A(1).

for a time order and that he wishes to make a proposal for the making of payments under the agreement, with details of the proposal.[64]

When s 16 of the CCA 2006 comes into force, probably on 6 April 2008, it will be fully retrospective and will apply to agreements whenever made.[65] **7.72**

Note that the remainder of s 16 makes consequential procedural amendments to the law of Northern Ireland and Scotland. **7.73**

L. INTEREST PAYABLE ON JUDGMENT DEBTS

Section 17 inserts a new s 130A into the CCA 1974 which applies to all regulated agreements except non-commercial and small agreements.[66] **7.74**

Under s 74 of the County Courts Act 1974 interest is payable on judgment debts as of right in cases covered by orders made by the Lord Chancellor. The County Courts (Interest on Debts) Order 1991 (as amended) essentially covers judgments of over £5,000 and judgments to which the Late Payment of Commercial Debts (Interest) Act 1998 applies. This interest will continue to be payable and is unaffected by s 130A.[67] **7.75**

Under the new s 130A, if a creditor wants to recover interest on the judgment sum he must give the debtor a notice under s 130A and further notices at intervals of not more than six months. The debtor is not required to pay post-judgment interest for any period before the day he receives the first such notice[68] and if the creditor lets six months slip without giving a repeat notice, the debtor's obligation to pay interest ceases on the expiry of the six months and does not revive until another notice is served.[69] **7.76**

As with the other notices introduced by this part of the CCA 2006, the creditor is not entitled to charge for preparing and serving the notice,[70] the notice can be combined with other notices,[71] and regulations will be made prescribing the form and content of the notices.[72] **7.77**

Section 130A will apply to agreements whenever made but only to sums due on judgments given after the commencement of s 17 of the CCA 2006, which is expected in April 2008.[73] **7.78**

---

[64] Ibid s 129A(2).
[65] CCA 2006 Sch 3 para 12.
[66] CCA 1974 as inserted by CCA 2006 s 130A(8).
[67] Ibid s 130(7)(c).
[68] Ibid s 130A(2).
[69] Ibid s 130A(5).
[70] Ibid s 130A(4).
[71] Ibid s 130A(5).
[72] Ibid s 130A(6).
[73] CCA 2006 Sch 3 para 13.

8

EARLY SETTLEMENT

A. FORMER RULES ON EARLY SETTLEMENT

Even before the Consumer Credit Act 1974 (CCA 1974), the common law **8.01** recognized that, when a credit agreement is paid off prematurely (whether voluntarily or compulsorily on breach), the debtor should receive a discount for early repayment, being a rebate of the credit charges which would not be paid because of the premature termination.[1]

Section 95 of the CCA 1974 formalized that concept by providing for the **8.02** making of regulations governing the calculation of the rebate of charges for credit to the debtor under a regulated agreement 'where, under s 94, on refinancing, on breach of the agreement, or for any other reason, his indebtedness is discharged or becomes payable before the time fixed by the agreement, or any sum becomes payable before the time so fixed'.

These rebates were originally covered by the Consumer Credit (Rebate on **8.03** Early Settlement) Regulations 1983 (the 1983 Regulations). The subject of rebates has been left untouched by the Consumer Credit Act 2006 (CCA 2006) but the 1983 Rebate Regulations have been replaced by the Consumer Credit (Early Settlement) Regulations 2004 (the 2004 Regulations). The 2004 Regulations came into force on 31 May 2005 and revoked the 1983 Regulations[2] but, as

---

[1] See, for example, *Interoffice Telephones Ltd v Robert Freeman Co Ltd* [1958] 1 QB 190.
[2] 1983 Regulations Reg 8.

will be seen, the provisions of the 1983 Regulations were preserved in relation to agreements made before 31 May 2005.[3]

8.04   The right of the debtor to obtain a settlement figure on request was contained in the Consumer Credit (Settlement Information) Regulations 1983. These have been retained, subject to amendments consequential on the coming into force of the 2004 Regulations.[4]

8.05   The 1983 Regulations applied a minimum rebate in the situations listed in s 95.[5] It was open to the parties to agree a more generous rebate but the regulations prescribed the minimum. The regulations did not cover agreements where no payment of items included in the total charge for credit remained to be made after the settlement date, nor agreements for running-account credit.[6] Termination of hire-purchase and conditional sale agreements by the debtor or hirer under s 99 are also governed by their own regime outside the scope of the 1983 Regulations.[7]

8.06   The rebate is to be calculated by reference to all sums paid or payable in connection with the agreement and included in the total charge for credit.[8] Excluded from this category are:

(a) taxes and other official duties fees or charges;

(b) sums paid or payable under linked transactions (save for certain advance payments);

(c) certain other sums payable under linked transactions specifically exempted from the operation of s 96;

(d) credit brokerage fees or commissions.[9]

8.07   Regulation 4 of the 1983 Regulations provided for the calculation of the rebate in four different situations and the formula was set out in Schedules 1 to 4 accordingly. Schedule 5 provided a method of determining whether the repayment of credit was to be regarded as being in equal or unequal instalments for the purposes of applying the formulae in Schedules 2 to 4.

8.08   The formulae contained in Schedules 1 to 4, which will not be transliterated in the text, had what was, at the time, seen to be the merit of being extremely simple. A reasonably numerate person could calculate them with a pencil and the back of an envelope. As will be seen, *nous avons changé tout cela*.

8.09   Schedule 1 gave a very basic formula for the calculation of a rebate where fixed-sum credit is repayable in a single sum at the end of a specified period.

8.10   Schedule 2 enshrined the 'rule of 78'. This had been the rule from time immemorial for calculating rebates. Schedule 2 itself describes it in Part I as a

---

[3] 1983 Regulations Reg 10.
[4] See Reg 9 of the 2004 Regulations.
[5] 1983 Regulations Reg 2(1).
[6] Ibid Reg 2(2).
[7] Ibid Reg 2(3).
[8] Ibid Reg 3(1).   [9] Ibid Reg 3(2).

'simple formula for calculation of rebate where credit is repayable in equal instalments at equal intervals'. 78 is the sum of the numbers 1 to 12 (taking 12 monthly payments as the model). The rule assumed that the charges for credit were paid off on a descending scale over the lifetime of the agreement. Thus in the first month the debtor paid 12/78 of the charges, in the second 11/78, and so on down to the last month when he paid 1/78. If the agreement were paid off, say, after eight instalments the rebate would be the proportion of the final four instalments of charges in relation to the total charges thus 10/78 (10 being $1 + 2 + 3 + 4$).

The operation of the rule of 78 where the instalments were unequal or the **8.11** intervals for payment were unequal necessarily involved a more complex formula, set out in Schedule 2 Part II, but the principles were the same.

Schedule 3 gave the formula where settlement took place between two instal- **8.12** ment dates and the credit was payable at intervals of greater than a month and Schedule 4 the formula where a sum less than the total remaining indebtedness of the debtor is to be paid early.

Regulation 6 legislated for the determination of the 'settlement date'. Where **8.13** the agreement provides for the payment of instalments at intervals of one month or less and settlement occurs between two instalment dates, the settlement date is to be the instalment date immediately following:

(a) the date of service of notice by the debtor under s 94 but only if accompanied by payment of the amount due less the rebate or such later date as is specified in the s 94 notice (again if accompanied by payment on that date);

(b) the date specified as the date for payment in any creditor's notice under s 76, s 87, or s 98, if the debtor actually pays on that date;

(c) in all other cases the date on which the debtor pays the settlement sum.[10]

Where the credit is to be repaid at intervals greater than a month and settle- **8.14** ment takes place between two instalments, the settlement day is 14 days after the date set out in (a) to (c) above.[11] If the creditor has given a notice under s 97 and the Settlement Information Regulations, then, provided the debtor pays on the date specified in the notice, that date is the settlement date.

In all other cases, settlement date is the date of actual payment by the debtor **8.15** of the rebated sum.

Creditors were afforded a measure of protection against forced early settle- **8.16** ment by Regulation 5. This enables the creditor to defer the settlement date:

(a) where the agreement provided for the credit to be repaid over or at the end of five years, by two months;

---

[10] Ibid Reg 6(1).
[11] Ibid Reg 6(2).

(b) where the credit was to be repaid over or at the end of a period greater than five years, by one month.

8.17   These regulations were the subject of criticism by consumer groups who considered that the rule of 78 was unduly favourable to creditors and that the deferral provisions in Regulation 5 gave too much latitude to creditors. In meeting these concerns, the Department of Trade and Industry (DTI) and the Office of Fair Trading (OFT) did not go the whole way. The calculation formulae were changed and the deferral provisions made less favourable to creditors but the right to defer was not abolished completely.

B. ENTITLEMENT TO REBATE

8.18   In the following sections we shall discuss the provisions of the 2004 Regulations and indicate where changes have occurred from the 1983 Regulations.

8.19   Regulation 2 of the 2004 Regulations reproduces the corresponding regulation of the 1983 Regulations with one important change. In addition to agreements where no payment of items included in the total charge for credit remain to be made after the settlement date and agreements for running-account credit the category of exclusions now includes:

land mortgages under which no instalment repayments secured by the mortgage on the debtor's home, and no payment of interest on the credit (other than interest charged when all or part of the credit is repaid voluntarily by the debtor), are due or capable of becoming due while the debtor continues to occupy the mortgaged land as his main residence.[12]

8.20   This addition is clearly designed to cover a new type of mortgage of a kind which was virtually unknown in 1983.

C. ITEMS INCLUDED IN CALCULATION

8.21   The present version of Regulation 3 of the 2004 Regulations is that it is identical to Regulation 3 of the 1983 Regulations (see paragraph 8.06 above) but it was the subject of some feeble dithering on the part of the DTI. As originally made, Regulation 3(2)(d) excluded from the calculation of rebate:

any fee or commission paid by the debtor or a relative of his under a credit brokerage contract relating to the agreement, *other than a fee or commission financed by the agreement*.

8.22   The italicized words had been added to the words of the identical provision in the 1983 Regulations in order cater for the situation where the fee or commission

---

[12]   2004 Regulations Reg 2(2)(c).

is added to the credit and subject to charges accordingly. Before the 2004 Regulations came into force on 31 May 2005, however, it dawned on the Department that this addition was undesirable. The fee or commission itself (ie the 'capital' amount) was not a charge for credit whether financed or not by the agreement and the *charges* for the part of the credit which financed the fee or commission would be caught by the general rebate provisions without the need to legislate separately for them. Consequently, before the 2004 Regulations came into force they were amended by the removal of the offending words.

Thus the items included in the calculation of rebate remain the same as under **8.23** the 1983 Regulations.

D. CHANGES TO THE BASIS OF CALCULATION

It is here that there is a fundamental departure from the 1983 Regulations. Out **8.24** goes the rule of 78 and in comes a formula designed to apply an actuarial calculation to rebates. What was previously possible with the pencil and the envelope now requires the employment of a computer in the hands of a highly numerate operator.

The different formulae for the different categories of agreement contained in **8.25** Schedules 1 to 4 to the 1983 Regulations have been swept away, to be replaced by a single formula contained in Regulation 4:

$$\sum_{i=1}^{m} A_i(1 + r)^{a_i} \quad - \quad \sum_{j=1}^{n} B_j(1 + r)^{b_j}$$

where:

A_i = the amount of the ith advance of credit
B_j = the amount of the jth repayment of credit
r = the periodic rate equivalent of the APR/100
m = the number of advances of credit made before the settlement date
n = the number of repayments of credit made before the settlement date
a_i = the time between the ith advance of credit and the settlement date, expressed in periods
b_j = the time between the jth repayment of credit and the settlement date, expressed in periods, and
Σ represents the sum of all the terms indicated.

Regulation 4(2) provides that if a repayment of credit is made at a time or at a **8.26** rate other than that provided for by the agreement, the creditor can choose to treat it for the purposes of calculating the rebate as if it had been made in accordance with the agreement.

There is only one Schedule to the 2004 Regulations and that contains **8.27** examples of the application of the actuarial formula. These are merely illustrative and, if in conflict with the regulations themselves, the latter are to prevail.[13]

E. SETTLEMENT DATE AND DEFERRAL

8.28   In contrast to the calculation of the rebate, the provisions concerning settlement date have been simplified from the 1983 Regulations.

8.29   The settlement date is to be taken as:

(a) where the debtor has given notice under s 94, the settlement date is 28 days after service of the notice or any later date specified in the notice, provided in either case the debtor pays the settlement sum (subject to rebate) not later than that date;

(b) the date specified for payment in any creditor's notice served under s 76, s 87, or s 98 provided the debtor pays the settlement sum (subject to rebate) not later than that date;

(c) in all other cases, the date on which the debtor pays the settlement sum (subject to rebate).[14]

8.30   This eliminates the differences between categories of agreement based on the intervals for payment while retaining the basic concept of the 1983 Regulations that the debtor only receives his rebate if he actually pays on time.

8.31   Deferment of the settlement date by the creditor has been much curtailed by Regulation 6. Deferral is now only possible where the agreement provides for the credit to be repaid over or at the end of a period which is 'more than a year after the relevant date'. 'Relevant date' is defined by Regulation 1(2) as being defined by reference to the Consumer Credit (Total Charge for Credit) Regulations 1980.

8.32   The 'relevant date' under Regulation 1(2) of the 1980 Regulations means: 'in a case where a date is specified in or determinable under an agreement at the date of its making as that on which the debtor is entitled to require provision of anything the subject of the agreement, the earliest such date and, in any other case, the date of the making of the agreement'. The former provision is designed to apply where the provision of the fixed-sum credit or the provision of goods financed by the agreement post-dates the date of the agreement.

8.33   Where deferral is permitted, the creditor may defer the settlement date for calculation of the rebate by one month or, if this would be less than 30 days, 30 days at the option of the creditor.

8.34   The operation of Regulations 5 and 6 remains a matter of some controversy between the OFT and the Competition Commission in relation to cases where

---

[13] 2004 Regulations Reg 4(3).
[14] Ibid Reg 5.

credit is refinanced. In these cases, the debtor serves a s 94 notice terminating his existing credit agreement and enters into a new credit agreement to borrow sufficient money to pay off the old credit and obtain additional money for other purposes. The creditor exercises his right of deferral under Regulation 6 so that the settlement date for calculation of the rebate is one month after the s 94 notice takes effect (itself 28 days after the notice itself under Regulation 5(a)). The balance of the old credit is in fact paid off in total by the new credit and the rebate is then repaid to the debtor once the rebate has been calculated on this basis.

The view of both the OFT and the finance industry is that this is a permissible **8.35** transaction and the rebate is correctly calculated on the basis that the s 94 notice defers the settlement date 28 days and the creditor's deferral a further month. The Competition Commission has raised concerns that such a case may be caught by Regulation 5(c) and the settlement date is the date of actual payment, namely the date of the refinancing itself and not the later date under Regulations 5(a) and 6. For the time being the reader is invited to assume that the view of the OFT and the finance industry is correct but to note that it may be tested in the courts at some future date.

F. SAVINGS

The 2004 Regulations revoke the 1983 Regulations but with substantial savings. **8.36** In respect of regulated agreements made before 31 May 2005 when the 2004 Regulations came into force, the new rules contained in Regulations 1 to 7 of the 2004 Regulations will not apply:

(a) in the case of agreements for 10 years or less, until 31 May 2007;

(b) in the case of agreements for more than 10 years, until 31 May 2010.[15]

For these purposes the term of the agreement is the original term provided **8.37** for or, if the agreement was varied before the date on which the Regulations were *made* (5 June 2004), the term as so varied. In other words, once the new regulations were made, creditors could not thereafter postpone the application of the new provisions by extending the length of the credit term.

---

[15] Ibid Reg 10(1).

9

UNFAIR RELATIONSHIPS

A. INTRODUCTION

Sections 19 to 22 of the Consumer Credit Act 2006 (CCA 2006) repeal and **9.01** replace ss 137 to 140 of the Consumer Credit Act 1974 (CCA 1974). They are expected to come into force on 6 April 2007.

The old provisions empowered the court to reopen any credit bargain if, at the **9.02** time that it was made, it required the debtor to make payments which were 'grossly exorbitant or otherwise grossly contravened ordinary principles of fair dealing'.

The new provisions introduce a new and less onerous test, allowing the court **9.03** to interfere if it considers that the 'relationship' between the creditor and the debtor is 'unfair'. The court will be entitled to take into account all matters of relevance relating to the creditor and the debtor in making such an assessment— and it is provided with a broad range of remedies to address the unfairness.

B. THE CURRENT SCHEME OF EXTORTIONATE CREDIT BARGAINS

1. Before the Consumer Credit Act 1974

Before the introduction of the CCA 1974, consumers were given limited protec- **9.04** tion against exorbitant interest rates by the Moneylenders Acts 1900 and 1927.

These statutes allowed the court, in proceedings brought by a moneylender **9.05** for the recovery of a loan or reinforcement of a security, to reopen the transactions where it found that the interest or other charges were excessive, and the transaction was therefore harsh and unconscionable. There was a presumption that a transaction was harsh and unconscionable if the rate of interest exceeded 48 per cent per year—above which rate, a lender was obliged to refute the presumption.

2. The Consumer Credit Act 1974

9.06 Sections 137 to 140 introduced a new power to reopen credit bargains. In summary:

(a) If a court finds that a credit bargain is extortionate, it may reopen the credit agreement so as to do justice between the parties.

(b) A credit bargain is 'extortionate' if it requires the debtor[1] to make payments which are grossly exorbitant, or if it otherwise grossly contravenes ordinary principles of fair dealing.

(c) The court is required to take into account certain factors in determining whether a credit bargain is 'extortionate' including:
 (i) the interest rates prevailing at the time the agreement was made;
 (ii) the debtor's age, experience, business capacity, and health;
 (iii) the financial pressure on the debtor at the time of the agreement;
 (iv) the degree of risk accepted by the lender having regard to any security; and
 (v) any other relevant considerations.

(d) The statutory power applies to all credit agreements[2] whether regulated, unregulated, or exempt, where the debtor is an individual.

(e) The power is discretionary, but may not be exercised of the court's own motion.

(f) Once an application is made by the debtor, the burden of proof rests with the creditor to prove that the credit bargain is not extortionate.

(g) The remedy is to set aside, whether in whole or in part, any obligation imposed by such a credit bargain, or to alter the terms of the agreement.

9.07 On their face, therefore, these sections provide a powerful remedy for a consumer who has been the victim of unscrupulous lending. Experience, however, has suggested that they provide little practical protection.

9.08 The Government's recent consultation process highlighted a widespread dissatisfaction with these provisions. Their efficacy was queried, and it was widely felt that they afforded little protection to the most vulnerable people in society, namely those on low incomes who are most likely to fall prey to non-status lenders on the margins of the market.

9.09 A number of explanations were offered for this poor performance.

---

[1] Or his/her relative.
[2] But not to hire agreements for obvious reasons.

First, the qualifying hurdles were seen as too high. Many consultees criticized **9.10** the fact that the current statutory test focuses primarily on the cost of the credit at the time the loan is taken out—and does not encourage the court to look at the parties' subsequent relationship, or their current financial situations. Recent cases, in which borrowers have been unsuccessful in challenges against lenders who failed to reduce their rates in line with falls in the market rate, have highlighted such concerns.[3]

Second, those cases that did reach the courts caused problems for many **9.11** judges. The judiciary confessed to finding it difficult to define the touchstone phrases 'grossly exorbitant' and 'grossly contravenes ordinary principles of fair dealing', a difficulty made no easier by the fact that they rarely had to deal with such applications, and compounded by the fact that they were not assisted by authoritative guidance from decisions in the higher courts. As a result, there was an inconsistency of approach—and a tendency to apply a restricted interpretation to the provisions.

Finally, the complexity of the law and the unpredictability of outcome, the **9.12** potential costs liability of a failed application, and the fact that many borrowers are unaware of their rights, have combined to discourage borrowers from using the courts—particularly those most vulnerable to unscrupulous lenders.

The proof of the pudding has been in its eating. The White Paper *Fair, Clear* **9.13** *and Competitive—The Consumer Credit Market in the 21st Century* (the White Paper) suggested that only 30 or so cases had been reported since the Act came into force. When it has been used, the borrower has rarely benefited.[4]

In summary, challenges under the current legislation are difficult to maintain, **9.14** unpredictable, and potentially expensive for the litigant. The number of cases that go to court is small. In a growing credit market place, in which there are increasing numbers of vulnerable people who are exposed to unlicensed and non-status credit providers, the Government felt that there was a need for an improved legislative shield.

It is in these circumstances that the new Act has radically overhauled the **9.15** court's powers.

C. THE NEW SCHEME OF UNFAIR RELATIONSHIPS

1. The Repeal of Sections 137 to 140

Section 22(3) of the CCA 2006 provides that 'sections 137–140 of that Act **9.16** (extortionate credit bargains) shall cease to have effect'. As stated above, the commencement date for this provision is expected to be 6 April 2007.

---

[3] *Paragon Finance plc v Nash & Staunton* [2001] EWCA Civ 1466; *Broadwick Financial Services Ltd v Spencer & Another* [2002] EWCA Civ 35.
[4] See, for example, *A Tetley Limited v Scott* [1980] CCLR 36.

2. New Section 140A: Unfair Relations between Creditors and Debtors

9.17 Section 19 of the CCA 2006 inserts a new s 140A into the CCA 1974. This new section provides the power to make orders in relation to unfair relationships, and sets out the test for such intervention.

9.18 Section 140A (1) enables the court to make one of a number of orders under the new s 140B (see below) in relation to any credit agreement if it finds that 'the relationship between the creditor and the debtor arising out of the agreement (or the agreement taken with any related agreement[5]) is unfair to the debtor'.

9.19 The section goes on to stipulate that a relationship may be unfair to the debtor because of one or more of the following:

(a) any of the terms of the agreement or any related agreement;
(b) the way in which the creditor has exercised or enforced any of his rights under the agreement, or any related agreement;
(c) any other thing done (or not done) by—or on behalf of—the creditor—whether before or after the making of the agreement or any related agreement.

9.20 Section 140A(2) provides that, when determining whether an agreement is unfair, the court 'shall have regard to all matters it thinks relevant (including matters relating to the creditor and matters relating to the debtor)'. This may include 'anything done (or not done) by, or on behalf of, or in relation to, an associate or a former associate of the creditor'.[6]

9.21 Section 140A(5) states that the section does not apply to agreements that are exempt under s 16(6C) of the CCA 1974—namely consumer credit agreements secured on land that are regulated by the Financial Services Authority under the Financial Services and Markets Act 2000.

3. Section 140B: Powers of Court in Relation to Unfair Relationships

9.22 Section 20 of the CCA 2006 inserts a new s 140B after new s 140A. This sets out the types of orders that a court may make in relation to any relationship between a creditor and a debtor that has been found to be unfair.

9.23 Section 140B(1) provides that an order under this section may do one, or more, of the following:

(a) require the creditor, or any associate or former associate of his, to repay (in whole or in part) any sum paid by the debtor, or by a surety, by virtue of the agreement or any related agreement (whether paid to the creditor, the associate or former associate or to any other person);

---

[5] As defined by CCA 1974 s 140C(4) and paragraph 9.29 below.
[6] As defined by CCA 1974 s 184.

(b) require the creditor, or any associate or former associate of his, to do or not to do (or to cease from doing) anything specified in the order in connection with the agreement or any related agreement;

(c) reduce or discharge any sum payable by the debtor, or by a surety, by virtue of the agreement or any related agreement;

(d) direct the return to a surety of any property provided by him for the purposes of a security;

(e) otherwise set aside (in whole or in part) any duty imposed on the debtor or on a surety by virtue of the agreement or any related agreement;

(f) alter the terms of the agreement, or of any related agreement;

(g) direct accounts to be taken, or (in Scotland) an accounting to be made, between any persons.

Section 140B(2) specifies that such an order may only be made in the following circumstances: **9.24**

(a) 'on an application by the debtor or surety'. Such an application may only be made to the county court in England and Wales, or to the sheriff court in Scotland, or to the High Court in Northern Ireland;[7] or

(b) 'at the instance of the debtor (or surety) in any Court proceedings to which the debtor and creditor are parties, and in the course of which the agreement or any agreement is to be enforced'; or

(c) 'at the instance of the debtor (or surety) in any other proceedings where the amount paid or payable under the agreement or any related agreement is relevant'.

In short, such an order may only be made at the debtor's request. Note that there is no power given to the court to make such an order of its own motion.

The burden of proof rests on the creditor. Section 140B(9) stipulates that, once such an allegation is made by a debtor or surety, it is for the creditor to prove that the relationship is not unfair to the debtor. **9.25**

4. Section 140C: Interpretation of Sections 140A and 140B

Section 140C defines the types of agreements that are covered by ss 140A and 140B. **9.26**

Section 140C(1) provides that 'credit agreement' in s 140A(1) means 'any agreement between an individual (the "debtor") and any other person (the "creditor")[8] by which the creditor provides the debtor with credit of any **9.27**

---

[7] CCA 1974 as inserted by CCA 2006 s 140A(4)–(6). In Northern Ireland, such an application may be made to the county court if the credit agreement is an agreement under which the creditor provides the debtor with fixed-sum credit not exceeding £15,000 or running-account credit on which the credit limit does not exceed £15,000: see s 140B(6).

[8] References in these sections to the 'creditor' or the 'debtor' under such agreements are to include references to their assigns: s 189(1).

amount'. These provisions apply, therefore, to any credit agreement with an individual, whether or not it is regulated by, or exempt from, the CCA 1974.[9]

9.28 Section 140C(3) provides that the restrictive definition of 'court' in s 189(1)—which is limited to the county court in England and Wales, the sheriff court in Scotland—does not apply to these provisions. Such applications may therefore be determined in the higher courts.

9.29 Section 140C(4) defines a 'related agreement' as being any agreement that is consolidated by the main agreement;[10] or is a linked transaction in relation to the main (or consolidated) agreement;[11] or is security provided in relation to the main agreement,[12] a consolidated agreement, or a linked transaction.

9.30 The corollary is that, through this definition of a 'related agreement', these provisions also cover the practice where the creditor enters into successive credit agreements with the debtor for the purpose for example of increasing the total amount of the debt or obtaining multiple fees from the debtor setting up each loan.

9.31 Further, in the case of any credit agreement which is not a regulated consumer credit agreement, such references to a credit agreement shall include any transaction that, if the agreement were a regulated consumer credit agreement, would fall into the definition of a linked transaction. This is to ensure consistency of approach between regulated and unregulated credit agreements.

9.32 In short, the various definitions in this section seek to extend the ambit of these sanctions to all credit agreements and their related transactions.

5. Section 140D: Advice and Information Published by the Office of Fair Trading

9.33 Section 22 of the CCA 2006 makes various consequential amendments to the CCA 1974.

9.34 In particular, it inserts a new s 140D which requires the Office of Fair Trading (OFT) to give advice and information about the interaction between these new provisions on unfair relationships, and Part 8 of the Enterprise Act 2002. The latter allows the OFT to bring proceedings against a person who, as a consequence of a breach of statutory obligation, harms the collective interests of consumers in the United Kingdom. It is anticipated[13] that this advice and information will include examples of the circumstances, conduct, or practices that, in the opinion of the OFT, could give rise to an unfair relationship between creditors and debtors.

---

[9] Save for exempt agreements by virtue of s 16(6C): see s 140A(5).
[10] See also s 140C(7).
[11] See also s 140C(5).
[12] See also s 140C(6).
[13] See the Explanatory Notes to the legislation published at <http://www.opsi.gov.uk>.

While not binding on the courts, it is probable that such guidance from the OFT will provide a useful pointer to the sort of criteria that might apply when considering the fairness of credit transactions. **9.35**

D. THE COURT'S APPROACH IN FUTURE

The statutory test provided by s 140A(1) is very widely drawn. In deciding whether a relationship is unfair, the court must look at all the circumstances pertaining to the terms of the agreement, and the history of the relationship between the parties. Unlike the current provisions in ss 137 to 140, the amended legislation makes it clear that in determining whether a relationship is unfair, consideration must be given to events after its making that may have led to unfairness. **9.36**

The vagueness of the statutory test, and the absence of any legislative guidance on its application, means that this is an area ripe for judicial interpretation. It is unlikely that case law decided under the old provisions will be relevant, as the statutory wording is so different. **9.37**

Although each case will be decided on its own facts, the following factors may be considered relevant in such applications. **9.38**

(a) The way in which the agreement is drafted. The more open and clear its terms, the less likely is a finding that the relationship is unfair. It is unlikely that an agreement that complies with all of the formalities will be the subject of much criticism on this ground.

(b) Whether the lender or any broker has engaged in an unfair commercial practice, such as misleading, harassing, coercing, or otherwise unduly influencing the borrower to enter into the transaction.

(c) The steps taken by the lender to ensure that the consumer was suited to this financial product, including any assessment of creditworthiness.

(d) The circumstances of the borrower, including his/her age, experience, business capacity, and state of health, and the extent to which he/she may have been under any pressure to enter into the agreement.

(e) Whether the borrower provided accurate, full, and honest information to the lender.

(f) Whether the rate of interest reflects the degree of risk taken by the lender, having regard to the personal characteristics of the debtor and the nature and value of any security offered.

(g) Whether ancillary or linked transactions (such as insurance policies) are reasonably required or have been unnecessarily included.

(h) The relevant practices in the current market, and in particular the level of interest charged throughout the term of the agreement.

9.39 In essence, the court is likely to be striving to find a balance between the lender's duty to behave fairly and responsibly, and the need for borrowers to provide accurate information about their circumstances, to borrow sensibly, and to take responsibility for their own financial decisions.

9.40 The breadth of remedies afforded by s 140B(1)—which allow a judge to strike down an agreement or simply to tinker with its form or effect—may encourage judges to make findings of unfairness—particularly as each case is likely to be decided on its own facts. There is, therefore, an increased possibility for judicial intervention in such agreements.

9.41 The legislature having failed to provide any proper guidance, practitioners will have to await guidance from the courts on the proper principles governing the exercise of this power.

10

ADVERTISEMENTS

A. THE PREVIOUS RULES AND THE NEED FOR CHANGE

Advertising and the Consumer Credit Act 1974 (CCA 1974) make uneasy bed- **10.01**
fellows. Advertising is about making bold, clear assertions about the superiority
of one's products, designed to catch the eye or the ear of the potential customer.
The potential customer is seen by the advertiser as a fairly sophisticated fellow,
capable of being tickled by witty or cheeky advertisements or of appreciating
allusion and reference. The CCA 1974, by contrast, works on the premise that
the potential customer is as a little child who will not understand the concepts
and pitfalls of credit unless everything is spelled out in *Janet and John* language
replete with warnings in capital letters to the effect that credit will severely
damage your financial health. In short, credit advertising is a battle between the
admen and the nannies.

This has made it very difficult to create a regime for advertising credit and hire **10.02**
which will combine the needs of the credit providers to bring their products to
public notice and the obsession of the regulators that every conceivable danger
should be emphasized.

The CCA 1974 controls three categories of credit or hire advertisement: **10.03**

(a) advertising by consumer credit or consumer hire businesses;

(b) advertising by those providing credit to individuals secured on land;

(c) advertising by those carrying on a business which would comprise regulated agreements but for the fact that the agreements are governed by the law of a non-UK country.[1]

10.04 Under the CCA 1974 as originally passed, two categories of advertisement were excluded from control:

(a) credit advertisements where the advertisement stated that the credit must exceed the financial limit and that no security was required or that any security would not be on land;

(b) advertisements for credit only available to a body corporate.

10.05 As we have seen in Chapter 2, s 2(3) of the Consumer Credit Act 2006 (CCA 2006) has removed the first of these exemptions.

10.06 Section 44 of the CCA 1974 contains the power for the Secretary of State to make regulations as to the form and content of regulations. The Consumer Credit (Advertisements) Regulations 1989 (the 1989 Regulations) came into force on 1 February 1990 and were not a happy document. They represented a triumph of bureaucratic ingenuity over common sense. We shall not waste the reader's time with a long disquisition on the provisions of the 1989 Regulations because they have been swept away by the Consumer Credit (Advertisements) Regulations 2004 (in this chapter the 2004 Regulations).

10.07 Suffice it to say that the 1989 Regulations distinguished between four categories of advertisement for each of credit and hire advertisements. There were simple advertisements, intermediate advertisements, full advertisements, and full variation advertisements. Each of these eight categories had its own requirements which had to be met with absolute strictness—substantial compliance was not enough.[2]

10.08 There were complicated provisions for stating what were described as 'representative terms' and equally complicated rules for stating the APR. The giving of warnings about the consequences of default were not entirely appropriate to any form of broadcast advertisement: listeners to commercial radio will be familiar with the gabbled statutory warnings read at breakneck speed at the end of credit advertisements.

10.09 Clearly the 1989 Regulations were not working adequately and they had certainly not kept pace with the enormous changes in the credit industry in the intervening period. The White Paper *Fair, Clear and Competitive—The Consumer Credit Market in the 21st Century* (the White Paper) recognized this: 'current rules have resulted in a highly technical and complex regime, creating confusion for lenders, enforcers and customers'.[3] The White Paper therefore stated the intention to 'ensure greater consistency and transparency in credit

---

[1] CCA 1974 s 43(2).
[2] See *Carrington Carr Ltd v Leicestershire County Council* [1993] Crim LR 938.
[3] Paragraph 2.5 of the White Paper.

advertising, so that consumers can compare financial products with confidence and make informed purchasing decisions'.[4]

In particular, the Department of Trade and Industry (DTI) proposed to **10.10** harmonize credit advertisements with the Financial Services Authority regime on mortgage regulation and to simplify the rules relating to the statement of the APR in advertisements.[5] The principal change proposed was the abolition of the four categories of advertisement for each type of advertisement and the creation of a single set of rules for credit and hire respectively.

The upshot was the 2004 Regulations which came into force on 31 October **10.11** 2004.

B. THE 2004 REGULATIONS—SCOPE AND GENERAL

The 2004 Regulations apply to credit advertisements and to hire advertise- **10.12** ments.[6] Both terms are defined by reference to s 43 of the CCA 1974 and the definitions are unaffected by the new Regulations.

Regulation 2 provides that 'a person who causes a credit advertisement or a **10.13** hire advertisement to be published shall ensure that the advertisement complies with all applicable requirements of these Regulations'. As before, this is a duty enforced by criminal sanctions, particularly under s 46 of the CCA 1974 which relates to 'false or misleading advertisements' and s 47 which criminalizes breaches of the Regulations.

In addition to the general exemption of credit advertisements targeted only **10.14** at bodies corporate created by s 43(3) there are specific exemptions created by Regulation 10 of the 2004 Regulations.

Regulation 10(1) excludes an advertisement which: **10.15**

(a) whether expressly or by implication indicates clearly that a person is willing—
  (i) to provide credit, or
  (ii) to enter into an agreement for the bailment of goods for the purposes of another person's business and
(b) does not indicate (whether expressly or by implication) that a person is willing to do either of those things otherwise than for the purposes of such a business.

Regulation 10(2), however, provides that the reference to a 'business' in **10.16** Regulation 10(1) does not include a business carried on by the advertiser or any person acting as a credit broker in respect of the credit or hire mentioned in the advertisement.

---

[4] Paragraph 2.7 of the White Paper.
[5] Paragraphs 2.8–2.12 of the White Paper.
[6] 2004 Regulations Reg 2.

10.17 The 2004 Regulations also exclude advertisements which consist of the communication of an invitation or inducement to engage in an investment activity under s 21 of the Financial Services and Markets Act 2000.[7]

10.18 The Regulations also, however, exclude advertisements which consist of the communication of an invitation or inducement to enter into a regulated mortgage contract as defined by Article 61 of the Financial Services and Markets Act 2000 (Regulated Activities) Order 2001.[8] This is quite far-reaching. A 'regulated mortgage contract' is defined[9] as follows:

a 'regulated mortgage contract' means a contract under which—
(i) a person ('the lender') provides credit to an individual or to trustees ('the borrower'); and
(ii) the obligation of the borrower to repay is secured by a first legal mortgage on land (other than timeshare accommodation) in the United Kingdom, at least 40% of which is used, or is intended to be used, as or in connection with a dwelling by the borrower or (in the case of credit provided to trustees) by an individual who is a beneficiary of the trust, or by a related person.[10]

10.19 Consequently, in contrast to the 1989 Regulations, advertisements offering house-purchase mortgages will not be regulated by the 2004 Regulations but by the 2000 Act and its associated Regulations.

10.20 In addition to the specific requirements as to content, Regulation 3 makes three general requirements. An advertisement shall:

(a) use plain and intelligible language;

(b) be easily legible (or in the case of any information given orally, clearly audible); and

(c) specify the name of the advertiser.

C. CONTENT OF ADVERTISEMENTS—CREDIT AGREEMENTS

10.21 As stated above, the 2004 Regulations have replaced the former complicated categories of advertisement with a single category for each of credit and hire advertisements.

10.22 Schedule 2 lists the information to be contained in a credit advertisement. As will be seen, not all the information need be given in all advertisements but the seven requirements are listed.

10.23 *1. Amount of credit.* This means the amount of credit which 'may be provided'

---

[7] 2004 Regulations Reg 10(3) and (4).
[8] Ibid Reg 10(5).
[9] By Art 61(3)(a) of the 2001 Order.
[10] 'Related person' includes spouse, partner (gender irrelevant), parent, child, grandparent, grandchild, or sibling—Art 61(4)(c).

under a consumer credit agreement or an indication of either or both of a maximum and minimum amount.

2. Deposit of money in an account. Where this is a requirement of the credit, it must be stated. **10.24**

3. Cash price. In advertisements for debtor–creditor–supplier agreements relating to the acquisition of goods, services, land, or anything else with a cash price, the cash price must be stated. **10.25**

4. Advance payment. If an advance payment is required, this must be stated, together with the amount or a minimum amount, in either case expressed as a sum or as a percentage. **10.26**

5. Frequency, number, and amount of repayments of credit. In advertisements relating to running-account credit there must be a statement of the frequency of repayments of credit and the amount (stating whether it is a fixed or minimum amount or one calculated by reference to a stated formula). With other credit advertisements, there must be a statement of the frequency, number, and amounts of repayments of credit. Note, this does not refer to interest—only to the repayment of the credit itself. **10.27**

6. Other payments and charges. A credit advertisement must list the description and amount of any other payments or charges payable under the credit transaction advertised: if the amount cannot be ascertained in advance, a description alone will suffice. This does not include sums payable on default. **10.28**

7. Total amount payable by the debtor. Credit advertisements for fixed-sum credit repayable at specified intervals which specify goods, services, land, or other things having a particular cash price to be acquired with the credit must state the total amount payable by the debtor, being the aggregate of the advance payments, the amount of the credit, and the amount of the total charge for credit. **10.29**

In general, the advertiser is to be at liberty to choose which of the seven items he includes in his credit advertisement but Regulation 4(1) provides that if the advertisement contains any of the amounts in items 5, 6, or 7, the advertisement must contain *all* the remaining items in the entire list (unless clearly inapplicable). It must also, in that case, contain the postal address of the advertiser, except for broadcast advertisements or where the advertisements are displayed at the premises of the creditor or dealer, or contain the name and address of a dealer or a credit broker. **10.30**

The items in the list must be shown together as a whole and given equal prominence.[11] Information in a book, catalogue, or leaflet likely to vary from time to time can comply with this requirement if it is set out in a separate document issued with the book, catalogue, or leaflet or is identified in it or if all the material is actually contained in the book, catalogue, or leaflet.[12] **10.31**

---

[11] 2004 Regulations Reg 4(2).
[12] Ibid Reg 4(3).

10.32   There are special rules in Regulation 6 for advertisements in dealers' publications relating to credit under a debtor–creditor–supplier agreement where such publications concern goods or services being offered by the dealer. The requirement of Regulation 4(2) that the necessary information must be shown together as a whole is not easy to comply with in such publications and the rules are somewhat relaxed.

10.33   In such a publication, therefore, the Regulation 4 information is to be taken as shown together as a whole if:

(a) the advertisement clearly indicates—
    (i) the cash price alone, or
    (ii) the cash price, any advance payment and the information in items 5 to 7 of Schedule 2 and (in general) the APR,
    in close proximity to every description of or specific reference to the goods and services, and
(b) the remaining information in the advertisement is so presented as to be readily comprehensible as a whole and an indication is given in close proximity to any of the information that it relates to all or specified descriptions of the goods or services, and
(c) except as set out in (a), no information relating to the provision of credit is shown together with the cash price.

D. CONTENT OF ADVERTISEMENTS—HIRE AGREEMENTS

10.34   The rules relating to hire advertisements are identical to those concerning credit advertisements save that, of course, the information requirements are different.

10.35   There are six items of information for hire advertisements contained in Schedule 3 to the 2004 Regulations.

10.36   *1. Deposit of money in an account*. Where this is a requirement of the credit, it must be stated.

10.37   *2. Advance payment*. If an advance payment is required, this must be stated, together with the amount or a minimum amount, in either case expressed as a sum or as a percentage.

10.38   *3. Duration of hire*. Where goods are hired for a fixed period or a maximum or minimum period, there must be a statement indicating this is the case and the duration of the period.

10.39   *4. Frequency and amount of hire payments*. The frequency and amount of hire payments must be stated, indicating whether the amount is a minimum amount and, if any amount is variable, a statement that it is variable and of the circumstances in which that would occur.

10.40   *5. Other payments and charges*. As with credit advertisements, a hire advertisement must list the description and amount of any other payments or charges payable under the transaction advertised: if the amount cannot be ascertained in advance, a description alone will suffice. Again, this does not include sums payable on default.

6. Variable payments or charges. If any hire payment or other payment may be **10.41** varied other than for a change in VAT, there must be a statement to that effect. This overlaps with item 4 to some extent.

As with credit advertisements, there is some flexibility about content but **10.42** Regulation 4(1) provides that, if the hire advertisement contains any of the amounts in items 4 and 5, it must contain all the six items in the list (so far as applicable) and must also contain the name and address of the advertiser (subject to the exceptions concerning broadcast advertisements, advertisements at the creditor's or dealer's premises, and advertisements stating the name and address of the dealer or credit broker).

Again, the rules concerning the display of the information together and as a **10.43** whole and with equal prominence apply to hire advertisements as do the rules concerning books, catalogues, and leaflets noted above.

E. CALENDAR OR SEASONAL PERIODS

Even the 1989 Regulations recognized that special rules were appropriate for **10.44** credit advertisements relating to seasonal promotions. Regulation 5 applies where a credit advertisement is contained in or is issued in a separate document supplied with a publication published by or on behalf of a dealer relating to goods or services to be offered in a specified calendar or season period.

In that case, the advertiser is relieved of the requirements of Regulation 4 (set **10.45** out in paragraphs 10.21 to 10.33 above) provided that the advertisement contains the information in Regulation 5(2) and 'no other indication that a person is willing to provide credit'. The information in paragraph (2) is:

(a) the name of the creditor, credit-broker or dealer and a postal address of his with or without his occupation or a statement of the general nature of his occupation; and
(b) an indication that individuals may obtain on request details of the terms on which the advertiser is prepared to do business.

F. SECURITY

As with past regulations, the 2004 Regulations remain desperately worried about **10.46** secured lending and firmly wedded to the health warning in block capitals.

Regulation 7(1) provides that where either a credit advertisement or a hire **10.47** advertisement is a facility for which security is or may be required, the advertisement must state that security is or may be required and the nature of such security.

Special treatment is afforded to credit agreements secured on mortgages **10.48** which are not repayable while the debtor continues to occupy the land as his main residence. These fall into two categories:

(a) mortgages where no instalment repayment of the credit and no payment of interest (other than on voluntary repayment of all or part of the credit) is payable while the debtor continues in occupation;

(b) mortgages where the creditor cannot enforce by taking possession or by selling while the debtor continues in occupation, and no full or partial repayment of the credit becomes payable while he continues in occupation (although interest may be payable in that period).[13]

10.49   With credit agreements of this type, the advertisement must contain the warning:

CHECK THAT THIS MORTGAGE WILL MEET YOUR NEEDS IF YOU WANT TO MOVE OR SELL YOUR HOME OR YOU WANT YOUR FAMILY TO INHERIT IT. IF YOU ARE IN ANY DOUBT, SEEK INDEPENDENT ADVICE.

10.50   In all other cases of credit secured by a mortgage on the debtor's home, the warning must read:

YOUR HOME MAY BE REPOSSESSED IF YOU DO NOT KEEP UP REPAYMENTS ON A MORTGAGE OR ANY OTHER DEBT SECURED ON IT.

10.51   A similar warning is to be given in the case of a hire advertisement where the payments are or may be secured by a mortgage on the hirer's home.[14]

10.52   Where the advertisement indicates that credit is available to pay off debts to other creditors, it must say:

THINK CAREFULLY BEFORE SECURING OTHER DEBTS AGAINST YOUR HOME.

10.53   Where the mortgage secures credit whose repayments are to be made in a currency other than sterling, the advertisement must contain a warning that changes in exchange rates may increase the debt.[15]

10.54   The warnings are to be given no less prominence than the information required to be given under Regulation 4 and Schedules 2 and 3[16] and, in the case of credit advertisements, must be given greater prominence than is given to any rate of charge other than the typical APR or any 'indication or incentive' within Regulation 8(1)(c) or (d) (see below).

10.55   Relief, however, is given from the gabbled rubric on commercial radio. Regulation 7(8) exempts advertisers from all the requirements of Regulation 7, except for Regulation 7(1) (statement that security is required) in the case of an advertisement which:

---

[13] 2004 Regulations Reg 7(3).
[14] Ibid Reg 7(5).
[15] Ibid Reg 7(4).
[16] Ibid Reg 6(b) for credit advertisements and 6(7) for hire advertisements.

(a) is published by means of a television or radio broadcast in the course of programming the primary purpose of which is not advertising;

(b) is published by exhibition of a film (other than on television); or

(c) contains only the name of the advertiser.

It is to be assumed that (a) will exempt an advertisement contained in a 'commercial break' but not an advertisement forming part of a promotional broadcast, as, for example, on a shopping channel. **10.56**

The third exception is designed to exempt the most basic forms of 'brand recognition' advertising, for example a matchbook or beer mat which simply says 'Offered by Bloggs Mortgages plc'. **10.57**

G. THE APR

1. What Governs the Stated APR ?

The requirements with regard to stating the APR have been simplified from those of the 1989 Regulations but are still not entirely straightforward. **10.58**

The APR is defined as meaning the annualized percentage rate of charge for credit determined in accordance with the Total Charge for Credit Regulations 1980 and Schedule 1 to the 2004 Regulations. **10.59**

Schedule 1 sets out particular rules for the statement of the APR in credit advertisements. **10.60**

1. Assumptions about running-account credit. These assumptions replace those in Part 4 of the 1980 Regulations and apply notwithstanding the terms of the transaction. In summary, the calculation is to assume: **10.61**

(a) the credit is the lower of £1,500 or the maximum credit offered;

(b) the credit is provided for one year;

(c) the credit is provided in full at the outset;

(d) where the interest rate will change within three years of the outset, the rate taken is the highest during that period;

(e) where the credit is provided to finance the purchase of goods, service, land, or other things and also provides a cash loan, refinancing credit, or credit for any other purpose and different rates of interest or different charges are payable depending on the purpose, the rate is assumed to be that relating to the credit for the purchase;

(f) the credit is repaid in 12 equal instalments at monthly intervals.

2. Permissible tolerances in disclosure of an APR. Other than when rules 3 and 4 apply, the permissible tolerances are expressing a rate which exceeds the APR by not more than 1 per cent or a rate which falls short of the APR by not more than 0.1 per cent. **10.62**

3. Tolerance where repayments are nearly equal. If all repayments but one are equal and the odd man out does not differ from the others by 'more whole pence **10.63** than there are repayments of credit', the rate may be calculated as if that one payment were equal to the others.

10.64   *4. Tolerance where the interval between the relevant date and the first repayment is greater than the interval between repayments.* Where there are more than three repayments to be made at equal intervals but there is a gap between the making of the agreement[17] and the first of those repayments which is longer than the interval between the repayments, then the calculation is to assume that the gap is reduced to that interval.

10.65   In general, what is to be stated is a 'typical APR'. This is defined by Regulation 1(2) as:

an APR at or below which an advertiser reasonably expects, at the date on which an advertisement is published that credit would be provided under at least 66% of the agreements he will enter into as a result of the advertisement.

10.66   This is clearly aimed at the advertiser who is minded to quote a very favourable APR without disclosing that it will be available in only a tiny handful of cases. The phenomenon, familiar in advertisements, of saying 'Prices from . . .' or 'Prices start at only . . .' when, in reality, these prices are unrepresentative, is banned with credit and hire advertisements.

2. When must the APR be Stated?

10.67   A credit advertisement must specify the typical APR in any of four situations,[18] namely where the advertisement:

(a) specifies any other rate of charge;

(b) includes any of the items of information in items 5, 6, or 7 of Schedule 2 (see above);

(c) indicates in any way (including the use of a business name or an electronic address[19]) that:
   (i)   credit is available to persons who might otherwise consider their access to credit restricted; or
   (ii) any of the terms on which credit is available is more favourable than corresponding terms applied in any other case or by any other creditors; or

(d) includes any incentive to apply for credit or to enter into an agreement under which credit is provided.

10.68   The first two categories are self-explanatory but the third is very wide-

---

[17] Or the date of its being put into effect, if later—see Reg 1(2) of the 2004 Regulations.
[18] 2004 Regulations Reg 8(1).
[19] For example 'statusfreeloans.com' (assumed by the authors not to be a genuine name).

ranging. Many advertisements target what are sometimes described as 'non-status' customers, that is to say customers who might find it difficult in the light of their financial or credit record to obtain credit. For obvious reasons they are considered (rightly) as vulnerable and possibly of less financial sophistication than other borrowers. Given that credit rates are understandably somewhat higher for such borrowers, it is not unreasonable that advertisements that target them should state a typical APR.

The other limb of (c) is equally reasonable. If an advertiser is saying that his terms for a particular type of transaction are more favourable than those available for others of his agreements or those available generally in the market, or are more favourable than those offered by other creditors (whether named or not), it is fair that he should make good his assertions by publishing a typical APR.   **10.69**

The problems arise with (d) and they have been compounded by the Office of Fair Trading (OFT) itself. In its role as, so to speak, guardian of the CCA 1974, the OFT publishes a great deal of guidance on the Act and its Regulations, often in the form of 'Frequently Asked Questions' (FAQs) to which the OFT supplies what may be considered to be the official answers. The FAQs published by the OFT in relation to Regulations in 2005 marked a considerable hardening of the OFT's views from those published in 2004 and the OFT may well be trying to work towards a position where (d) is construed so widely as to apply to *any* credit advertisement.   **10.70**

To come within paragraph (d), the credit advertisement must include 'any incentive to apply for credit or to enter into an agreement under which credit is provided'. Patently any credit advertisement must, of its very nature, invite the prospective customer to use the credit of the advertiser in preference to that offered by its competitors (even if the competitors are nowhere mentioned). An advertisement inviting you to shop at Tesco necessarily implies that you should do so in preference to shopping at Sainsbury, Asda, or your corner shop.   **10.71**

If that was all paragraph (d) meant, however, both the paragraph and the whole of Regulation 8(1) would be unnecessary. All credit advertisements would be caught by the requirement to state the typical APR. Paragraph (d) must, therefore, be more restricted than the general exhortation to the public to 'come to us and not our competitors'.   **10.72**

If paragraph (d) were construed objectively, it must surely mean that the customer is being offered an incentive to use *credit* rather than some other form of agreement (cash purchase or hire being the obvious alternatives). This construction is, in my view, strengthened by looking at paragraph (d) in its context. Paragraphs (a) and (b) are designed to ensure that if the advertiser gives some financial information he must also state a typical APR. Paragraph (c)(i) applies to advertisements which target non-status borrowers and paragraph (c)(ii) those which make actual comparisons with competitors. This leaves paragraph (d), as part of a logical scheme, to sweep up those who are inviting customers to apply for credit rather than acquire goods or services in some other way.   **10.73**

10.74   This has the merit of viewing Regulation 8(1) as a coherent list of triggers and avoids:

(a) any unnecessary overlap between the triggers; and

(b) the consequence that Regulation 8(1) is construed so as to include all credit advertisements of any kind.

10.75   Clearly, an offer of gifts or other financial benefits if the customer signs up for credit as opposed to doing nothing or making a cash purchase is an inducement within paragraph (d).

10.76   Thus paragraph (d) would apply to statements such as: '2% off our usual rates', 'pay nothing for 6 months', 'buy now, pay next June', 'no fee on loans over £10,000' or 'no deposit on orders before 1 May'.

10.77   With paragraph (d), therefore, the correct questions to be asked are:

(a) is the inducement an inducement to apply for credit rather than use some other method of acquiring goods and services; or

(b) is it an inducement to apply for the advertisers' credit rather than anyone else's?

If the answer is (a), the advertisement is caught: if (b), it is not.

3. A Range of APRs

10.78   Advertisers often like to display a range of APRs, no doubt hoping that the potential customer will see himself as coming at the bottom of the range rather than the top and be attracted to apply. This is permissible, but only if the advertisement specifies with equal prominence both:

(a) the APR which the advertiser reasonably expects at the date of publication of the advertisement would be the lowest APR at which credit would be provided under not less than 10 per cent of agreements entered into as a result of the advertisement, and

(b) the APR which the advertiser reasonably expects at that date to be the highest APR under any of the agreements thus entered into.[20]

4. Obligatory Wording

10.79   An APR must be denoted in an advertisement as '%APR'.[21]

10.80   When an APR is subject to change, it must say 'variable'.[22]

10.81   A typical APR must be described as 'typical', presented together with the obligatory information under Schedule 2, and be given greater prominence than

---

[20] 2004 Regulations Reg 8(2).
[21] Ibid Reg 8(3).
[22] Ibid Reg 8(4).

any other rate of charge, any of the Schedule 2 items, and any indication or incentive under paragraphs (c) and (d) of Regulation 8(1) (above). It must, in any printed or electronic form which includes any Schedule 2 items, be printed in characters at least 150 per cent the size of the characters in which those items are shown.

5. Special Cases

Where the advertisement relates to a debtor–creditor agreement for a current account overdraft where the creditor is the Bank of England or an authorized deposit taker,[23] the advertisement may give, in place of a typical APR, a statement of a rate, expressed as a rate of interest, determined as the rate of the total charge for credit on the assumption that it only includes interest and the nature and a statement of the amount of any other charge included in the total charge for credit. **10.82**

H. WHAT NOT TO SAY

One hangover (one is tempted to say 'hangup') from the 1989 Regulations is a list of banned expressions or, more precisely, expressions that may only be used in a very narrow context.[24] **10.83**

Running-account credit may not be referred to as an '*overdraft*' unless it is an agreement enabling the debtor to overdraw on a current account. **10.84**

'*Interest free*' or any similar expression is banned for transactions financed by credit except where the total amount payable by the debtor does not exceed the cash price. **10.85**

'*No deposit*' must mean that no advance payments are to be made whatsoever. **10.86**

'*Loan guaranteed*' or '*pre-approved*' can only be used where the agreement is free from any conditions regarding the credit status of the debtor. **10.87**

Only use '*gift*', '*present*', or similar when there are no conditions which might require the debtor to have to give the present back to the creditor. **10.88**

Neither credit advertisements nor hire advertisements may use the expression '*weekly equivalent*' (or any other periodical equivalent) unless weekly payments (or the stated periodical payments) are provided for under the agreement.[25] **10.89**

---

[23] As defined by the Financial Services and Markets Act 2000 Part 4 and Sch 3.
[24] 2004 Regulations Reg 9(1).
[25] Ibid Reg 9(2).

11

ELECTRONIC COMMUNICATIONS

A. SCOPE OF THIS CHAPTER

When the Consumer Credit Act 1974 (CCA 1974) was passed computers were in **11.01** their infancy and certainly not available to the average seeker of credit at the levels at which the Act applied. The intervening three decades, however, have seen a revolution in communications and widespread access to and use of the Internet. The scheme of the original CCA 1974 was very much based on paper transactions, almost always involving face-to-face communication between the debtor and the creditor or his agent.

There has been an understandable reluctance on the part of those responsible **11.02** for the CCA 1974 to rush into legislating for the concluding of consumer credit or consumer hire agreements electronically, but it has formed part of the drive to modernize consumer credit spearheaded by the White Paper *Fair, Clear and Competitive—The Consumer Credit Market in the 21st Century* (the White Paper).

A general discussion of the rules relating to electronic signatures and distance **11.03** marketing would be inappropriate to a book dealing principally with changes to consumer credit law so we shall simply give an indication of the relevant provisions of the legislation on these topics while emphasizing that this is not a substitute for a detailed study of that legislation if a particular distance marketing problem arises.

We shall then describe the amendments to the CCA 1974 itself and to **11.04** its dependent regulations brought about by the Consumer Credit Act 1974 (Electronic Communications) Order 2004.

B. ELECTRONIC SIGNATURES

11.05 Electronic communication eliminates the need for paper. Any agreement, however, requires some sort of acknowledgment by the parties that they agree to be bound by the obligations mutually undertaken. In the case of the CCA 1974 and other legislation, there is a statutory requirement for agreements within certain categories to be signed by what may loosely be called 'the customer'. Consequently, if such agreements are to be concluded electronically, there must be a mechanism for something which operates in the same way electronically as the signature written on the physical document.

11.06 The issue of electronic signatures has been tackled at European level. The Electronic Signatures Directive 1999 came into force on 19 January 2000 and required implementation by Member States by 19 July 2001. In 2002 Parliament passed the Electronic Communications Act 2000 (the 2000 Act) which came into force on 25 June 2000. The Act was later supplemented by the Electronic Signatures Regulations 2002 which came into force on 8 March 2002 (the 2002 Regulations).

11.07 The Directive and the subsequent UK legislation distinguishes between an 'electronic signature' and an 'advanced electronic signature'. Both are defined in Regulation 2 of the 2002 Regulations:

'electronic signature' means data in electronic form which are attached to or logically associated with other electronic data and which serve as a method of authentication;
  'advanced electronic signature' means an electronic signature—
(a) which is uniquely linked to the signatory,
(b) which is capable of identifying the signatory,
(c) which is created using means that the signatory can maintain under his sole control, and
(d) which is linked to the data to which it relates in such a manner that any subsequent change of the data is detectable.

11.08 Section 7 of the Electronic Communications Act 2000 provides that in any legal proceedings an electronic signature incorporated into or logically associated with a particular electronic communication or particular electronic data together with the certification by any person of such a signature shall be admissible in evidence in relation to any question as to the authenticity or integrity of the communication or data.[1]

11.09 An electronic signature is 'certified' for the purposes of s 7(1) by a person if that person (whether before or after the making of the communication) has made a statement confirming that the signature or the means of producing, communicating, or verifying the signature or a procedure applied to the signature is a valid means of establishing the authenticity or integrity of the

---

[1] The 2000 Act s 7(1).

communication or data.[2] In this context, 'authenticity' refers to whether the communication or data comes from a particular person and/or whether it is accurately timed and dated and/or whether it is intended to have legal effect; and 'integrity' refers to whether there has been any tampering with or other modification of the communication or data.[3]

Certificate is defined as meaning 'an electronic attestation which links signature-verification data to a person and confirms the identity of that person'. The key to certification is the provision of the services of reliable certification service providers. Such providers are to be controlled by the Department of Trade and Industry (DTI) and subject to registration.[4] To be registered the provider must satisfy the criteria set out in Schedule 2 to the 2002 Regulations. **11.10**

Once a provider is approved, then that provider can issue a qualified certificate, being a certificate which meets the requirements of Schedule 1 to the 2002 Regulations. This certificate acts to make the certification service provider liable if loss is suffered by reliance on a certified electronic signature and to place the provider under a duty of care to the public, breach of which is actionable.[5] **11.11**

The way was thus paved for electronic signatures to be treated as sufficient for legal purposes, including those of contracting under the CCA 1974. **11.12**

C. DISTANCE MARKETING

Distance marketing of financial products, including credit agreements, is largely governed by the Financial Services (Distance Marketing) Regulations 2004 (the FS (DM) Regulations). **11.13**

'Distance contract' means 'any contract concerning one or more financial services concluded between a supplier and a consumer under an organized distance sales or service-provision scheme run by the supplier or by an intermediary, who, for the purpose of that contract, makes exclusive use of one or more means of distance communication up to and including the time at which the contract is concluded'.[6] **11.14**

'Financial service' includes any service of a credit nature. **11.15**

Interestingly, the FS (DM) Regulations protect the 'consumer' who is defined in the standard EU Directive manner as 'an individual who . . . is acting for purposes which are outside any business he may carry on'. This definition is obviously more restrictive than that in the amended s 189(1) of the CCA 1974.[7] **11.16**

---

[2] Ibid s 7(3).
[3] Ibid s 15.
[4] 2002 Regulations Reg 3.
[5] Ibid Reg 4.
[6] FS (DM) Regulations Reg 2(1).
[7] See Chap 2 above.

11.17   The salient points to note about the FS (DM) Regulations are as follows. Whether or not a contract is regulated by the CCA 1974, the obligations of the Regulations must be complied with in addition to any CCA obligations.

11.18   'In good time prior to the consumer being bound by any distance contract', the supplier or, where appropriate, the intermediary (ie broker) must provide a list of (up to 21) separate pieces of information set out in Schedule 1 to the Regulations.[8] That information must be clear and comprehensible with 'due regard to the principles of good faith in commercial transactions' and the supplier must 'make clear his commercial purpose'.

11.19   Under Regulation 8 of the FS (DM) Regulations, the supplier must also communicate to the consumer on paper or some other 'durable medium' all the contractual terms and conditions and the Schedule 1 information in good time prior to the consumer being bound or immediately after conclusion of the contract if it has been concluded at the consumer's request using a means of distance communication which does not enable the written document to be sent out in advance.

11.20   Regulation 9 gives the consumer a right to cancel which, if exercised, terminates the contract. Notice of cancellation can be given orally (if previously authorized by the supplier) or in writing or any other durable medium and can itself be given electronically. Regulation 10 specifies the cancellation period (essentially 14 days from the happening of a named event, normally the day the contract is concluded).

11.21   There are exceptions to the right to cancel under Regulation 11. The principal exceptions applicable to consumer credit agreements are:

(a) a contract which has been fully performed before cancellation;

(b) a contract under which a supplier provides credit to a consumer secured by a legal mortgage on land;

(c) a 'related credit agreement' automatically cancelled on cancellation of the principal agreement under Regulation 15(1) of the Consumer Protection (Distance Selling) Regulations 2000;

(d) a credit agreement cancelled under s 6A of the Timeshare Act 1992;

(e) a restricted-use credit agreement to finance the purchase of land or an existing building or an agreement for a bridging loan in connection with such a purchase.

11.22   These exemptions do not, however, apply in certain circumstances where the supplier has failed to comply with Regulations 7 and 8 and a right of cancellation is preserved in these cases.

11.23   It must be emphasized that these rights of cancellation are additional to those conferred by the CCA 1974 itself.

---

[8] FS (DM) Regulations Reg 7 and Sch 1.

There are provisions for automatic cancellation of 'attached' contracts[9] and **11.24** for payment for services provided before cancellation.[10] Protection is also given to credit or debit card holders where the card or its details have been made fraudulently or without authority[11].

Enforcement of the FS (DM) Regulations is by criminal sanction or civil **11.25** injunction brought by the enforcement authority.[12] A breach of the Regulations does not render a distance contract for the provision of credit unenforceable as such or even enforceable with leave of the court as under s 127 of the CCA 1974. An aggrieved customer has the right to complain and the enforcement authority can extract undertakings or seek an injunction to compel compliance by the supplier.[13] Certain breaches of the FS (DM) Regulations are criminal offences.[14]

D. CHANGES TO THE CONSUMER CREDIT ACT 1974

The necessary changes to the CCA 1974 and the Regulations was brought about **11.26** by the Consumer Credit Act 1974 (Electronic Communications) Order 2004 (the Electronic Communications Order) which came into force on 31 December 2004.

Article 2(8) introduces a new concept to the definition section of the CCA **11.27** 1974, s 189(1):

'appropriate method' means—
(a) post, or
(b) transmission in the form of an electronic communication in accordance with section 176A(1).

A document is to be treated as electronically transmitted under s 176A if: **11.28**

(a) the person to whom it is transmitted agrees that it may be delivered to him by being transmitted to a particular electronic address in a particular electronic form,
(b) it is transmitted to that address in that form, and
(c) the form in which the document is transmitted is such that any information in the document which is addressed to the person to whom the document is transmitted is capable of being stored for future reference for an appropriate period in a way which allows the information to be reproduced without change.[15]

---

[9] Ibid Reg 12.
[10] Ibid Reg 13.
[11] Ibid Reg 14.
[12] Principally the Financial Services Authority (FSA), but for some local authority contracts it is the Office of Fair Trading (OFT) and for minor breaches the authority is either the OFT or the local weights and measures authority—see Reg 17 of the FS (DM) Regulations.
[13] FS (DM) Regulations Regs 18 and 19.
[14] See ibid Reg 22.
[15] Electronic Communications Order Art 2(7).

11.29   Except for a communication under s 69 (notice of cancellation), any electronic document is to be treated as having been delivered the following day (subject to proof to the contrary).[16]

11.30   The substitution of 'by an appropriate method' for 'by post' is effected throughout the CCA 1974 and the Regulations.

11.31   Thus changes are made to s 61(2) (signing of the agreement), s 63(3) (duty to supply copy of executed agreement), s 64 (duty to give notice of cancellation rights), and s 176 (service of documents).

11.32   The exception is s 69(7) where Article 2(5) substitutes a new subsection providing:

Whether or not it is actually received by him, a notice of cancellation sent to a person shall be deemed to be served on him—
(a) in the case of a notice sent by post, at the time of posting, and
(b) in the case of a notice transmitted in the form of an electronic communication in accordance with section 176A(1), at the time of the transmission.

E. CHANGES TO THE REGULATIONS

11.33   The regulations need to legislate for a number of mundane but necessary matters such as the definition of 'postal address' and the colour of paper used in agreements.

11.34   The only change to **the Consumer Credit (Termination of Licences) Regulations 1976** is the substitution of 'by an appropriate method' for 'by post'.[17]

11.35   Several changes are made to **the Consumer Credit (Agreements) Regulations 1983**.[18] 'Colour of paper' becomes 'background medium upon which the information is displayed' and provisions are made for the creditor or owner to insert an electronic address in addition to the postal address at various places in the agreement.

11.36   Changes very similar to those for the Agreements Regulations are made to **the Consumer Credit (Guarantees and Indemnities) Regulations 1983**.[19]

11.37   Most of the changes to **the Consumer Credit (Cancellation Notices and Copies of Documents) Regulations 1983** involve the substitution of 'by an appropriate method' for 'by post' but they also provide for cancellation notices to be given electronically in certain cases.[20]

11.38   **The Consumer Credit (Settlement Information) Regulations 1983, the Consumer Credit (Conduct of Business) (Pawn Records) Regulations 1983** and **the Consumer Credit (Realisation of Pawn) Regulations 1983** only have the addition of 'other

---

[16] CCA 1974 as inserted by CCA 2006 s 176A(2).
[17] Electronic Communications Order Art 3.
[18] By Art 4 of the Electronic Communications Order and see Chapter 6 above.
[19] Electronic Communications Order Art 5.
[20] Ibid Art 7.

address' to 'postal address'.[21] **The Consumer Credit (Pawn Receipts) Regulations 1983**[22] have these changes and the change relating to 'colour of paper' set out in paragraph 11.35 above.

Finally the 'colour of paper' changes are made to **the Consumer Credit (Running Account Information) Regulations 1983**.[23]   **11.39**

---

[21] Ibid Arts 8, 9, and 11.
[22] Ibid Art 10.
[23] Ibid Art 12.

APPENDIX 1

Consumer Credit Act 2006

An Act to amend the Consumer Credit Act 1974; to extend the ombudsman scheme under the Financial Services and Markets Act 2000 to cover licensees under the Consumer Credit Act 1974; and for connected purposes.

[30th March 2006]

BE IT ENACTED by the Queen's most Excellent Majesty, by and with the advice and consent of the Lords Spiritual and Temporal, and Commons, in this present Parliament assembled, and by the authority of the same, as follows:—

Agreements regulated under the 1974 Act etc.

1 Definition of "individual"

In section 189(1) of the 1974 Act (definitions) for the definition of "individual" substitute—

" 'individual' includes—
  (a) a partnership consisting of two or three persons not all of whom are bodies corporate; and
  (b) an unincorporated body of persons which does not consist entirely of bodies corporate and is not a partnership;".

2 Removal of financial limits etc.

(1) In section 8 of the 1974 Act (which defines consumer credit agreements)—
  (a) in subsection (1) for "personal" substitute "consumer";
  (b) subsection (2) shall cease to have effect.
(2) In section 15(1) of that Act (which defines consumer hire agreements) paragraph (c) and the "and" immediately preceding it shall cease to have effect.
(3) In section 43(3) of that Act (financial and other limits relating to regulation of advertisements) paragraph (a) and the "or" immediately after it shall cease to have effect.

3 Exemption relating to high net worth debtors and hirers

After section 16 of the 1974 Act insert—

"16A Exemption relating to high net worth debtors and hirers

(1) The Secretary of State may by order provide that this Act shall not regulate a consumer credit agreement or a consumer hire agreement where—
  (a) the debtor or hirer is a natural person;

   (b) the agreement includes a declaration made by him to the effect that he agrees to forgo the protection and remedies that would be available to him under this Act if the agreement were a regulated agreement;

   (c) a statement of high net worth has been made in relation to him; and

   (d) that statement is current in relation to the agreement and a copy of it was provided to the creditor or owner before the agreement was made.

(2) For the purposes of this section a statement of high net worth is a statement to the effect that, in the opinion of the person making it, the natural person in relation to whom it is made—

   (a) received during the previous financial year income of a specified description totalling an amount of not less than the specified amount; or

   (b) had throughout that year net assets of a specified description with a total value of not less than the specified value.

(3) Such a statement—

   (a) may not be made by the person in relation to whom it is made;

   (b) must be made by a person of a specified description; and

   (c) is current in relation to an agreement if it was made during the period of one year ending with the day on which the agreement is made.

(4) An order under this section may make provision about—

   (a) how amounts of income and values of net assets are to be determined for the purposes of subsection (2)(a) and (b);

   (b) the form, content and signing of—

     (i) statements of high net worth;

     (ii) declarations for the purposes of subsection (1)(b).

(5) Where an agreement has two or more debtors or hirers, for the purposes of paragraph (c) of subsection (1) a separate statement of high net worth must have been made in relation to each of them; and paragraph (d) of that subsection shall have effect accordingly.

(6) In this section—

'previous financial year' means, in relation to a statement of high net worth, the financial year immediately preceding the financial year during which the statement is made;

'specified' means specified in an order under this section.

(7) In subsection (6) 'financial year' means a period of one year ending with 31st March.

(8) Nothing in this section affects the application of sections 140A to 140C."

4 Exemption relating to businesses

Before section 17 of the 1974 Act insert—

"16B Exemption relating to businesses

(1) This Act does not regulate—

   (a) a consumer credit agreement by which the creditor provides the debtor with credit exceeding £25,000, or

   (b) a consumer hire agreement that requires the hirer to make payments exceeding £25,000,

if the agreement is entered into by the debtor or hirer wholly or predominantly for the purposes of a business carried on, or intended to be carried on, by him.

(2) If an agreement includes a declaration made by the debtor or hirer to the effect that the agreement is entered into by him wholly or predominantly for the purposes of a business carried on, or intended to be carried on, by him, the agreement shall be presumed to have been entered into by him wholly or predominantly for such purposes.

(3) But that presumption does not apply if, when the agreement is entered into—

    (a) the creditor or owner, or

    (b) any person who has acted on his behalf in connection with the entering into of the agreement,

knows, or has reasonable cause to suspect, that the agreement is not entered into by the debtor or hirer wholly or predominantly for the purposes of a business carried on, or intended to be carried on, by him.

(4) The Secretary of State may by order make provision about the form, content and signing of declarations for the purposes of subsection (2).

(5) Where an agreement has two or more creditors or owners, in subsection (3) references to the creditor or owner are references to any one or more of them.

(6) Nothing in this section affects the application of sections 140A to 140C."

5 Consequential amendments relating to ss. 1 to 4

(1) In section 8(3) of the 1974 Act (which defines regulated consumer credit agreements) after "16" insert ", 16A or 16B".

(2) In section 10 of that Act (running-account credit and fixed-sum credit)—

    (a) in subsection (1) for "personal" wherever occurring substitute "consumer";

    (b) in subsection (3)—

        (i) for "section 8(2)" substitute "paragraph (a) of section 16B(1)";

        (ii) for "subsection" substitute "paragraph".

(3) In section 17(2) of that Act (small agreements) for "8(2)" substitute "16B(1)(a)".

(4) In section 145(4) of that Act (types of hire businesses relevant to credit brokerage) after paragraph (a) insert—

        "(aa) a business which comprises or relates to consumer hire agreements being, otherwise than by virtue of section 16(6), exempt agreements;".

(5) In subsection (1) of section 158 of that Act (duty of credit reference agency to disclose filed information) for paragraph (a) substitute—

    "(a) a request in writing to that effect from a consumer,".

(6) After subsection (4) of that section insert—

    "(4A) In this section 'consumer' means—

        (a) a partnership consisting of two or three persons not all of whom are bodies corporate; or

        (b) an unincorporated body of persons which does not consist entirely of bodies corporate and is not a partnership."

(7) In section 181(1) and (2) of that Act (power to alter monetary limits etc.) for "8(2), 15(1)(c)" substitute "16B(1)".

(8) In subsection (5) of section 185 of that Act (agreement with more than one debtor or hirer)—

    (a) in paragraph (b) for "a body corporate" substitute "not an individual";

    (b) for "the body corporate or bodies corporate" substitute "each person within paragraph (b)".

(9) In subsection (6) of that section after "a body corporate" insert "within paragraph (b) of that subsection".

(10) In section 189(1) of that Act (definitions) in the definition of "exempt agreement" after "16" insert ", 16A or 16B".

Statements to be provided in relation to regulated credit agreements

6 Statements to be provided in relation to fixed-sum credit agreements

After section 77 of the 1974 Act insert—

"77A Statements to be provided in relation to fixed-sum credit agreements

(1) The creditor under a regulated agreement for fixed-sum credit—
  (a) shall, within the period of one year beginning with the day after the day on which the agreement is made, give the debtor a statement under this section; and
  (b) after the giving of that statement, shall give the debtor further statements under this section at intervals of not more than one year.
(2) Regulations may make provision about the form and content of statements under this section.
(3) The debtor shall have no liability to pay any sum in connection with the preparation or the giving to him of a statement under this section.
(4) The creditor is not required to give the debtor any statement under this section once the following conditions are satisfied—
  (a) that there is no sum payable under the agreement by the debtor; and
  (b) that there is no sum which will or may become so payable.
(5) Subsection (6) applies if at a time before the conditions mentioned in subsection (4) are satisfied the creditor fails to give the debtor—
  (a) a statement under this section within the period mentioned in subsection (1)(a); or
  (b) such a statement within the period of one year beginning with the day after the day on which such a statement was last given to him.
(6) Where this subsection applies in relation to a failure to give a statement under this section to the debtor—
  (a) the creditor shall not be entitled to enforce the agreement during the period of non-compliance;
  (b) the debtor shall have no liability to pay any sum of interest to the extent calculated by reference to the period of non-compliance or to any part of it; and
  (c) the debtor shall have no liability to pay any default sum which (apart from this paragraph)—
    (i) would have become payable during the period of non-compliance; or
    (ii) would have become payable after the end of that period in connection with a breach of the agreement which occurs during that period (whether or not the breach continues after the end of that period).
(7) In this section 'the period of non-compliance' means, in relation to a failure to give a statement under this section to the debtor, the period which—
  (a) begins immediately after the end of the period mentioned in paragraph (a) or (as the case may be) paragraph (b) of subsection (5); and
  (b) ends at the end of the day on which the statement is given to the debtor or on which the conditions mentioned in subsection (4) are satisfied, whichever is earlier.

(8) This section does not apply in relation to a non-commercial agreement or to a small agreement."

7 Further provision relating to statements

(1) In section 78 of the 1974 Act (duty to give information to debtor under running-account credit agreement) after subsection (4) insert—

"(4A) Regulations may require a statement under subsection (4) to contain also information in the prescribed terms about the consequences of the debtor—
  (a) failing to make payments as required by the agreement; or
  (b) only making payments of a prescribed description in prescribed circumstances."

(2) In subsection (7) of that section for "(4) and (5)" substitute "(4) to (5)".

(3) In section 185 of that Act (agreement with more than one debtor or hirer) for subsection (2) substitute—

"(2) Notwithstanding subsection (1)(a), where credit is provided under an agreement to two or more debtors jointly, in performing his duties—
  (a) in the case of fixed-sum credit, under section 77A, or
  (b) in the case of running-account credit, under section 78(4),
  the creditor need not give statements to any debtor who has signed and given to him a notice (a 'dispensing notice') authorising him not to comply in the debtor's case with section 77A or (as the case may be) 78(4).

(2A) A dispensing notice given by a debtor is operative from when it is given to the creditor until it is revoked by a further notice given to the creditor by the debtor.

(2B) But subsection (2) does not apply if (apart from this subsection) dispensing notices would be operative in relation to all of the debtors to whom the credit is provided.

(2C) Any dispensing notices operative in relation to an agreement shall cease to have effect if any of the debtors dies.

(2D) A dispensing notice which is operative in relation to an agreement shall be operative also in relation to any subsequent agreement which, in relation to the earlier agreement, is a modifying agreement."

Default under regulated agreements

8 OFT to prepare information sheets on arrears and default

At the beginning of Part 7 of the 1974 Act insert—

"Information sheets

86A OFT to prepare information sheets on arrears and default

(1) The OFT shall prepare, and give general notice of, an arrears information sheet and a default information sheet.

(2) The arrears information sheet shall include information to help debtors and hirers who receive notices under section 86B or 86C.

(3) The default information sheet shall include information to help debtors and hirers who receive default notices.

(4) Regulations may make provision about the information to be included in an information sheet.

(5) An information sheet takes effect for the purposes of this Part at the end of the period of three months beginning with the day on which general notice of it is given.

(6) If the OFT revises an information sheet after general notice of it has been given, it shall give general notice of the information sheet as revised.

(7) A revised information sheet takes effect for the purposes of this Part at the end of the period of three months beginning with the day on which general notice of it is given."

9 Notice of sums in arrears under fixed-sum credit agreements etc.

After section 86A of the 1974 Act (inserted by section 8 of this Act) insert—

"Sums in arrears and default sums

86B Notice of sums in arrears under fixed-sum credit agreements etc.

(1) This section applies where at any time the following conditions are satisfied—
   (a) that the debtor or hirer under an applicable agreement is required to have made at least two payments under the agreement before that time;
   (b) that the total sum paid under the agreement by him is less than the total sum which he is required to have paid before that time;
   (c) that the amount of the shortfall is no less than the sum of the last two payments which he is required to have made before that time;
   (d) that the creditor or owner is not already under a duty to give him notices under this section in relation to the agreement; and
   (e) if a judgment has been given in relation to the agreement before that time, that there is no sum still to be paid under the judgment by the debtor or hirer.

(2) The creditor or owner—
   (a) shall, within the period of 14 days beginning with the day on which the conditions mentioned in subsection (1) are satisfied, give the debtor or hirer a notice under this section; and
   (b) after the giving of that notice, shall give him further notices under this section at intervals of not more than six months.

(3) The duty of the creditor or owner to give the debtor or hirer notices under this section shall cease when either of the conditions mentioned in subsection (4) is satisfied; but if either of those conditions is satisfied before the notice required by subsection (2)(a) is given, the duty shall not cease until that notice is given.

(4) The conditions referred to in subsection (3) are—
   (a) that the debtor or hirer ceases to be in arrears;
   (b) that a judgment is given in relation to the agreement under which a sum is required to be paid by the debtor or hirer.

(5) For the purposes of subsection (4)(a) the debtor or hirer ceases to be in arrears when—
   (a) no sum, which he has ever failed to pay under the agreement when required, is still owing;
   (b) no default sum, which has ever become payable under the agreement in connection with his failure to pay any sum under the agreement when required, is still owing;
   (c) no sum of interest, which has ever become payable under the agreement in connection with such a default sum, is still owing; and

(d) no other sum of interest, which has ever become payable under the agreement in connection with his failure to pay any sum under the agreement when required, is still owing.

(6) A notice under this section shall include a copy of the current arrears information sheet under section 86A.

(7) The debtor or hirer shall have no liability to pay any sum in connection with the preparation or the giving to him of a notice under this section.

(8) Regulations may make provision about the form and content of notices under this section.

(9) In the case of an applicable agreement under which the debtor or hirer must make all payments he is required to make at intervals of one week or less, this section shall have effect as if in subsection (1)(a) and (c) for 'two' there were substituted 'four'.

(10) If an agreement mentioned in subsection (9) was made before the beginning of the relevant period, only amounts resulting from failures by the debtor or hirer to make payments he is required to have made during that period shall be taken into account in determining any shortfall for the purposes of subsection (1)(c).

(11) In subsection (10) 'relevant period' means the period of 20 weeks ending with the day on which the debtor or hirer is required to have made the most recent payment under the agreement.

(12) In this section 'applicable agreement' means an agreement which—

(a) is a regulated agreement for fixed-sum credit or a regulated consumer hire agreement; and

(b) is neither a non-commercial agreement nor a small agreement."

10 Notice of sums in arrears under running-account credit agreements

After section 86B of the 1974 Act (inserted by section 9 of this Act) insert—

"86C Notice of sums in arrears under running-account credit agreements

(1) This section applies where at any time the following conditions are satisfied—

(a) that the debtor under an applicable agreement is required to have made at least two payments under the agreement before that time;

(b) that the last two payments which he is required to have made before that time have not been made;

(c) that the creditor has not already been required to give a notice under this section in relation to either of those payments; and

(d) if a judgment has been given in relation to the agreement before that time, that there is no sum still to be paid under the judgment by the debtor.

(2) The creditor shall, no later than the end of the period within which he is next required to give a statement under section 78(4) in relation to the agreement, give the debtor a notice under this section.

(3) The notice shall include a copy of the current arrears information sheet under section 86A.

(4) The notice may be incorporated in a statement or other notice which the creditor gives the debtor in relation to the agreement by virtue of another provision of this Act.

(5) The debtor shall have no liability to pay any sum in connection with the preparation or the giving to him of the notice.

(6) Regulations may make provision about the form and content of notices under this section.

(7) In this section 'applicable agreement' means an agreement which—

(a) is a regulated agreement for running-account credit; and

(b) is neither a non-commercial agreement nor a small agreement."

11 Failure to give notice of sums in arrears

After section 86C of the 1974 Act (inserted by section 10 of this Act) insert—

"86D Failure to give notice of sums in arrears

(1) This section applies where the creditor or owner under an agreement is under a duty to give the debtor or hirer notices under section 86B but fails to give him such a notice—

(a) within the period mentioned in subsection (2)(a) of that section; or

(b) within the period of six months beginning with the day after the day on which such a notice was last given to him.

(2) This section also applies where the creditor under an agreement is under a duty to give the debtor a notice under section 86C but fails to do so before the end of the period mentioned in subsection (2) of that section.

(3) The creditor or owner shall not be entitled to enforce the agreement during the period of non-compliance.

(4) The debtor or hirer shall have no liability to pay—

(a) any sum of interest to the extent calculated by reference to the period of non-compliance or to any part of it; or

(b) any default sum which (apart from this paragraph)—

(i) would have become payable during the period of non-compliance; or

(ii) would have become payable after the end of that period in connection with a breach of the agreement which occurs during that period (whether or not the breach continues after the end of that period).

(5) In this section 'the period of non-compliance' means, in relation to a failure to give a notice under section 86B or 86C to the debtor or hirer, the period which—

(a) begins immediately after the end of the period mentioned in (as the case may be) subsection (1)(a) or (b) or (2); and

(b) ends at the end of the day mentioned in subsection (6).

(6) That day is—

(a) in the case of a failure to give a notice under section 86B as mentioned in subsection (1)(a) of this section, the day on which the notice is given to the debtor or hirer;

(b) in the case of a failure to give a notice under that section as mentioned in subsection (1)(b) of this section, the earlier of the following—

(i) the day on which the notice is given to the debtor or hirer;

(ii) the day on which the condition mentioned in subsection (4)(a) of that section is satisfied;

(c) in the case of a failure to give a notice under section 86C, the day on which the notice is given to the debtor."

12 Notice of default sums

After section 86D of the 1974 Act (inserted by section 11 of this Act) insert—

"86E Notice of default sums

(1) This section applies where a default sum becomes payable under a regulated agreement by the debtor or hirer.

(2) The creditor or owner shall, within the prescribed period after the default sum becomes payable, give the debtor or hirer a notice under this section.

(3) The notice under this section may be incorporated in a statement or other notice which the creditor or owner gives the debtor or hirer in relation to the agreement by virtue of another provision of this Act.

(4) The debtor or hirer shall have no liability to pay interest in connection with the default sum to the extent that the interest is calculated by reference to a period occurring before the 29th day after the day on which the debtor or hirer is given the notice under this section.

(5) If the creditor or owner fails to give the debtor or hirer the notice under this section within the period mentioned in subsection (2), he shall not be entitled to enforce the agreement until the notice is given to the debtor or hirer.

(6) The debtor or hirer shall have no liability to pay any sum in connection with the preparation or the giving to him of the notice under this section.

(7) Regulations may—

    (a) provide that this section does not apply in relation to a default sum which is less than a prescribed amount;

    (b) make provision about the form and content of notices under this section.

(8) This section does not apply in relation to a non-commercial agreement or to a small agreement."

13 Interest on default sums

After section 86E of the 1974 Act (inserted by section 12 of this Act) insert—

"86F Interest on default sums

(1) This section applies where a default sum becomes payable under a regulated agreement by the debtor or hirer.

(2) The debtor or hirer shall only be liable to pay interest in connection with the default sum if the interest is simple interest."

14 Default notices

(1) In subsections (2) and (3) of section 88 of the 1974 Act (contents and effect of default notice) for "seven" wherever occurring substitute "14".

(2) In subsection (4) of that section after "it" insert "and any other prescribed matters relating to the agreement".

(3) After that subsection insert—

    "(4A) The default notice must also include a copy of the current default information sheet under section 86A."

15 Enforceability of regulated agreements

In section 127 of the 1974 Act (enforcement orders in cases of infringement) subsections (3) to (5) shall cease to have effect.

16 Time orders

(1) In subsection (1) of section 129 of the 1974 Act (time orders) before paragraph (c) insert—

"(ba) on an application made by a debtor or hirer under this paragraph after he has been given a notice under section 86B or 86C; or".

(2) After that section insert—

"129A Debtor or hirer to give notice of intent etc. to creditor or owner

(1) A debtor or hirer may make an application under section 129(1)(ba) in relation to a regulated agreement only if—

(a) following his being given the notice under section 86B or 86C, he gave a notice within subsection (2) to the creditor or owner; and

(b) a period of at least 14 days has elapsed after the day on which he gave that notice to the creditor or owner.

(2) A notice is within this subsection if it—

(a) indicates that the debtor or hirer intends to make the application;

(b) indicates that he wants to make a proposal to the creditor or owner in relation to his making of payments under the agreement; and

(c) gives details of that proposal."

(3) In section 143(b) of that Act (provision which may be made by rules of court in Northern Ireland) after "129(1)(b)" insert "or (ba)".

(4) In section 32(1) of the Sheriff Courts (Scotland) Act 1971 (c. 58) (regulation of civil procedure in sheriff court) after paragraph (l) insert—

"(m) permitting the debtor or hirer in proceedings for—

(i) a time order under section 129 of the Consumer Credit Act 1974 (time orders), or

(ii) variation or revocation, under section 130(6) of that Act (variation and revocation of time orders), of a time order made under section 129,

to be represented by a person who is neither an advocate nor a solicitor."

(5) In section 32(2B) of the Solicitors (Scotland) Act 1980 (c. 46) (offence for unqualified persons to prepare certain documents)—

(a) after "represent" insert "—(a)";

(b) after "cause" insert—

"(b) a debtor or hirer in proceedings for—

(i) a time order under section 129 of the Consumer Credit Act 1974 (time orders); or

(ii) variation or revocation, under section 130(6) of that Act (variation and revocation of time orders), of a time order made under section 129".

17 Interest payable on judgment debts etc.

After section 130 of the 1974 Act insert—

"Interest

130A Interest payable on judgment debts etc.

(1) If the creditor or owner under a regulated agreement wants to be able to recover from the debtor or hirer post-judgment interest in connection with a sum that is

required to be paid under a judgment given in relation to the agreement (the 'judgment sum'), he—

(a) after the giving of that judgment, shall give the debtor or hirer a notice under this section (the 'first required notice'); and

(b) after the giving of the first required notice, shall give the debtor or hirer further notices under this section at intervals of not more than six months.

(2) The debtor or hirer shall have no liability to pay post-judgment interest in connection with the judgment sum to the extent that the interest is calculated by reference to a period occurring before the day on which he is given the first required notice.

(3) If the creditor or owner fails to give the debtor or hirer a notice under this section within the period of six months beginning with the day after the day on which such a notice was last given to the debtor or hirer, the debtor or hirer shall have no liability to pay post-judgment interest in connection with the judgment sum to the extent that the interest is calculated by reference to the whole or to a part of the period which—

(a) begins immediately after the end of that period of six months; and

(b) ends at the end of the day on which the notice is given to the debtor or hirer.

(4) The debtor or hirer shall have no liability to pay any sum in connection with the preparation or the giving to him of a notice under this section.

(5) A notice under this section may be incorporated in a statement or other notice which the creditor or owner gives the debtor or hirer in relation to the agreement by virtue of another provision of this Act.

(6) Regulations may make provision about the form and content of notices under this section.

(7) This section does not apply in relation to post-judgment interest which is required to be paid by virtue of any of the following—

(a) section 4 of the Administration of Justice (Scotland) Act 1972;

(b) Article 127 of the Judgments Enforcement (Northern Ireland) Order 1981;

(c) section 74 of the County Courts Act 1984.

(8) This section does not apply in relation to a non-commercial agreement or to a small agreement.

(9) In this section 'post-judgment interest' means interest to the extent calculated by reference to a period occurring after the giving of the judgment under which the judgment sum is required to be paid."

18 Definition of "default sum"

(1) After section 187 of the 1974 Act insert—

"187A Definition of 'default sum'

(1) In this Act 'default sum' means, in relation to the debtor or hirer under a regulated agreement, a sum (other than a sum of interest) which is payable by him under the agreement in connection with a breach of the agreement by him.

(2) But a sum is not a default sum in relation to the debtor or hirer simply because, as a consequence of his breach of the agreement, he is required to pay it earlier than he would otherwise have had to."

(2) In section 189(1) of that Act (definitions) after the definition of "default notice" insert—

" 'default sum' has the meaning given by section 187A;".

Unfair relationships

19 Unfair relationships between creditors and debtors

After section 140 of the 1974 Act insert—

"Unfair relationships

140A Unfair relationships between creditors and debtors

(1) The court may make an order under section 140B in connection with a credit agreement if it determines that the relationship between the creditor and the debtor arising out of the agreement (or the agreement taken with any related agreement) is unfair to the debtor because of one or more of the following—

    (a) any of the terms of the agreement or of any related agreement;

    (b) the way in which the creditor has exercised or enforced any of his rights under the agreement or any related agreement;

    (c) any other thing done (or not done) by, or on behalf of, the creditor (either before or after the making of the agreement or any related agreement).

(2) In deciding whether to make a determination under this section the court shall have regard to all matters it thinks relevant (including matters relating to the creditor and matters relating to the debtor).

(3) For the purposes of this section the court shall (except to the extent that it is not appropriate to do so) treat anything done (or not done) by, or on behalf of, or in relation to, an associate or a former associate of the creditor as if done (or not done) by, or on behalf of, or in relation to, the creditor.

(4) A determination may be made under this section in relation to a relationship notwithstanding that the relationship may have ended.

(5) An order under section 140B shall not be made in connection with a credit agreement which is an exempt agreement by virtue of section 16(6C)."

20 Powers of court in relation to unfair relationships

After section 140A of the 1974 Act (inserted by section 19 of this Act) insert—

"140B Powers of court in relation to unfair relationships

(1) An order under this section in connection with a credit agreement may do one or more of the following—

    (a) require the creditor, or any associate or former associate of his, to repay (in whole or in part) any sum paid by the debtor or by a surety by virtue of the agreement or any related agreement (whether paid to the creditor, the associate or the former associate or to any other person);

    (b) require the creditor, or any associate or former associate of his, to do or not to do (or to cease doing) anything specified in the order in connection with the agreement or any related agreement;

    (c) reduce or discharge any sum payable by the debtor or by a surety by virtue of the agreement or any related agreement;

    (d) direct the return to a surety of any property provided by him for the purposes of a security;

    (e) otherwise set aside (in whole or in part) any duty imposed on the debtor or on a surety by virtue of the agreement or any related agreement;

    (f) alter the terms of the agreement or of any related agreement;

    (g) direct accounts to be taken, or (in Scotland) an accounting to be made, between any persons.

(2) An order under this section may be made in connection with a credit agreement only—

    (a) on an application made by the debtor or by a surety;

    (b) at the instance of the debtor or a surety in any proceedings in any court to which the debtor and the creditor are parties, being proceedings to enforce the agreement or any related agreement; or

    (c) at the instance of the debtor or a surety in any other proceedings in any court where the amount paid or payable under the agreement or any related agreement is relevant.

(3) An order under this section may be made notwithstanding that its effect is to place on the creditor, or any associate or former associate of his, a burden in respect of an advantage enjoyed by another person.

(4) An application under subsection (2)(a) may only be made—

    (a) in England and Wales, to the county court;

    (b) in Scotland, to the sheriff court;

    (c) in Northern Ireland, to the High Court (subject to subsection (6)).

(5) In Scotland such an application may be made in the sheriff court for the district in which the debtor or surety resides or carries on business.

(6) In Northern Ireland such an application may be made to the county court if the credit agreement is an agreement under which the creditor provides the debtor with—

    (a) fixed-sum credit not exceeding £15,000; or

    (b) running-account credit on which the credit limit does not exceed £15,000.

(7) Without prejudice to any provision which may be made by rules of court made in relation to county courts in Northern Ireland, such rules may provide that an application made by virtue of subsection (6) may be made in the county court for the division in which the debtor or surety resides or carries on business.

(8) A party to any proceedings mentioned in subsection (2) shall be entitled, in accordance with rules of court, to have any person who might be the subject of an order under this section made a party to the proceedings.

(9) If, in any such proceedings, the debtor or a surety alleges that the relationship between the creditor and the debtor is unfair to the debtor, it is for the creditor to prove to the contrary."

21 Interpretation of ss. 140A and 140B of the 1974 Act

After section 140B of the 1974 Act (inserted by section 20 of this Act) insert—

"140C Interpretation of ss. 140A and 140B

(1) In this section and in sections 140A and 140B 'credit agreement' means any agreement between an individual (the 'debtor') and any other person (the 'creditor') by which the creditor provides the debtor with credit of any amount.

(2) References in this section and in sections 140A and 140B to the creditor or to the debtor under a credit agreement include—

    (a) references to the person to whom his rights and duties under the agreement have passed by assignment or operation of law;

    (b) where two or more persons are the creditor or the debtor, references to any one or more of those persons.

(3) The definition of 'court' in section 189(1) does not apply for the purposes of sections 140A and 140B.

(4) References in sections 140A and 140B to an agreement related to a credit agreement (the 'main agreement') are references to—

    (a) a credit agreement consolidated by the main agreement;

    (b) a linked transaction in relation to the main agreement or to a credit agreement within paragraph (a);

    (c) a security provided in relation to the main agreement, to a credit agreement within paragraph (a) or to a linked transaction within paragraph (b).

(5) In the case of a credit agreement which is not a regulated consumer credit agreement, for the purposes of subsection (4) a transaction shall be treated as being a linked transaction in relation to that agreement if it would have been such a transaction had that agreement been a regulated consumer credit agreement.

(6) For the purposes of this section and section 140B the definitions of 'security' and 'surety' in section 189(1) apply (with any appropriate changes) in relation to—

    (a) a credit agreement which is not a consumer credit agreement as if it were a consumer credit agreement; and

    (b) a transaction which is a linked transaction by virtue of subsection (5).

(7) For the purposes of this section a credit agreement (the 'earlier agreement') is consolidated by another credit agreement (the 'later agreement') if—

    (a) the later agreement is entered into by the debtor (in whole or in part) for purposes connected with debts owed by virtue of the earlier agreement; and

    (b) at any time prior to the later agreement being entered into the parties to the earlier agreement included—

        (i) the debtor under the later agreement; and

        (ii) the creditor under the later agreement or an associate or a former associate of his.

(8) Further, if the later agreement is itself consolidated by another credit agreement (whether by virtue of this subsection or subsection (7)), then the earlier agreement is consolidated by that other agreement as well."

22 Further provision relating to unfair relationships

(1) After section 140C of the 1974 Act (inserted by section 21 of this Act) insert—

"140D Advice and information

The advice and information published by the OFT under section 229 of the Enterprise Act 2002 shall indicate how the OFT expects sections 140A to 140C of this Act to interact with Part 8 of that Act."

(2) In section 16 of that Act (exempt agreements) before subsection (8) insert—

    "(7A) Nothing in this section affects the application of sections 140A to 140C."

(3) Sections 137 to 140 of that Act (extortionate credit bargains) shall cease to have effect.

(4) In section 181 of that Act (power to alter monetary limits etc.)—

    (a) in subsection (1) before "155(1)" insert "140B(6),";

    (b) in subsection (2) before "shall" insert "or 140B(6)".

Businesses requiring a licence and consequences of not being licensed

23 Definitions of "consumer credit business" and "consumer hire business"

In section 189(1) of the 1974 Act (definitions)—

    (a) for the definition of "consumer credit business" substitute—

        " 'consumer credit business' means any business being carried on by a person so far as it comprises or relates to—

        (a) the provision of credit by him, or

        (b) otherwise his being a creditor,

    under regulated consumer credit agreements;"

    (b) for the definition of "consumer hire business" substitute—

        " 'consumer hire business' means any business being carried on by a person so far as it comprises or relates to—

        (a) the bailment or (in Scotland) the hiring of goods by him, or

        (b) otherwise his being an owner,

    under regulated consumer hire agreements;".

24 Debt administration etc.

(1) In subsection (1) of section 145 of the 1974 Act (types of ancillary credit business) for the "or" after paragraph (d) substitute—

    "(da) debt administration,".

(2) After subsection (7) of that section insert—

    "(7A) Subject to section 146(7), debt administration is the taking of steps—

        (a) to perform duties under a consumer credit agreement or a consumer hire agreement on behalf of the creditor or owner, or

        (b) to exercise or to enforce rights under such an agreement on behalf of the creditor or owner,

    so far as the taking of such steps is not debt-collecting."

(3) In subsection (6) of section 146 of that Act (persons who are to be treated as not carrying on types of ancillary credit businesses)—

    (a) after "an agreement if" insert "any of the following conditions is satisfied";

    (b) for paragraphs (a) and (b) substitute—

        "(aa) that he is the creditor or owner under the agreement, or";

    (c) at the beginning of each of paragraphs (c) to (e) insert "that".

(4) After that subsection insert—

    "(7) It is not debt administration for a person to take steps to perform duties, or to exercise or enforce rights, under an agreement on behalf of the creditor or owner if any of the conditions mentioned in subsection (6)(aa) to (e) is satisfied in relation to that person."

(5) In subsection (3) of section 177 of that Act (saving for registered charges) and in the subsection (3) applied by virtue of subsection (5) of that section for "a business of debt-collecting" substitute "a consumer credit business, a consumer hire business or a business of debt-collecting or debt administration".

(6) In section 189(1) of that Act (definitions) after the definition of "debt-adjusting" insert—

    " 'debt administration' has the meaning given by section 145(7A);".

25 Credit information services

(1) In subsection (1) of section 145 of the 1974 Act (types of ancillary credit business) before paragraph (e) insert—
"(db) the provision of credit information services, or".

(2) Before subsection (8) of that section insert—
"(7B) A person provides credit information services if—
    (a) he takes any steps mentioned in subsection (7C) on behalf of an individual; or
    (b) he gives advice to an individual in relation to the taking of any such steps.
(7C) Those steps are steps taken with a view—
    (a) to ascertaining whether a credit information agency (other than that person himself if he is one) holds information relevant to the financial standing of an individual;
    (b) to ascertaining the contents of such information held by such an agency;
    (c) to securing the correction of, the omission of anything from, or the making of any other kind of modification of, such information so held; or
    (d) to securing that such an agency which holds such information—
        (i) stops holding it; or
        (ii) does not provide it to another person.
(7D) In subsection (7C) 'credit information agency' means—
    (a) a person carrying on a consumer credit business or a consumer hire business;
    (b) a person carrying on a business so far as it comprises or relates to credit brokerage, debt-adjusting, debt-counselling, debt-collecting, debt administration or the operation of a credit reference agency;
    (c) a person carrying on a business which would be a consumer credit business except that it comprises or relates to consumer credit agreements being, otherwise than by virtue of section 16(5)(a), exempt agreements; or
    (d) a person carrying on a business which would be a consumer hire business except that it comprises or relates to consumer hire agreements being, otherwise than by virtue of section 16(6), exempt agreements."

(3) In section 151 of that Act (advertisements relating to ancillary credit businesses)—
    (a) in subsection (2) for "or" substitute "to" and after "liquidation of debts" insert "or to provide credit information services";
    (b) in subsection (3) for "or debt-counselling" substitute ", debt-counselling or the provision of credit information services";
    (c) in subsection (4) after "advertisement" insert "(other than one for credit information services)".

(4) In each of the following provisions of that Act for "or debt-counselling" substitute ", debt-counselling or the provision of credit information services"—
    (a) section 152(1) (application of sections 52 to 54 to ancillary credit businesses);
    (b) section 154 (prohibition of canvassing ancillary credit business off trade premises);
    (c) section 156 (regulations about agreements entered into for ancillary credit businesses).

(5) In section 189(1) of that Act (definitions) after the definition of "credit brokerage" insert—
" 'credit information services' has the meaning given by section 145(7B)."

26 Enforcement of agreements by unlicensed trader etc.

(1) In section 40 of the 1974 Act (enforcement of regulated agreements made by unlicensed trader) for subsections (1) and (2) substitute—

"(1) A regulated agreement is not enforceable against the debtor or hirer by a person acting in the course of a consumer credit business or a consumer hire business (as the case may be) if that person is not licensed to carry on a consumer credit business or a consumer hire business (as the case may be) of a description which covers the enforcement of the agreement.

(1A) Unless the OFT has made an order under subsection (2) which applies to the agreement, a regulated agreement is not enforceable against the debtor or hirer if—

(a) it was made by the creditor or owner in the course of a consumer credit business or a consumer hire business (as the case may be); and

(b) at the time the agreement was made he was not licensed to carry on a consumer credit business or a consumer hire business (as the case may be) of a description which covered the making of the agreement.

(2) Where—

(a) during any period a person (the 'trader' has made regulated agreements in the course of a consumer credit business or a consumer hire business (as the case may be), and

(b) during that period he was not licensed to carry on a consumer credit business or a consumer hire business (as the case may be) of a description which covered the making of those agreements,

he or his successor in title may apply to the OFT for an order that the agreements are to be treated for the purposes of subsection (1A) as if he had been licensed as required."

(2) In subsection (4) of that section—

(a) in paragraph (a) for "regulated agreements made by the trader during that period" substitute "the regulated agreements in question";

(b) in paragraph (b) after "covering" insert "the making of those agreements during";

(c) in paragraph (c) for "obtain a licence" substitute "be licensed as required".

(3) In subsection (6) of that section after "This section" insert "(apart from subsection (1))".

(4) After that subsection insert—

"(7) Subsection (1) does not apply to the enforcement of a regulated agreement by a consumer credit EEA firm unless that firm is precluded from enforcing it as a result of a prohibition or restriction mentioned in subsection (6)(a) or (b).

(8) This section (apart from subsection (1)) does not apply to a regulated agreement made by a person if by virtue of section 21(2) or (3) he was not required to be licensed to make the agreement.

(9) Subsection (1) does not apply to the enforcement of a regulated agreement by a person if by virtue of section 21(2) or (3) he is not required to be licensed to enforce the agreement."

Applications for licences and fitness to hold a licence etc.

27 Charge on applicants for licences etc.

(1) After section 6 of the 1974 Act insert—

"6A Charge on applicants for licences etc.

(1) An applicant for a licence, or for the renewal of a licence, shall pay the OFT a charge towards the costs of carrying out its functions under this Act.

(2) The amount of the charge payable by an applicant shall be determined in accordance with provision made by the OFT by general notice.

(3) The provision that may be made by the OFT under subsection (2) includes—

(a) different provision in relation to persons of different descriptions;

(b) provision for no charge at all to be payable by persons of specified descriptions.

(4) The approval of the Secretary of State and the Treasury is required for a general notice under subsection (2)."

(2) In section 6 of that Act (which contains provision relating to applications) after subsection (2) insert—

"(2A) The application must also be accompanied—

(a) in the case of an application for a licence or for the renewal of a licence, by the charge payable by virtue of section 6A;

(b) in any other case, by the specified fee."

(3) In section 189 of that Act (definitions) after subsection (1) insert—

"(1A) In sections 36E(3), 70(4), 73(4) and 75(2) and paragraphs 14 and 15 of Schedule A1 'costs', in relation to proceedings in Scotland, means expenses."

(4) In section 191(1)(a) of that Act (special provisions as to Northern Ireland) after "notices" insert ", charges".

28 Applications for standard licences

After section 24 of the 1974 Act insert—

"24A Applications for standard licences

(1) An application for a standard licence shall, in relation to each type of business which is covered by the application, state whether the applicant is applying—

(a) for the licence to cover the carrying on of that type of business with no limitation; or

(b) for the licence to cover the carrying on of that type of business only so far as it falls within one or more descriptions of business.

(2) An application within subsection (1)(b) in relation to a type of business shall set out the description or descriptions of business in question.

(3) References in this Part to a type of business are references to a type of business within subsection (4).

(4) The types of business within this subsection are—

(a) a consumer credit business;

(b) a consumer hire business;

(c) a business so far as it comprises or relates to credit brokerage;

(d) a business so far as it comprises or relates to debt-adjusting;

(e) a business so far as it comprises or relates to debt-counselling;

(f) a business so far as it comprises or relates to debt-collecting;

(g) a business so far as it comprises or relates to debt administration;

(h) a business so far as it comprises or relates to the provision of credit information services;

(i) a business so far as it comprises or relates to the operation of a credit reference agency.

(5) The OFT—

(a) shall by general notice specify the descriptions of business which can be set out in an application for the purposes of subsection (2) in relation to a type of business;

(b) may by general notice provide that applications within subsection (1)(b) cannot be made in relation to one or more of the types of business within subsection (4)(c) to (i).

(6) The power of the OFT under subsection (5) includes power to make different provision for different cases or classes of case."

29 Issue of standard licences

(1) In section 25 of the 1974 Act (licensee to be a fit person) for subsection (1) substitute—

"(1) If an applicant for a standard licence—

(a) makes an application within section 24A(1)(a) in relation to a type of business, and

(b) satisfies the OFT that he is a fit person to carry on that type of business with no limitation,

he shall be entitled to be issued with a standard licence covering the carrying on of that type of business with no limitation.

(1AA) If such an applicant—

(a) makes an application within subsection (1)(b) of section 24A in relation to a type of business, and

(b) satisfies the OFT that he is a fit person to carry on that type of business so far as it falls within the description or descriptions of business set out in his application in accordance with subsection (2) of that section,

he shall be entitled to be issued with a standard licence covering the carrying on of that type of business so far as it falls within the description or descriptions in question.

(1AB) If such an applicant makes an application within section 24A(1)(a) or (b) in relation to a type of business but fails to satisfy the OFT as mentioned in subsection (1) or (1AA) (as the case may be), he shall nevertheless be entitled to be issued with a standard licence covering the carrying on of that type of business so far as it falls within one or more descriptions of business if—

(a) he satisfies the OFT that he is a fit person to carry on that type of business so far as it falls within the description or descriptions in question;

(b) he could have applied for the licence to be limited in that way; and

(c) the licence would not cover any activity which was not covered by his application.

(1AC) In this section 'description of business' means, in relation to a type of business, a description of business specified in a general notice under section 24A(5)(a).

(1AD) An applicant shall not, by virtue of this section, be issued with a licence unless he satisfies the OFT that the name or names under which he would be licensed is or are not misleading or otherwise undesirable."

(2) For subsection (2) of that section substitute—

"(2) In determining whether an applicant for a licence is a fit person for the purposes of this section the OFT shall have regard to any matters appearing to it to be relevant including (amongst other things)—

(a) the applicant's skills, knowledge and experience in relation to consumer credit businesses, consumer hire businesses or ancillary credit businesses;

(b) such skills, knowledge and experience of other persons who the applicant proposes will participate in any business that would be carried on by him under the licence;

(c) practices and procedures that the applicant proposes to implement in connection with any such business;

(d) evidence of the kind mentioned in subsection (2A).

(2A) That evidence is evidence tending to show that the applicant, or any of the applicant's employees, agents or associates (whether past or present) or, where the applicant is a body corporate, any person appearing to the OFT to be a controller of the body corporate or an associate of any such person, has—

(a) committed any offence involving fraud or other dishonesty or violence;

(b) contravened any provision made by or under—

(i) this Act;

(ii) Part 16 of the Financial Services and Markets Act 2000 so far as it relates to the consumer credit jurisdiction under that Part;

(iii) any other enactment regulating the provision of credit to individuals or other transactions with individuals;

(c) contravened any provision in force in an EEA State which corresponds to a provision of the kind mentioned in paragraph (b);

(d) practised discrimination on grounds of sex, colour, race or ethnic or national origins in, or in connection with, the carrying on of any business; or

(e) engaged in business practices appearing to the OFT to be deceitful or oppressive or otherwise unfair or improper (whether unlawful or not).

(2B) For the purposes of subsection (2A)(e), the business practices which the OFT may consider to be deceitful or oppressive or otherwise unfair or improper include practices in the carrying on of a consumer credit business that appear to the OFT to involve irresponsible lending."

(3) In subsection (3) of that section for "(2)" substitute "(2A)".

30 Guidance on fitness test

After section 25 of the 1974 Act insert—

"25A Guidance on fitness test

(1) The OFT shall prepare and publish guidance in relation to how it determines, or how it proposes to determine, whether persons are fit persons as mentioned in section 25.

(2) If the OFT revises the guidance at any time after it has been published, the OFT shall publish it as revised.

(3) The guidance shall be published in such manner as the OFT thinks fit for the purpose of bringing it to the attention of those likely to be affected by it.

(4) In preparing or revising the guidance the OFT shall consult such persons as it thinks fit.

(5) In carrying out its functions under this Part the OFT shall have regard to the guidance as most recently published."

31 Variation of standard licences etc.

(1) In section 30 of the 1974 Act (variation of licences by request) for subsection (1) substitute—

"(1) If it thinks fit, the OFT may by notice to the licensee under a standard licence—

(a) in the case of a licence which covers the carrying on of a type of business only so far as it falls within one or more descriptions of business, vary the licence by—

(i) removing that limitation;

(ii) adding a description of business to that limitation; or

(iii) removing a description of business from that limitation;

(b) in the case of a licence which covers the carrying on of a type of business with no limitation, vary the licence so that it covers the carrying on of that type of business only so far as it falls within one or more descriptions of business;

(c) vary the licence so that it no longer covers the carrying on of a type of business at all;

(d) vary the licence so that a type of business the carrying on of which is not covered at all by the licence is covered either—

(i) with no limitation; or

(ii) only so far as it falls within one or more descriptions of business; or

(e) vary the licence in any other way except for the purpose of varying the descriptions of activities covered by the licence.

(1A) The OFT may vary a licence under subsection (1) only in accordance with an application made by the licensee.

(1B) References in this section to a description of business in relation to a type of business—

(a) are references to a description of business specified in a general notice under section 24A(5)(a); and

(b) in subsection (1)(a) (apart from sub-paragraph (ii)) include references to a description of business that was, but is no longer, so specified."

(2) In subsection (1) of section 31 of that Act (compulsory variation of licences) for "the licence should be varied" substitute "it should take steps mentioned in subsection (1A)".

(3) After that subsection insert—

"(1A) Those steps are—

(a) in the case of a standard licence, steps mentioned in section 30(1)(a)(ii) and (iii), (b), (c) and (e);

(b) in the case of a group licence, the varying of terms of the licence."

(4) After subsection (7) of that section insert—

"(8) Subsection (1) shall have effect in relation to a standard licence as if an application could be made for the renewal or further renewal of the licence on the same terms (except as to expiry) even if such an application could not be made because of provision made in a general notice under section 24A(5).

(9) Accordingly, in applying subsection (1AA) of section 25 in relation to the licence for the purposes of this section, the OFT shall treat references in that subsection to the description or descriptions of business in relation to a type of business as references to the description or descriptions of business included in the licence in relation to that type of business, notwithstanding that provision under section 24A(5)."

(5) In section 32 of that Act (suspension and revocation of licences) after subsection (8) insert—

"(9) The OFT has no power to revoke or to suspend a standard licence simply because, by virtue of provision made in a general notice under section 24A(5), a person cannot apply for the renewal of such a licence on terms which are the same as the terms of the licence in question."

32 Winding-up of standard licensee's business

(1) After section 34 of the 1974 Act insert—

"34A Winding-up of standard licensee's business

(1) If it thinks fit, the OFT may, for the purpose of enabling the licensee's business, or any part of his business, to be transferred or wound up, include as part of a determination to which subsection (2) applies provision authorising the licensee to carry on for a specified period—

(a) specified activities, or

(b) activities of specified descriptions,

which, because of that determination, the licensee will no longer be licensed to carry on.

(2) This subsection applies to the following determinations—

(a) a determination to refuse to renew a standard licence in accordance with the terms of the application for its renewal;

(b) a determination to vary such a licence under section 31;

(c) a determination to suspend or revoke such a licence.

(3) Such provision—

(a) may specify different periods for different activities or activities of different descriptions;

(b) may provide for persons other than the licensee to carry on activities under the authorisation;

(c) may specify requirements which must be complied with by a person carrying on activities under the authorisation in relation to those activities;

and, if a requirement specified under paragraph (c) is not complied with, the OFT may by notice to a person carrying on activities under the authorisation terminate the authorisation (in whole or in part) from a specified date.

(4) Without prejudice to the generality of paragraph (c) of subsection (3), a requirement specified under that paragraph may have the effect of—

(a) preventing a named person from being an employee of a person carrying on activities under the authorisation, or restricting the activities he may engage in as an employee of such a person;

    (b) preventing a named person from doing something, or restricting his doing something, in connection with activities being carried on by a person under the authorisation;

    (c) securing that access to premises is given to officers of the OFT for the purpose of enabling them to inspect documents or to observe the carrying on of activities.

  (5) Activities carried on under an authorisation shall be treated for the purposes of sections 39(1), 40, 148 and 149 as if carried on under a standard licence."

(2) In section 29 of that Act (renewal of licences) after subsection (3) insert—

    "(3A) In its application to the renewal of standard licences by virtue of subsection (3) of this section, section 27(1) shall have effect as if for paragraph (b) there were substituted—

      '(b) invite the applicant to submit to the OFT in accordance with section 34 representations—

        (i) in support of his application; and

        (ii) about the provision (if any) that should be included under section 34A as part of the determination were the OFT to refuse the application or grant it in terms different from those applied for.' "

(3) Subsection (5) of that section (which gives the OFT power to give directions allowing licensees to carry agreements into effect) shall cease to have effect.

(4) In section 31(2) of that Act (procedure to be followed in case of proposed compulsory variation of a standard licence) for paragraph (b) substitute—

    "(b) invite him to submit to the OFT in accordance with section 34 representations—

      (i) as to the proposed variations; and

      (ii) about the provision (if any) that should be included under section 34A as part of the determination were the OFT to vary the licence."

(5) In subsection (2) of section 32 of that Act (procedure to be followed in case of proposed revocation or suspension of a standard licence) for paragraph (b) substitute—

    "(b) invite him to submit to the OFT in accordance with section 34 representations—

      (i) as to the proposed revocation or suspension; and

      (ii) about the provision (if any) that should be included under section 34A as part of the determination were the OFT to revoke or suspend the licence."

(6) Subsection (5) of that section (which gives the OFT power to give directions allowing licensees to carry agreements into effect) shall cease to have effect.

33 Consequential amendments relating to ss. 27 to 32

(1) In section 21(1) of the 1974 Act (businesses needing a licence) for "consumer hire business" substitute "a consumer hire business or an ancillary credit business".

(2) In section 22 of that Act (standard and group licences) after subsection (5) insert—

    "(5A) A group licence to carry on a business may limit the activities it covers in any way the OFT thinks fit."

(3) In subsection (1) of section 23 of that Act (authorisation of specific activities) for "this section" substitute "the terms of the licence".

(4) In subsection (4) of that section for "Regulations may be made specifying" substitute "The OFT may by general notice specify".

(5) After section 27 of that Act insert—

"27A Consumer credit EEA firms

(1) Where—

    (a) a consumer credit EEA firm makes an application for a standard licence, and

    (b) the activities covered by the application are all permitted activities,

the OFT shall refuse the application.

(2) Subsection (3) applies where—

    (a) a consumer credit EEA firm makes an application for a standard licence; and

    (b) some (but not all) of the activities covered by the application are permitted activities.

(3) In order to be entitled to be issued with a standard licence in accordance with section 25(1) to (1AB) in relation to a type of business, the firm need not satisfy the OFT that it is a fit person to carry on that type of business so far as it would involve any of the permitted activities covered by the application.

(4) A standard licence held by a consumer credit EEA firm does not at any time authorise the carrying on of an activity which is a permitted activity at that time.

(5) In this section 'permitted activity' means, in relation to a consumer credit EEA firm, an activity for which the firm has, or could obtain, permission under paragraph 15 of Schedule 3 to the Financial Services and Markets Act 2000."

(6) In the Table in section 41 of that Act (appeals) in the entry relating to "refusal to make order under section 40(2) in accordance with terms of application" after "40(2)" insert ", 148(2) or 149(2)".

(7) In sections 194(3) and 203(4) of the 2000 Act (powers of intervention and prohibition) for "(a) to (d) of section 25(2)" substitute "(a) to (e) of section 25(2A)".

(8) In section 203(10) of that Act (definitions relating to Consumer Credit Act businesses) in the definition of "associate" for "25(2)" substitute "25(2A)".

(9) In paragraph 15(3) of Schedule 3 to that Act (EEA passport rights) for "21, 39(1) and 147(1)" substitute "21 and 39(1)".

(10) In paragraph 23 of that Schedule in sub-paragraph (1) for "Sub-paragraph (2) applies" substitute "Sub-paragraphs (2) and (2A) apply".

(11) In sub-paragraph (2) of that paragraph for "(a) to (d) of section 25(2)" substitute "(a) to (e) of section 25(2A)".

(12) After that sub-paragraph insert—

    "(2A) The Authority may also exercise its power under section 45 in respect of the firm if the Office of Fair Trading has informed the Authority that it has concerns about any of the following—

        (a) the firm's skills, knowledge and experience in relation to Consumer Credit Act businesses;

        (b) such skills, knowledge and experience of other persons who are participating in any Consumer Credit Act business being carried on by the firm;

        (c) practices and procedures that the firm is implementing in connection with any such business."

Duration of licences and charges

34 Definite and indefinite licences

(1) In subsection (1) of section 22 of the 1974 Act (definitions of standard and group licences)—

    (a) in paragraph (a) for "during the prescribed period" substitute "whilst the licence is in effect";

    (b) in paragraph (b) for the words from "during" to "indefinitely" substitute "whilst the licence is in effect".

(2) After that subsection insert—

    "(1A) The terms of a licence shall specify—

        (a) whether it has effect indefinitely or only for a limited period; and

        (b) if it has effect for a limited period, that period.

    (1B) For the purposes of subsection (1A)(b) the period specified shall be such period not exceeding the prescribed period as the OFT thinks fit (subject to subsection (1E)).

    (1C) A standard licence shall have effect indefinitely unless—

        (a) the application for its issue requests that it have effect for a limited period only; or

        (b) the OFT otherwise thinks there is good reason why it should have effect for such a period only.

    (1D) A group licence shall have effect for a limited period only unless the OFT thinks there is good reason why it should have effect indefinitely.

    (1E) Where a licence which has effect indefinitely is to be varied under section 30 or 31 for the purpose of limiting the licence's duration, the variation shall provide for the licence to expire—

        (a) in the case of a variation under section 30, at the end of such period from the time of the variation as is set out in the application for the variation; or

        (b) in the case of a variation under section 31, at the end of such period from the time of the variation as the OFT thinks fit;

    but a period mentioned in paragraph (a) or (b) shall not exceed the prescribed period."

(3) In section 29 of that Act (renewal of licences)—

    (a) in subsection (1) after "standard licence" insert "of limited duration";

    (b) in subsection (4) for "in force" substitute "to have effect".

(4) In subsection (1) of section 31 of that Act (compulsory variation of licences) after "that time" insert "(assuming, in the case of a licence which has effect indefinitely, that it were a licence of limited duration)".

(5) Before subsection (2) of that section insert—

    "(1B) The OFT shall also proceed as follows if, having regard to section 22(1B) to (1E), it is of the opinion—

        (a) that a licence which has effect indefinitely should have its duration limited; or

        (b) in the case of a licence of limited duration, that the period during which it has effect should be shortened."

(6) In section 32(1) of that Act (suspension and revocation of licences) after "that time" insert "(assuming, in the case of a licence which has effect indefinitely, that it were a licence of limited duration)".

(7) In section 35(1)(b) of that Act (particulars to be kept in register maintained by OFT) for "force" substitute "effect".

(8) In section 37 of that Act (circumstances giving rise to termination of a licence) after subsection (1) insert—

"(1A) A licence terminates if the licensee gives the OFT a notice under subsection (1B).

(1B) A notice under this subsection shall—

    (a) be in such form as the OFT may by general notice specify;

    (b) contain such information as may be so specified;

    (c) be accompanied by the licence or give reasons as to why it is not accompanied by the licence; and

    (d) be signed by or on behalf of the licensee."

(9) In subsection (3)(a) of that section after "(1)" insert "or (1A)".

35 Charges for indefinite licences

After section 28 of the 1974 Act insert—

"Charges for indefinite licences

28A Charges to be paid by licensees etc. before end of payment periods

(1) The licensee under a standard licence which has effect indefinitely shall, before the end of each payment period of his, pay the OFT a charge towards the costs of carrying out its functions under this Act.

(2) The original applicant for a group licence which has effect indefinitely shall, before the end of each payment period of his, pay the OFT such a charge.

(3) The amount of the charge payable by a person under subsection (1) or (2) before the end of a payment period shall be determined in accordance with provision which—

    (a) is made by the OFT by general notice; and

    (b) is current on such day as may be determined in accordance with provision made by regulations.

(4) The provision that may be made by the OFT under subsection (3)(a) includes—

    (a) different provision in relation to persons of different descriptions (including persons whose payment periods end at different times);

    (b) provision for no charge at all to be payable by persons of specified descriptions.

(5) The approval of the Secretary of State and the Treasury is required for a general notice under subsection (3)(a).

(6) For the purposes of this section a person's payment periods are to be determined in accordance with provision made by regulations."

36 Extension of period to pay charge for indefinite licence

After section 28A of the 1974 Act (inserted by section 35 of this Act) insert—

"28B Extension of period to pay charge under s. 28A

(1) A person who is required under section 28A to pay a charge before the end of a period may apply once to the OFT for that period to be extended.

(2) The application shall be made before such day as may be determined in accordance with provision made by the OFT by general notice.

(3) If the OFT is satisfied that there is a good reason—
    (a) why the applicant has not paid that charge prior to his making of the application, and
    (b) why he cannot pay that charge before the end of that period,
it may, if it thinks fit, by notice to him extend that period by such time as it thinks fit having regard to that reason.

(4) The power of the OFT under this section to extend a period in relation to a charge—
    (a) includes the power to extend the period in relation to a part of the charge only;
    (b) may be exercised even though the period has ended."

37 Failure to pay charge for indefinite licence

(1) After section 28B of the 1974 Act (inserted by section 36 of this Act) insert—

"28C Failure to pay charge under s. 28A

(1) This section applies if a person (the 'defaulter') fails to pay a charge—
    (a) before the end of a period (the 'payment period') as required under section 28A; or
    (b) where the payment period is extended under section 28B, before the end of the payment period as extended (subject to subsection (2)).

(2) Where the payment period is extended under section 28B in relation to a part of the charge only, this section applies if the defaulter fails—
    (a) to pay so much of the charge as is not covered by the extension before the end of the payment period disregarding the extension; or
    (b) to pay so much of the charge as is covered by the extension before the end of the payment period as extended.

(3) Subject to subsection (4), if the charge is a charge under section 28A(1), the defaulter's licence terminates.

(4) If the defaulter has applied to the OFT under section 28B for the payment period to be extended and that application has not been determined—
    (a) his licence shall not terminate before the application has been determined and the OFT has notified him of the determination; and
    (b) if the OFT extends the payment period on that application, this section shall have effect accordingly.

(5) If the charge is a charge under section 28A(2), the charge shall be recoverable by the OFT."

(2) In section 35(1)(b) of that Act (particulars to be kept in register maintained by OFT) after "revoked" insert "or terminated by section 28C".

Further powers of OFT to regulate conduct of licensees etc.

38 Power of OFT to impose requirements on licensees

After section 33 of the 1974 Act insert—

"Further powers of OFT to regulate conduct of licensees etc.

33A Power of OFT to impose requirements on licensees

(1) This section applies where the OFT is dissatisfied with any matter in connection with—
    (a) a business being carried on, or which has been carried on, by a licensee or by an associate or a former associate of a licensee;

(b) a proposal to carry on a business which has been made by a licensee or by an associate or a former associate of a licensee; or

(c) any conduct not covered by paragraph (a) or (b) of a licensee or of an associate or a former associate of a licensee.

(2) The OFT may by notice to the licensee require him to do or not to do (or to cease doing) anything specified in the notice for purposes connected with—

(a) addressing the matter with which the OFT is dissatisfied; or

(b) securing that matters of the same or a similar kind do not arise.

(3) A requirement imposed under this section on a licensee shall only relate to a business which the licensee is carrying on, or is proposing to carry on, under the licence under which he is a licensee.

(4) Such a requirement may be framed by reference to a named person other than the licensee.

(5) For the purposes of subsection (1) it is immaterial whether the matter with which the OFT is dissatisfied arose before or after the licensee became a licensee.

(6) If—

(a) a person makes an application for a standard licence, and

(b) while dealing with that application the OFT forms the opinion that, if such a licence were to be issued to that person, it would be minded to impose on him a requirement under this section,

the OFT may, before issuing such a licence to that person, do (in whole or in part) anything that it must do under section 33D or 34(1) or (2) in relation to the imposing of the requirement.

(7) In this section 'associate', in addition to the persons specified in section 184, includes a business associate."

39 Power of OFT to impose requirements on supervisory bodies

After section 33A of the 1974 Act (inserted by section 38 of this Act) insert—

"33B Power of OFT to impose requirements on supervisory bodies

(1) This section applies where the OFT is dissatisfied with the way in which a responsible person in relation to a group licence—

(a) is regulating or otherwise supervising, or has regulated or otherwise supervised, persons who are licensees under that licence; or

(b) is proposing to regulate or otherwise to supervise such persons.

(2) The OFT may by notice to the responsible person require him to do or not to do (or to cease doing) anything specified in the notice for purposes connected with—

(a) addressing the matters giving rise to the OFT's dissatisfaction; or

(b) securing that matters of the same or a similar kind do not arise.

(3) A requirement imposed under this section on a responsible person in relation to a group licence shall only relate to practices and procedures for regulating or otherwise supervising licensees under the licence in connection with their carrying on of businesses under the licence.

(4) For the purposes of subsection (1) it is immaterial whether the matters giving rise to the OFT's dissatisfaction arose before or after the issue of the group licence in question.

(5) If—

(a) a person makes an application for a group licence, and

(b) while dealing with that application the OFT forms the opinion that, if such a licence were to be issued to that person, it would be minded to impose on him a requirement under this section,

the OFT may, before issuing such a licence to that person, do (in whole or in part) anything that it must do under section 33D or 34(1) or (2) in relation to the imposing of the requirement.

(6) For the purposes of this Part a person is a responsible person in relation to a group licence if—

   (a) he is the original applicant for it; and

   (b) he has a responsibility (whether by virtue of an enactment, an agreement or otherwise) for regulating or otherwise supervising persons who are licensees under the licence."

40 Supplementary provision relating to requirements

After section 33B of the 1974 Act (inserted by section 39 of this Act) insert—

"33C Supplementary provision relating to requirements

(1) A notice imposing a requirement under section 33A or 33B may include provision about the time at or by which, or the period during which, the requirement is to be complied with.

(2) A requirement imposed under section 33A or 33B shall not have effect after the licence by reference to which it is imposed has itself ceased to have effect.

(3) A person shall not be required under section 33A or 33B to compensate, or otherwise to make amends to, another person.

(4) The OFT may by notice to the person on whom a requirement has been imposed under section 33A or 33B vary or revoke the requirement (including any provision made under subsection (1) of this section in relation to it) with effect from such date as may be specified in the notice.

(5) The OFT may exercise its power under subsection (4) in relation to a requirement either on its own motion or on the application of a person falling within subsection (6) or (7) in relation to the requirement.

(6) A person falls within this subsection in relation to a requirement if he is the person on whom the requirement is imposed.

(7) A person falls within this subsection in relation to a requirement if—

   (a) the requirement is imposed under section 33A;

   (b) he is not the person on whom the requirement is imposed;

   (c) the requirement is framed by reference to him by name; and

   (d) the effect of the requirement is—

      (i) to prevent him being an employee of the person on whom the requirement is imposed;

      (ii) to restrict the activities that he may engage in as an employee of that person; or

      (iii) otherwise to prevent him from doing something, or to restrict his doing something, in connection with a business being carried on by that person."

41 Procedure in relation to requirements

After section 33C of the 1974 Act (inserted by section 40 of this Act) insert—

"33D Procedure in relation to requirements

(1) Before making a determination—
  (a) to impose a requirement on a person under section 33A or 33B,
  (b) to refuse an application under section 33C(5) in relation to a requirement imposed under either of those sections, or
  (c) to vary or to revoke a requirement so imposed,
  the OFT shall proceed as follows.

(2) The OFT shall give a notice to every person to whom subsection (3) applies in relation to the determination—
  (a) informing him, with reasons, that it is minded to make the determination; and
  (b) inviting him to submit to it representations as to the determination under section 34.

(3) This subsection applies to a person in relation to the determination if he falls within, or as a consequence of the determination would fall within, section 33C(6) or (7) in relation to the requirement in question.

(4) This section does not require the OFT to give a notice to a person if the determination in question is in the same terms as a proposal made to the OFT by that person (whether as part of an application under this Part or otherwise)."

42 Guidance on requirements

After section 33D of the 1974 Act (inserted by section 41 of this Act) insert—

"33E Guidance on requirements

(1) The OFT shall prepare and publish guidance in relation to how it exercises, or how it proposes to exercise, its powers under sections 33A to 33C.

(2) If the OFT revises the guidance at any time after it has been published, the OFT shall publish it as revised.

(3) The guidance shall be published in such manner as the OFT thinks fit for the purpose of bringing it to the attention of those likely to be affected by it.

(4) In preparing or revising the guidance the OFT shall consult such persons as it thinks fit.

(5) In exercising its powers under sections 33A to 33C the OFT shall have regard to the guidance as most recently published."

43 Consequential amendments relating to requirements

(1) In section 35(1) of the 1974 Act (particulars to be kept in register maintained by OFT) after paragraph (b) insert—
  "(ba) requirements imposed under section 33A or 33B which are in effect or which have been in effect, with details of any variation of such a requirement;".

(2) In the Table in section 41 of that Act (appeals) after the entry relating to "refusal to end suspension of licence in accordance with terms of application" insert the following entry—
  "Determination—
    (a) to impose a requirement under section 33A or 33B;

(b) to refuse an application under section 33C(5) in relation to a requirement imposed under either of those sections; or

(c) to vary or revoke a requirement so imposed.

A person who falls within section 33C(6) or (7) in relation to the requirement unless the OFT was not required to give a notice to him in relation to the determination by virtue of section 33D(4)."

Powers and duties in relation to information

44 Provision of information etc. by applicants

(1) In subsection (2) of section 6 of the 1974 Act (which contains provision relating to applications)—

(a) for "particulars" substitute "information and documents";

(b) for "by" in the second place where it occurs substitute "or describe in a".

(2) For subsection (3) of that section substitute—

"(3)Where the OFT receives an application, it may by notice to the applicant at any time before the determination of the application require him to provide such information or documents relevant to the application as may be specified or described in the notice."

(3) After subsection (4) of that section insert—

"(5) Subsection (6) applies where a general notice under subsection (2) comes into effect—

(a) after an application has been made; but

(b) before its determination.

(6) The applicant shall, within such period as may be specified in the general notice, provide the OFT with any information or document—

(a) which he has not previously provided in relation to the application by virtue of this section;

(b) which he would have been required to provide with his application had it been made after the general notice came into effect; and

(c) which the general notice requires to be provided for the purposes of this subsection.

(7) An applicant shall notify the OFT, giving details, if before his application is determined—

(a) any information or document provided by him in relation to the application by virtue of this section is, to any extent, superseded or otherwise affected by a change in circumstances; or

(b) he becomes aware of an error in or omission from any such information or document.

(8) A notification for the purposes of subsection (7) shall be given within the period of 28 days beginning with the day on which (as the case may be)—

(a) the information or document is superseded;

(b) the change in circumstances occurs; or

(c) the applicant becomes aware of the error or omission.

(9) Subsection (7) does not require an applicant to notify the OFT about—

(a) anything of which he is required to notify it under section 36; or

(b) an error in or omission from any information or document which is a clerical error or omission not affecting the substance of the information or document."

45 Duties to notify changes in information etc.

After section 36 of the 1974 Act insert—

"36A Further duties to notify changes etc.

(1) Subsections (2) to (4) apply where a general notice under section 6(2) comes into effect.

(2) A person who is the licensee under a standard licence or who is the original applicant for a group licence shall, in relation to each relevant application which he has made and which was determined before the general notice came into effect, provide the OFT with any information or document—

   (a) which he would have been required to provide with the application had the application been made after the general notice came into effect; and

   (b) which the general notice requires to be provided for the purposes of this subsection.

(3) Any such information or document shall be provided within such period as may be specified in the general notice.

(4) Subsection (2) does not require a person to provide any information or document—

   (a) which he provided in relation to the application by virtue of section 6;

   (b) which he has previously provided in relation to the application by virtue of this section; or

   (c) which he would have been required to provide in relation to the application by virtue of subsection (5) but for subsection (6).

(5) A person who is the licensee under a standard licence or who is the original applicant for a group licence shall, in relation to each relevant application which he has made, notify the OFT giving details if, after the application is determined, any information or document which he—

   (a) provided in relation to the application by virtue of section 6, or

   (b) has so provided by virtue of this section,

   is, to any extent, superseded or otherwise affected by a change in circumstances.

(6) Subsection (5) does not require a person to notify the OFT about a matter unless it falls within a description of matters specified by the OFT in a general notice.

(7) A description may be specified for the purposes of subsection (6) only if the OFT is satisfied that the matters which would fall within that description are matters which would be relevant to the question of—

   (a) whether, having regard to section 25(2), a person is a fit person to carry on a business under a standard licence; or

   (b) whether the public interest is better served by a group licence remaining in effect than by obliging the licensees under it to apply separately for standard licences.

(8) A person who is the licensee under a standard licence or who is the original applicant for a group licence shall, in relation to each relevant application which he has made, notify the OFT about every error or omission—

   (a) in or from any information or document which he provided by virtue of section 6, or which he has provided by virtue of this section, in relation to the application; and

   (b) of which he becomes aware after the determination of the application.

(9) A notification for the purposes of subsection (5) or (8) shall be given within the period of 28 days beginning with the day on which (as the case may be)—
  (a) the information or document is superseded;
  (b) the change in circumstances occurs; or
  (c) the licensee or the original applicant becomes aware of the error or omission.
(10) This section does not require a person to notify the OFT about—
  (a) anything of which he is required to notify it under section 36; or
  (b) an error in or omission from any information or document which is a clerical error or omission not affecting the substance of the information or document.
(11) In this section 'relevant application' means, in relation to a person who is the licensee under a standard licence or who is the original applicant for a group licence—
  (a) the original application for the licence; or
  (b) an application for its renewal or for its variation."

46 Power of OFT to require information generally

After section 36A of the 1974 Act (inserted by section 45 of this Act) insert—

"36B Power of OFT to require information generally

(1) The OFT may by notice to a person require him—
  (a) to provide such information as may be specified or described in the notice; or
  (b) to produce such documents as may be so specified or described.
(2) The notice shall set out the reasons why the OFT requires the information or documents to be provided or produced.
(3) The information or documents shall be provided or produced—
  (a) before the end of such reasonable period as may be specified in the notice; and
  (b) at such place as may be so specified.
(4) A requirement may be imposed under subsection (1) on a person who is—
  (a) the licensee under a standard licence, or
  (b) the original applicant for a group licence,
only if the provision or production of the information or documents in question is reasonably required for purposes connected with the OFT's functions under this Act.
(5) A requirement may be imposed under subsection (1) on any other person only if—
  (a) an act or omission mentioned in subsection (6) has occurred or the OFT has reason to suspect that such an act or omission has occurred; and
  (b) the provision or production of the information or documents in question is reasonably required for purposes connected with—
    (i) the taking by the OFT of steps under this Part as a consequence; or
    (ii) its consideration of whether to take such steps as a consequence.
(6) Those acts or omissions are acts or omissions which—
  (a) cast doubt on whether, having regard to section 25(2), a person is a fit person to carry on a business under a standard licence;
  (b) cast doubt on whether the public interest is better served by a group licence remaining in effect, or being issued, than by obliging the persons who are licensees under it, or who would be licensees under it, to apply separately for standard licences;

    (c) give rise, or are likely to give rise, to dissatisfaction for the purposes of section 33A(1) or 33B(1); or

    (d) constitute or give rise to a failure of the kind mentioned in section 39A(1)."

47 Power of OFT to require access to premises

After section 36B of the 1974 Act (inserted by section 46 of this Act) insert—

"36C Power of OFT to require access to premises

(1) The OFT may by notice to a licensee under a licence require him to secure that access to the premises specified or described in the notice is given to an officer of an enforcement authority in order for the officer—

    (a) to observe the carrying on of a business under the licence by the licensee; or

    (b) to inspect such documents of the licensee relating to such a business as are—

        (i) specified or described in the notice; and

        (ii) situated on the premises.

(2) The notice shall set out the reasons why the access is required.

(3) The premises which may be specified or described in the notice—

    (a) include premises which are not premises of the licensee if they are premises from which he carries on activities in connection with the business in question; but

    (b) do not include premises which are used only as a dwelling.

(4) The licensee shall secure that the required access is given at such times as the OFT reasonably requires.

(5) The OFT shall give reasonable notice of those times.

(6) Where an officer is given access to any premises by virtue of this section, the licensee shall also secure that persons on the premises give the officer such assistance or information as he may reasonably require in connection with his observation or inspection of documents (as the case may be).

(7) The assistance that may be required under subsection (6) includes (amongst other things) the giving to the officer of an explanation of a document which he is inspecting.

(8) A requirement may be imposed under subsection (1) on a person who is—

    (a) the licensee under a standard licence, or

    (b) the original applicant for a group licence,

only if the observation or inspection in question is reasonably required for purposes connected with the OFT's functions under this Act.

(9) A requirement may be imposed under subsection (1) on any other person only if—

    (a) an act or omission mentioned in section 36B(6) has occurred or the OFT has reason to suspect that such an act or omission has occurred; and

    (b) the observation or inspection in question is reasonably required for purposes connected with—

        (i) the taking by the OFT of steps under this Part as a consequence; or

        (ii) its consideration of whether to take such steps as a consequence.

(10) In this section—

    (a) references to a licensee under a licence include, in relation to a group licence issued on application, references to the original applicant; and

    (b) references to a business being carried on under a licence by a licensee include, in relation to the original applicant for a group licence, activities being carried on by him for the purpose of regulating or otherwise supervising (whether by virtue of an enactment, an agreement or otherwise) licensees under that licence in connection with their carrying on of businesses under that licence."

48 Entry to premises under warrant

After section 36C of the 1974 Act (inserted by section 47 of this Act) insert—

"36D Entry to premises under warrant

(1) A justice of the peace may issue a warrant under this section if satisfied on information on oath given on behalf of the OFT that there are reasonable grounds for believing that the following conditions are satisfied.

(2) Those conditions are—
    (a) that there is on the premises specified in the warrant information or documents in relation to which a requirement could be imposed under section 36B; and
    (b) that if such a requirement were to be imposed in relation to the information or documents—
        (i) it would not be complied with; or
        (ii) the information or documents would be tampered with.

(3) A warrant under this section shall authorise an officer of an enforcement authority—
    (a) to enter the premises specified in the warrant;
    (b) to search the premises and to seize and detain any information or documents appearing to be information or documents specified in the warrant or information or documents of a description so specified;
    (c) to take any other steps which may appear to be reasonably necessary for preserving such information or documents or preventing interference with them; and
    (d) to use such force as may be reasonably necessary.

(4) An officer entering premises by virtue of this section may take such persons and equipment with him as he thinks necessary.

(5) In the application of this section to Scotland—
    (a) the reference to a justice of the peace includes a reference to a sheriff;
    (b) for 'information on oath' there is substituted 'evidence on oath'.

(6) In the application of this section to Northern Ireland the reference to a justice of the peace shall be construed as a reference to a lay magistrate."

49 Failure to comply with information requirement

After section 36D of the 1974 Act (inserted by section 48 of this Act) insert—

"36E Failure to comply with information requirement

(1) If on an application made by the OFT it appears to the court that a person (the 'information defaulter') has failed to do something that he was required to do by virtue of section 36B or 36C, the court may make an order under this section.

(2) An order under this section may require the information defaulter—
    (a) to do the thing that it appears he failed to do within such period as may be specified in the order;
    (b) otherwise to take such steps to remedy the consequences of the failure as may be so specified.

(3) If the information defaulter is a body corporate, a partnership or an unincorporated body of persons which is not a partnership, the order may require any officer who is (wholly or partly) responsible for the failure to meet such costs of the application as are specified in the order.

(4) In this section—

'court' means—

(a) in England and Wales and Northern Ireland, the High Court or the county court;

(b) in Scotland, the Court of Session or the sheriff;

'officer' means—

(a) in relation to a body corporate, a person holding a position of director, manager or secretary of the body or any similar position;

(b) in relation to a partnership or to an unincorporated body of persons, a member of the partnership or body.

(5) In subsection (4) 'director' means, in relation to a body corporate whose affairs are managed by its members, a member of the body."

50 Officers of enforcement authorities other than OFT

After section 36E of the 1974 Act (inserted by section 49 of this Act) insert—

"36F Officers of enforcement authorities other than OFT

(1) A relevant officer may only exercise powers by virtue of section 36C or 36D in pursuance of arrangements made with the OFT by or on behalf of the enforcement authority of which he is an officer.

(2) Anything done or omitted to be done by, or in relation to, a relevant officer in the exercise or purported exercise of a power by virtue of section 36C or 36D shall be treated for all purposes as having been done or omitted to be done by, or in relation to, an officer of the OFT.

(3) Subsection (2) does not apply for the purposes of any criminal proceedings brought against the officer, the enforcement authority of which he is an officer or the OFT in respect of anything done or omitted to be done by the officer.

(4) A relevant officer shall not disclose to a person other than the OFT information obtained by his exercise of a power by virtue of section 36C or 36D unless—

(a) he has the approval of the OFT to do so; or

(b) he is under a duty to make the disclosure.

(5) In this section 'relevant officer' means an officer of an enforcement authority other than the OFT."

51 Consequential amendments relating to information

(1) For section 7 of the 1974 Act (penalty for false information) substitute—

"7 Penalty for false information

A person commits an offence if, for the purposes of, or in connection with, any requirement imposed or other provision made by or under this Act, he knowingly or recklessly gives information to the OFT, or to an officer of the OFT, which, in a material particular, is false or misleading."

(2) In subsection (1)(b)(ii) of section 162 of that Act (powers of entry and inspection) for the words from "recorded" onwards substitute "to provide him with that information;".

(3) At the end of that section insert—

"(8) References in this section to a breach of any provision of or under this Act do not include references to—

(a) a failure to comply with a requirement imposed under section 33A or 33B;

(b) a failure to comply with section 36A; or

(c) a failure in relation to which the OFT can apply for an order under section 36E."

(4) In section 165 of that Act (obstruction of authorised officers) after subsection (1) insert—

"(1A) A failure to give assistance or information shall not constitute an offence under subsection (1)(c) if it is also—

(a) a failure to comply with a requirement imposed under section 33A or 33B;

(b) a failure to comply with section 36A; or

(c) a failure in relation to which the OFT can apply for an order under section 36E."

(5) In Part 12 of that Act before section 175 insert—

"174A Powers to require provision of information or documents etc.

(1) Every power conferred on a relevant authority by or under this Act (however expressed) to require the provision or production of information or documents includes the power—

(a) to require information to be provided or produced in such form as the authority may specify, including, in relation to information recorded otherwise than in a legible form, in a legible form;

(b) to take copies of, or extracts from, any documents provided or produced by virtue of the exercise of the power;

(c) to require the person who is required to provide or produce any information or document by virtue of the exercise of the power—

(i) to state, to the best of his knowledge and belief, where the information or document is;

(ii) to give an explanation of the information or document;

(iii) to secure that any information provided or produced, whether in a document or otherwise, is verified in such manner as may be specified by the authority;

(iv) to secure that any document provided or produced is authenticated in such manner as may be so specified;

(d) to specify a time at or by which a requirement imposed by virtue of paragraph (c) must be complied with.

(2) Every power conferred on a relevant authority by or under this Act (however expressed) to inspect or to seize documents at any premises includes the power to take copies of, or extracts from, any documents inspected or seized by virtue of the exercise of the power.

(3) But a relevant authority has no power under this Act—

(a) to require another person to provide or to produce,

(b) to seize from another person, or

(c) to require another person to give access to premises for the purposes of the inspection of,

any information or document which the other person would be entitled to refuse to provide or produce in proceedings in the High Court on the grounds of legal professional privilege or (in Scotland) in proceedings in the Court of Session on the grounds of confidentiality of communications.

(4) In subsection (3) 'communications' means—

(a) communications between a professional legal adviser and his client;

(b) communications made in connection with or in contemplation of legal proceedings and for the purposes of those proceedings.

(5) In this section 'relevant authority' means—

(a) the OFT or an enforcement authority (other than the OFT);

(b) an officer of the OFT or of an enforcement authority (other than the OFT)."

(6) In section 189(1) of that Act (definitions) after the definition of "deposit" insert—
" 'documents' includes information recorded in any form;".

(7) In Part 1 of Schedule 1 to the Criminal Justice and Police Act 2001 (c. 16) (powers of seizure to which section 50 applies) before paragraph 19 insert—
"18A The power of seizure conferred by section 36D(3) of the Consumer Credit Act 1974."

Civil penalties

52 Power of OFT to impose civil penalties

After section 39 of the 1974 Act insert—

"39A Power of OFT to impose civil penalties

(1) Where the OFT is satisfied that a person (the 'defaulter') has failed or is failing to comply with a requirement imposed on him by virtue of section 33A, 33B or 36A, it may by notice to him (a 'penalty notice') impose on him a penalty of such amount as it thinks fit.

(2) The penalty notice shall—

(a) specify the amount of the penalty that is being imposed;

(b) set out the OFT's reasons for imposing a penalty and for specifying that amount;

(c) specify how the payment of the penalty may be made to the OFT; and

(d) specify the period within which the penalty is required to be paid.

(3) The amount of the penalty shall not exceed £50,000.

(4) The period specified in the penalty notice for the purposes of subsection (2)(d) shall not end earlier than the end of the period during which an appeal may be brought against the imposition of the penalty under section 41.

(5) If the defaulter does not pay the penalty to the OFT within the period so specified—

(a) the unpaid balance from time to time shall carry interest at the rate for the time being specified in section 17 of the Judgments Act 1838; and

(b) the penalty and any interest payable on it shall be recoverable by the OFT."

53 Further provision relating to civil penalties

(1) After section 39A of the 1974 Act (inserted by section 52 of this Act) insert—

"39B Further provision relating to civil penalties

(1) Before determining to impose a penalty on a person under section 39A the OFT shall give a notice to that person—

(a) informing him that it is minded to impose a penalty on him;

(b) stating the proposed amount of the penalty;

(c) setting out its reasons for being minded to impose a penalty on him and for proposing that amount;

(d) setting out the proposed period for the payment of the penalty; and

(e) inviting him to submit representations to it about the matters mentioned in the preceding paragraphs in accordance with section 34.

(2) In determining whether and how to exercise its powers under section 39A in relation to a person's failure, the OFT shall have regard to (amongst other things)—

(a) any penalty or fine that has been imposed on that person by another body in relation to the conduct giving rise to the failure;

(b) other steps that the OFT has taken or might take under this Part in relation to that conduct.

(3) General notice shall be given of the imposition of a penalty under section 39A on a person who is a responsible person in relation to a group licence.

(4) That notice shall include the matters set out in the notice imposing the penalty in accordance with section 39A(2)(a) and (b)."

(2) In the Table in section 41 of that Act (appeals) before the entry relating to "refusal to make order under section 40(2) in accordance with terms of application" insert the following entry—

"Imposition of penalty under section 39A.
The person on whom the penalty is imposed."

(3) In section 181 of that Act (power to alter monetary limits etc.)—

(a) in subsection (1) before "70(6)" insert "39A(3),";

(b) in subsection (2) before "75(3)(b)" insert "39A(3),".

54 Statement of policy in relation to civil penalties

After section 39B of the 1974 Act (inserted by section 53 of this Act) insert—

"39C Statement of policy in relation to civil penalties

(1) The OFT shall prepare and publish a statement of policy in relation to how it exercises, or how it proposes to exercise, its powers under section 39A.

(2) If the OFT revises the statement of policy at any time after it has been published, the OFT shall publish it as revised.

(3) No statement of policy shall be published without the approval of the Secretary of State.

(4) The statement of policy shall be published in such manner as the OFT thinks fit for the purpose of bringing it to the attention of those likely to be affected by it.

(5) In preparing or revising the statement of policy the OFT shall consult such persons as it thinks fit.

(6) In determining whether and how to exercise its powers under section 39A in relation to a person's failure, the OFT shall have regard to the statement of policy as most recently published at the time the failure occurred.

(7) The OFT shall not impose a penalty on a person under section 39A in relation to a failure occurring before it has published a statement of policy."

Appeals

55 The Consumer Credit Appeals Tribunal

(1) After section 40 of the 1974 Act insert—

"Appeals

40A The Consumer Credit Appeals Tribunal

(1) There shall be a tribunal known as the Consumer Credit Appeals Tribunal ('the Tribunal').

(2) The Tribunal shall have the functions conferred on it by or under this Part.

(3) The Lord Chancellor may by rules make such provision as he thinks fit for regulating the conduct and disposal of appeals before the Tribunal.

(4) Schedule A1 (which makes provision about the Tribunal and proceedings before it) shall have effect.

(5) But that Schedule does not limit the Lord Chancellor's powers under subsection (3)."

(2) Before Schedule 1 to that Act insert the Schedule A1 set out in Schedule 1 to this Act.

56 Appeals to the Consumer Credit Appeals Tribunal

(1) In subsection (1) of section 41 of the 1974 Act (appeals) for the words from "prescribed period" onwards substitute "specified period, appeal to the Tribunal".

(2) After that subsection insert—

"(1A) The means for making an appeal is by sending the Tribunal a notice of appeal.

(1B) The notice of appeal shall—

    (a) be in the specified form;

    (b) set out the grounds of appeal in the specified manner; and

    (c) include the specified information and documents.

(1C) An appeal to the Tribunal is to be by way of a rehearing of the determination appealed against.

(1D) In this section 'specified' means specified by rules under section 40A(3)."

(3) Subsections (2) to (5) of that section shall cease to have effect.

57 Appeals from the Consumer Credit Appeals Tribunal

In Part 3 of the 1974 Act after section 41 insert—

"41A Appeals from the Consumer Credit Appeals Tribunal

(1) A party to an appeal to the Tribunal may with leave appeal—

    (a) in England and Wales and Northern Ireland, to the Court of Appeal, or

    (b) in Scotland, to the Court of Session,

on a point of law arising from a decision of the Tribunal.

(2) For the purposes of subsection (1) leave to appeal may be given by—

    (a) the Tribunal; or

    (b) the Court of Appeal or the Court of Session.

(3) An application for leave to appeal may be made to the Court of Appeal or the Court of Session only if the Tribunal has refused such leave.

(4) If on an appeal under this section the court considers that the decision of the Tribunal was wrong in law, it may do one or more of the following—

    (a) quash or vary that decision;

    (b) substitute for that decision a decision of its own;

    (c) remit the matter to the Tribunal for rehearing and determination in accordance with the directions (if any) given to it by the court.

(5) An appeal may be brought from a decision of the Court of Appeal under this section only if leave to do so is given by the Court of Appeal or the House of Lords.

(6) Rules under section 40A(3) may make provision for regulating or prescribing any matters incidental to or consequential on an appeal under this section.

(7) In this section 'party' means, in relation to an appeal to the Tribunal, the appellant or the OFT."

58 Consequential amendments relating to appeals

(1) In section 2(7) of the 1974 Act (restriction on power to give directions to OFT) for "Secretary of State" substitute "the Tribunal".

(2) In section 182 of that Act (regulations and orders) after subsection (1) insert—

"(1A) The power of the Lord Chancellor to make rules under section 40A(3) shall be exercisable by statutory instrument subject to annulment in pursuance of a resolution of either House of Parliament."

(3) In subsection (2) of that section—

(a) after "orders" wherever occurring insert "or rules";

(b) after "by the Secretary of State" insert "or by the Lord Chancellor";

(c) in paragraph (c) for "Secretary of State" substitute "person making them".

(4) In section 189(1) of that Act (definitions)—

(a) in the definition of "appeal period" for "Secretary of State" substitute "Tribunal";

(b) after the definition of "total price" insert—

" 'the Tribunal' means the Consumer Credit Appeals Tribunal;".

(5) In Schedule 1 to the Tribunals and Inquiries Act 1992 (c. 53) (tribunals under supervision of Council on Tribunals) after paragraph 9A insert—

"Consumer credit
9B. The Consumer Credit Appeals Tribunal established by section 40A of the Consumer Credit Act 1974."

Ombudsman scheme

59 Financial services ombudsman scheme to apply to consumer credit licensees

(1) After section 226 of the 2000 Act insert—

"226A Consumer credit jurisdiction

(1) A complaint which relates to an act or omission of a person ("the respondent") is to be dealt with under the ombudsman scheme if the conditions mentioned in subsection (2) are satisfied.

(2) The conditions are that—

(a) the complainant is eligible and wishes to have the complaint dealt with under the scheme;

(b) the complaint falls within a description specified in consumer credit rules;

(c) at the time of the act or omission the respondent was the licensee under a standard licence or was authorised to carry on an activity by virtue of section 34A of the Consumer Credit Act 1974;

(d) the act or omission occurred in the course of a business being carried on by the respondent which was of a type mentioned in subsection (3);

(e) at the time of the act or omission that type of business was specified in an order made by the Secretary of State; and

    (f) the complaint cannot be dealt with under the compulsory jurisdiction.
  (3) The types of business referred to in subsection (2)(d) are—

    (a) a consumer credit business;

    (b) a consumer hire business;

    (c) a business so far as it comprises or relates to credit brokerage;

    (d) a business so far as it comprises or relates to debt-adjusting;

    (e) a business so far as it comprises or relates to debt-counselling;

    (f) a business so far as it comprises or relates to debt-collecting;

    (g) a business so far as it comprises or relates to debt administration;

    (h) a business so far as it comprises or relates to the provision of credit information services;

    (i) a business so far as it comprises or relates to the operation of a credit reference agency.

  (4) A complainant is eligible if—

    (a) he is—

      (i) an individual; or

      (ii) a surety in relation to a security provided to the respondent in connection with the business mentioned in subsection (2)(d); and

    (b) he falls within a class of person specified in consumer credit rules.

  (5) The approval of the Treasury is required for an order under subsection (2)(e).

  (6) The jurisdiction of the scheme which results from this section is referred to in this Act as the "consumer credit jurisdiction".

  (7) In this Act 'consumer credit rules' means rules made by the scheme operator with the approval of the Authority for the purposes of the consumer credit jurisdiction.

  (8) Consumer credit rules under this section may make different provision for different cases.

  (9) Expressions used in the Consumer Credit Act 1974 have the same meaning in this section as they have in that Act."

(2) In Schedule 17 to that Act (the ombudsman scheme) after Part 3 insert the Part 3A set out in Schedule 2 to this Act.

60 Funding of ombudsman scheme

In Part 16 of the 2000 Act after section 234 insert—

"234A Funding by consumer credit licensees etc.

  (1) For the purpose of funding—

    (a) the establishment of the ombudsman scheme so far as it relates to the consumer credit jurisdiction (whenever any relevant expense is incurred), and

    (b) its operation in relation to the consumer credit jurisdiction,

the scheme operator may from time to time with the approval of the Authority determine a sum which is to be raised by way of contributions under this section.

  (2) A sum determined under subsection (1) may include a component to cover the costs of the collection of contributions to that sum ("collection costs") under this section.

  (3) The scheme operator must notify the OFT of every determination under subsection (1).

  (4) The OFT must give general notice of every determination so notified.

  (5) The OFT may by general notice impose requirements on—

(a) licensees to whom this section applies, or

(b) persons who make applications to which this section applies,

to pay contributions to the OFT for the purpose of raising sums determined under subsection (1).

(6) The amount of the contribution payable by a person under such a requirement—

(a) shall be the amount specified in or determined under the general notice; and

(b) shall be paid before the end of the period or at the time so specified or determined.

(7) A general notice under subsection (5) may—

(a) impose requirements only on descriptions of licensees or applicants specified in the notice;

(b) provide for exceptions from any requirement imposed on a description of licensees or applicants;

(c) impose different requirements on different descriptions of licensees or applicants;

(d) make provision for refunds in specified circumstances.

(8) Contributions received by the OFT must be paid to the scheme operator.

(9) As soon as practicable after the end of—

(a) each financial year of the scheme operator, or

(b) if the OFT and the scheme operator agree that this paragraph is to apply instead of paragraph (a) for the time being, each period agreed by them,

the scheme operator must pay to the OFT an amount representing the extent to which collection costs are covered in accordance with subsection (2) by the total amount of the contributions paid by the OFT to it during the year or (as the case may be) the agreed period.

(10) Amounts received by the OFT from the scheme operator are to be retained by it for the purpose of meeting its costs.

(11) The Secretary of State may by order provide that the functions of the OFT under this section are for the time being to be carried out by the scheme operator.

(12) An order under subsection (11) may provide that while the order is in force this section shall have effect subject to such modifications as may be set out in the order.

(13) The licensees to whom this section applies are licensees under standard licences which cover to any extent the carrying on of a type of business specified in an order under section 226A(2)(e).

(14) The applications to which this section applies are applications for—

(a) standard licences covering to any extent the carrying on of a business of such a type;

(b) the renewal of standard licences on terms covering to any extent the carrying on of a business of such a type.

(15) Expressions used in the Consumer Credit Act 1974 have the same meaning in this section as they have in that Act."

61 Consequential amendments relating to ombudsman scheme

(1) In section 4 of the 1974 Act (OFT to disseminate information and advice) after "the operation of this Act," insert "the consumer credit jurisdiction under Part 16 of the Financial Services and Markets Act 2000,".

(2) In section 227(2)(e) of the 2000 Act (conditions for exercise of voluntary jurisdiction) after "jurisdiction" insert "or the consumer credit jurisdiction".

(3) In sections 228(1) and 229(1) of that Act (determinations and awards by ombudsman) after "jurisdiction" insert "and to the consumer credit jurisdiction".

(4) In subsection (4) of section 229 of that Act (awards by ombudsman) after "specify" insert "for the purposes of the compulsory jurisdiction".

(5) After that subsection insert—

"(4A) The scheme operator may specify for the purposes of the consumer credit jurisdiction the maximum amount which may be regarded as fair compensation for a particular kind of loss or damage specified under subsection (3)(b)."

(6) In subsection (8)(b) of that section after "17" insert "or (as the case may be) Part 3A of that Schedule".

(7) For subsection (11) of that section substitute—

"(11) "Specified" means—

   (a) for the purposes of the compulsory jurisdiction, specified in compulsory jurisdiction rules;

   (b) for the purposes of the consumer credit jurisdiction, specified in consumer credit rules.

(12) Consumer credit rules under this section may make different provision for different cases."

(8) In section 230 of that Act (costs)—

   (a) in subsection (1) after "jurisdiction" insert "or the consumer credit jurisdiction";

   (b) in subsection (7) after "17" insert "or (as the case may be) paragraph 16D of that Schedule".

(9) In section 353(1) of that Act (power to permit disclosure of information) after paragraph (b) insert—

   "(c) by the scheme operator to the Office of Fair Trading for the purpose of assisting or enabling that Office to discharge prescribed functions under the Consumer Credit Act 1974."

(10) In Schedule 17 to that Act (the ombudsman scheme)—

   (a) in paragraph 3(4) after "227" insert ", the function of making consumer credit rules, the function of making determinations under section 234A(1)";

   (b) in paragraph 7(2) after "compulsory jurisdiction" insert ", functions in relation to its consumer credit jurisdiction";

   (c) in paragraph 9(3) after "compulsory" insert ", consumer credit";

   (d) in paragraphs 10(1) and 11 after "jurisdiction" insert "or to the consumer credit jurisdiction".

Miscellaneous

62 Monitoring of businesses by OFT

In section 1(1) of the 1974 Act (general functions of OFT) after paragraph (b) insert—
   "(ba) to monitor, as it sees fit, businesses being carried on under licences;".

63 Disapplication of s.101 of the 1974 Act

(1) In section 101 of the 1974 Act (right of hirer to terminate regulated consumer hire agreement) after subsection (8) insert—

"(8A) If it appears to the OFT that it would be in the interests of hirers to do so, it may by general notice direct that, subject to such conditions (if any) as it may specify, this section shall not apply to a consumer hire agreement if the agreement falls within a specified description; and this Act shall have effect accordingly."

(2) In subsection (8) of that section for the words from "this section" onwards substitute, "subject to such conditions (if any) as it may specify, this section shall not apply to consumer hire agreements made by the applicant; and this Act shall have effect accordingly".

64 Determinations etc. by OFT

For section 183 of the 1974 Act (determinations etc. by OFT) substitute—

"183 Determinations etc. by OFT

(1) The OFT may vary or revoke any determination made, or direction given, by it under this Act.
(2) Subsection (1) does not apply to—
    (a) a determination to issue, renew or vary a licence;
    (b) a determination to extend a period under section 28B or to refuse to extend a period under that section;
    (c) a determination to end a suspension under section 33;
    (d) a determination to make an order under section 40(2), 148(2) or 149(2);
    (e) a determination mentioned in column 1 of the Table in section 41."

65 Sums received by OFT

In section 190(2) of the 1974 Act (fees received by OFT to be paid into the Consolidated Fund) after "fees" insert ", charges, penalties or other sums".

Final provisions

66 Financial provision

There shall be payable out of money provided by Parliament—
(a) any expenditure incurred by a Minister of the Crown or the Office of Fair Trading by virtue of this Act; and
(b) any increase attributable to this Act in the sums payable out of money so provided by virtue of any other Act.

67 Interpretation

In this Act—
"the 1974 Act" means the Consumer Credit Act 1974 (c. 39);
"the 2000 Act" means the Financial Services and Markets Act 2000 (c. 8).

68 Consequential amendments

(1) The Secretary of State may by order made by statutory instrument make such modifications of—
    (a) any Act or subordinate legislation (within the meaning of the Interpretation Act 1978 (c. 30)), or
    (b) any Northern Ireland legislation or instrument made under such legislation,
as he thinks fit in consequence of any provision of this Act.
(2) An order under this section may include transitional or transitory provisions and savings.

(3) A statutory instrument containing an order under this section may not be made by the Secretary of State unless a draft has been laid before and approved by a resolution of each House of Parliament.

69 Transitional provision and savings

(1) Schedule 3 (which sets out transitional provision and savings) has effect.
(2) The Secretary of State may by order made by statutory instrument make such transitional or transitory provisions and savings as he thinks fit in connection with the coming into force of any provision of this Act.
(3) An order under this section may (amongst other things)—
    (a) where a provision of this Act is brought into force for limited purposes only, make provision about how references in Schedule 3 to the commencement of that provision of this Act are to apply;
    (b) make provision for or in connection with the application of any provision of this Act in relation to—
        (i) things existing or done, or
        (ii) persons who have done something or in relation to whom something has been done,
    before the coming into force of that provision of this Act.
(4) An order under this section may—
    (a) modify any Act or any subordinate legislation (within the meaning of the Interpretation Act 1978);
    (b) modify any Northern Ireland legislation or any instrument made under such legislation;
    (c) make different provision for different cases.
(5) Schedule 3 does not restrict the power under this section to make transitional or transitory provisions or savings.

70 Repeals

The enactments and instruments set out in Schedule 4 are repealed or revoked to the extent shown in that Schedule.

71 Short title, commencement and extent

(1) This Act may be cited as the Consumer Credit Act 2006.
(2) This Act (apart from this section) shall come into force on such day as the Secretary of State may by order made by statutory instrument appoint; and different days may be appointed for different purposes.
(3) This Act extends to Northern Ireland.

SCHEDULES

SCHEDULE 1

SECTION 55

SCHEDULE A1 TO THE 1974 ACT

SCHEDULE A1

THE CONSUMER CREDIT APPEALS TRIBUNAL

PART 1

INTERPRETATION

1.—In this Schedule—

"the Deputy President" means the Deputy President of the Consumer Credit Appeals Tribunal;

"lay panel" means the panel established under paragraph 3(3);

"panel of chairmen" means the panel established under paragraph 3(1);

"party" means, in relation to an appeal, the appellant or the OFT;

"the President" means the President of the Consumer Credit Appeals Tribunal;

"rules" means rules under section 40A(3) of this Act;

"specified" means specified by rules.

PART 2

THE TRIBUNAL

The President and the Deputy President

2.—(1) The Lord Chancellor shall appoint one of the members of the panel of chairmen to preside over the discharge of the Tribunal's functions.

(2) The person so appointed shall be known as the President of the Consumer Credit Appeals Tribunal.

(3) The Lord Chancellor may appoint one of the members of the panel of chairmen to be the Deputy President of the Consumer Credit Appeals Tribunal.

(4) The Deputy President shall have such functions in relation to the Tribunal as the President may assign to him.

(5) If the President or the Deputy President ceases to be a member of the panel of chairmen, he shall also cease to be the President or (as the case may be) the Deputy President.

(6) The functions of the President may, if he is absent or is otherwise unable to act, be discharged—

(a) by the Deputy President; or

(b) if there is no Deputy President or he too is absent or otherwise unable to act, by a person appointed for that purpose from the panel of chairmen by the Lord Chancellor.

Panels

3.—(1) The Lord Chancellor shall appoint a panel of persons for the purpose of serving as chairmen of the Tribunal.

(2) A person shall not be appointed to the panel of chairmen unless he—

    (a) has a seven year general qualification within the meaning of section 71 of the Courts and Legal Services Act 1990;

    (b) is an advocate or solicitor in Scotland of at least seven years' standing; or

    (c) is a member of the Bar of Northern Ireland, or a solicitor of the Supreme Court of Northern Ireland, of at least seven years' standing.

(3) The Lord Chancellor shall also appoint a panel of persons who appear to him to be qualified by experience or otherwise to deal with appeals of the kind that may be made to the Tribunal.

Terms of office etc.

4.—(1) Each member of the panel of chairmen or the lay panel shall hold and vacate office in accordance with the terms of his appointment.

(2) The Lord Chancellor may remove a member of either panel from office on the ground of incapacity or misbehaviour.

(3) A member of either panel—

    (a) may at any time resign office by notice in writing to the Lord Chancellor;

    (b) is eligible for re-appointment if he ceases to hold office.

Remuneration and allowances

5.—The Lord Chancellor may pay to a person in respect of his service—

    (a) as the President or the Deputy President,

    (b) as a member of the Tribunal, or

    (c) as a person appointed under paragraph 7(4),

such remuneration and allowances as the Lord Chancellor may determine.

Staff and costs

6.—(1) The Lord Chancellor may appoint such staff for the Tribunal as he may determine.

(2) The Lord Chancellor shall defray—

    (a) the remuneration of the Tribunal's staff; and

    (b) such other costs of the Tribunal as he may determine.

PART 3

CONSTITUTION OF THE TRIBUNAL

7.—(1) On an appeal to the Tribunal, the persons to act as members of the Tribunal for the purposes of the appeal shall be selected from the panel of chairmen or the lay panel.

(2) The selection shall be in accordance with arrangements made by the President for the purposes of this paragraph.

(3) Those arrangements shall provide for at least one member to be a person selected from the panel of chairmen.

(4) If it appears to the Tribunal that a matter before it involves a question of fact of special difficulty, it may appoint one or more experts to provide assistance.

PART 4

TRIBUNAL POWERS AND PROCEDURE

Sittings

8.—The Tribunal shall sit at such times and in such places as the Lord Chancellor may direct.

Evidence

9.—(1) Subject to sub-paragraph (2), the Tribunal may, on an appeal, consider any evidence that it thinks relevant, whether or not it was available to the OFT at the time it made the determination appealed against.

(2) Rules may make provision restricting the evidence that the Tribunal may consider on an appeal in specified circumstances.

Rules on procedure

10.—Rules may include, amongst other things, provision—
   (a) about the withdrawal of appeals;
   (b) about persons who may appear on behalf of a party to an appeal;
   (c) about how an appeal is to be dealt with if a person acting as member of the Tribunal in respect of the appeal becomes unable to act;
   (d) setting time limits in relation to anything that is to be done for the purposes of an appeal or for such limits to be set by the Tribunal or a member of the panel of chairmen;
   (e) for time limits (including the period specified for the purposes of section 41(1) of this Act) to be extended by the Tribunal or a member of the panel of chairmen;
   (f) conferring powers on the Tribunal or a member of the panel of chairmen to give such directions to the parties to an appeal as it or he thinks fit for purposes connected with the conduct and disposal of the appeal;
   (g) about the holding of hearings by the Tribunal or a member of the panel of chairmen (including for such hearings to be held in private);
   (h) placing restrictions on the disclosure of information and documents or for such restrictions to be imposed by the Tribunal or a member of the panel of chairmen;
   (i) about the consequences of a failure to comply with a requirement imposed by or under any rule (including for the immediate dismissal or allowing of an appeal if the Tribunal or a member of the panel of chairmen thinks fit);
   (j) for proceedings on different appeals (including appeals with different appellants) to take place concurrently;
   (k) for the suspension of determinations of the OFT;
   (l) for the suspension of decisions of the Tribunal;
   (m) for the Tribunal to reconsider its decision disposing of an appeal where it has reason to believe that the decision was wrongly made because of an administrative error made by a member of its staff.

Council on Tribunals

11.—A member of the Council on Tribunals or of its Scottish Committee shall be entitled—
   (a) to attend any hearing held by the Tribunal or a member of the panel of chairmen whether or not it is held in public; and

167

(b) to attend any deliberations of the Tribunal in relation to an appeal.

Disposal of appeals

12.—(1) The Tribunal shall decide an appeal by reference to the grounds of appeal set out in the notice of appeal.

(2) In disposing of an appeal the Tribunal may do one or more of the following—
   (a) confirm the determination appealed against;
   (b) quash that determination;
   (c) vary that determination;
   (d) remit the matter to the OFT for reconsideration and determination in accordance with the directions (if any) given to it by the Tribunal;
   (e) give the OFT directions for the purpose of giving effect to its decision.

(3) In the case of an appeal against a determination to impose a penalty, the Tribunal—
   (a) has no power by virtue of sub-paragraph (2)(c) to increase the penalty;
   (b) may extend the period within which the penalty is to be paid (including in cases where that period has already ended).

(4) Sub-paragraph (3) does not affect—
   (a) the Tribunal's power to give directions to the OFT under sub-paragraph (2)(d); or
   (b) what the OFT can do where a matter is remitted to it under sub-paragraph (2)(d).

(5) Where the Tribunal remits a matter to the OFT, it may direct that the requirements of section 34 of this Act are not to apply, or are only to apply to a specified extent, in relation to the OFT's reconsideration of the matter.

(6) Subject to sub-paragraphs (7) and (8), where the Tribunal remits an application to the OFT, section 6(1) and (3) to (9) of this Act shall apply as if the application had not been previously determined by the OFT.

(7) In the case of a general notice which came into effect after the determination appealed against was made but before the application was remitted, the applicant shall provide any information or document which he is required to provide under section 6(6) within—
   (a) the period of 28 days beginning with the day on which the application was remitted; or
   (b) such longer period as the OFT may allow.

(8) In the case of—
   (a) any information or document which was superseded,
   (b) any change in circumstances which occurred, or
   (c) any error or omission of which the applicant became aware,
   after the determination appealed against was made but before the application was remitted, any notification that is required to be given by the applicant under section 6(7) shall be given within the period of 28 days beginning with the day on which the application was remitted.

Decisions of the Tribunal

13.—(1) A decision of the Tribunal may be taken by majority.

(2) A decision of the Tribunal disposing of an appeal shall—
   (a) state whether it was unanimous or taken by majority; and
   (b) be recorded in a document which—

(i) contains a statement of the reasons for the decision and any other specified information; and

(ii) is signed and dated by a member of the panel of chairmen.

(3) Where the Tribunal disposes of an appeal it shall—

(a) send to each party to the appeal a copy of the document mentioned in sub-paragraph (2)(b); and

(b) publish that document in such manner as it thinks fit.

(4) The Tribunal may exclude from what it publishes under sub-paragraph (3)(b) information of a specified description.

Costs

14.—(1) Where the Tribunal disposes of an appeal and—

(a) it decides that the OFT was wrong to make the determination appealed against, or

(b) during the course of the appeal the OFT accepted that it was wrong to make that determination,

it may order the OFT to pay to the appellant the whole or a part of the costs incurred by the appellant in relation to the appeal.

(2) In determining whether to make such an order, and the terms of such an order, the Tribunal shall have regard to whether it was unreasonable for the OFT to make the determination appealed against.

15.—Where—

(a) the Tribunal disposes of an appeal or an appeal is withdrawn before the Tribunal disposes of it, and

(b) the Tribunal thinks that a party to the appeal acted vexatiously, frivolously or unreasonably in bringing the appeal or otherwise in relation to the appeal,

it may order that party to pay to the other party the whole or a part of the costs incurred by the other party in relation to the appeal.

16.—An order of the Tribunal under paragraph 14 or 15 may be enforced—

(a) as if it were an order of the county court; or

(b) in Scotland, as if it were an interlocutor of the Court of Session.

SCHEDULE 2

SECTION 59

PART 3A OF SCHEDULE 17 TO THE 2000 ACT

PART 3A

THE CONSUMER CREDIT JURISDICTION

Introduction

16A.—This Part of this Schedule applies only in relation to the consumer credit jurisdiction.

Procedure for complaints etc.

16B.—(1)Consumer credit rules—

(a) must provide that a complaint is not to be entertained unless the complainant has referred it under the ombudsman scheme before the applicable time limit (determined in accordance with the rules) has expired;

    (b) may provide that an ombudsman may extend that time limit in specified circumstances;

    (c) may provide that a complaint is not to be entertained (except in specified circumstances) if the complainant has not previously communicated its substance to the respondent and given him a reasonable opportunity to deal with it;

    (d) may make provision about the procedure for the reference of complaints and for their investigation, consideration and determination by an ombudsman.

(2) Sub-paragraphs (2) and (3) of paragraph 14 apply in relation to consumer credit rules under sub-paragraph (1) of this paragraph as they apply in relation to scheme rules under that paragraph.

(3) Consumer credit rules may require persons falling within sub-paragraph (6) to establish such procedures as the scheme operator considers appropriate for the resolution of complaints which may be referred to the scheme.

(4) Consumer credit rules under sub-paragraph (3) may make different provision in relation to persons of different descriptions or to complaints of different descriptions.

(5) Consumer credit rules under sub-paragraph (3) may authorise the scheme operator to dispense with or modify the application of such rules in particular cases where the scheme operator—

    (a) considers it appropriate to do so; and

    (b) is satisfied that the specified conditions (if any) are met.

(6) A person falls within this sub-paragraph if he is licensed by a standard licence (within the meaning of the Consumer Credit Act 1974) to carry on to any extent a business of a type specified in an order under section 226A(2)(e) of this Act.

Fees

16C.—(1) Consumer credit rules may require a respondent to pay to the scheme operator such fees as may be specified in the rules.

(2) Sub-paragraph (2) of paragraph 15 applies in relation to consumer credit rules under this paragraph as it applies in relation to scheme rules under that paragraph.

Enforcement of money awards

16D.—A money award, including interest, which has been registered in accordance with consumer credit rules may—

    (a) if a county court so orders in England and Wales, be recovered by execution issued from the county court (or otherwise) as if it were payable under an order of that court;

    (b) be enforced in Northern Ireland as a money judgment under the Judgments Enforcement (Northern Ireland) Order 1981;

    (c) be enforced in Scotland as if it were a decree of the sheriff and whether or not the sheriff could himself have granted such a decree.

Procedure for consumer credit rules

16E.—(1) If the scheme operator makes any consumer credit rules, it must give a copy of them to the Authority without delay.

(2) If the scheme operator revokes any such rules, it must give written notice to the Authority without delay.

(3) The power to make such rules is exercisable in writing.

(4) Immediately after the making of such rules, the scheme operator must arrange for them to be printed and made available to the public.

(5) The scheme operator may charge a reasonable fee for providing a person with a copy of any such rules.

Verification of consumer credit rules

16F.—(1) The production of a printed copy of consumer credit rules purporting to be made by the scheme operator—

(a) on which there is endorsed a certificate signed by a member of the scheme operator's staff authorised by the scheme operator for that purpose, and

(b) which contains the required statements,

is evidence (or in Scotland sufficient evidence) of the facts stated in the certificate.

(2) The required statements are—

(a) that the rules were made by the scheme operator;

(b) that the copy is a true copy of the rules; and

(c) that on a specified date the rules were made available to the public in accordance with paragraph 16E(4).

(3) A certificate purporting to be signed as mentioned in sub-paragraph (1) is to be taken to have been duly signed unless the contrary is shown.

Consultation

16G.—(1) If the scheme operator proposes to make consumer credit rules, it must publish a draft of the proposed rules in the way appearing to it to be best calculated to bring the draft to the attention of the public.

(2) The draft must be accompanied by—

(a) an explanation of the proposed rules; and

(b) a statement that representations about the proposals may be made to the scheme operator within a specified time.

(3) Before making any consumer credit rules, the scheme operator must have regard to any representations made to it in accordance with sub-paragraph (2)(b).

(4) If consumer credit rules made by the scheme operator differ from the draft published under sub-paragraph (1) in a way which the scheme operator considers significant, the scheme operator must publish a statement of the difference.

SCHEDULE 3

SECTION 69

TRANSITIONAL PROVISION AND SAVINGS

Interpretation

1.—(1) Expressions used in the 1974 Act have the same meaning in this Schedule (apart from paragraphs 14 to 16 and 26) as they have in that Act.

(2) For the purposes of this Schedule an agreement becomes a completed agreement once—

(a) there is no sum payable under the agreement; and

(b) there is no sum which will or may become so payable.

Statements to be provided in relation to regulated agreements

2.—(1) Section 77A of the 1974 Act applies in relation to agreements whenever made.

(2) Section 77A shall have effect in relation to agreements made before the commencement of section 6 of this Act as if the period mentioned in subsection (1)(a) were the period of one year beginning with the day of the commencement of section 6.

3.—Regulations made under section 78(4A) of the 1974 Act may apply in relation to agreements regardless of when they were made.

4.—(1) Section 7(3) of this Act shall have effect in relation to agreements whenever made.

(2) A dispensing notice given under section 185(2) of the 1974 Act which is operative immediately before the commencement of section 7(3)—

(a) shall, on the commencement of section 7(3), be treated as having been given under section 185(2) as substituted by section 7(3); and

(b) shall continue to be operative accordingly.

Default under regulated agreements

5.—The OFT shall prepare, and give general notice of, the arrears information sheet and the default information sheet required under section 86A of the 1974 Act as soon as practicable after the commencement of section 8 of this Act.

6.—(1) Section 86B of the 1974 Act applies in relation to agreements whenever made.

(2) In the application of section 86B in relation to an agreement made before the commencement of section 9 of this Act, the conditions under subsection (1) can be satisfied only if the two payments mentioned in paragraph (c) were not required to have been made before the commencement of section 9.

(3) In the case of an agreement within subsection (9) of section 86B, sub-paragraph (2) has effect as if for "two" there were substituted "four".

7.—(1) Section 86C of the 1974 Act applies in relation to agreements whenever made.

(2) In the application of section 86C in relation to an agreement made before the commencement of section 10 of this Act, the conditions mentioned in subsection (1) can be satisfied only if the two payments mentioned in paragraph (b) were not required to have been made before the commencement of section 10.

8.—Section 86E of the 1974 Act applies in relation to agreements whenever made but only as regards default sums which become payable after the commencement of section 12 of this Act.

9.—(1) Section 86F of the 1974 Act applies in relation to agreements whenever made but only as regards default sums which become payable after the commencement of section 13 of this Act.

(2) Where section 86F applies in relation to an agreement made before the commencement of section 13, the agreement shall have effect as if any right of the creditor or owner to recover compound interest in connection with the default sum in question at a particular rate were a right to recover simple interest in that connection at that rate.

10.—Section 14 of this Act shall have effect in relation to any default notice served after the commencement of that section, regardless of—

(a) when the breach of the agreement in question occurred; or

(b) when that agreement was made.

11.—The repeal by this Act of—
  (a) the words "(subject to subsections (3) and (4))" in subsection (1) of section 127 of the 1974 Act,
  (b) subsections (3) to (5) of that section, and
  (c) the words "or 127(3)" in subsection (3) of section 185 of that Act,
  has no effect in relation to improperly-executed agreements made before the commencement of section 15 of this Act.
12.—A debtor or hirer under an agreement may make an application under section 129(1)(ba) of the 1974 Act regardless of when that agreement was made.
13.—Section 130A of the 1974 Act applies in relation to agreements whenever made but only as regards sums that are required to be paid under judgments given after the commencement of section 17 of this Act.

Unfair relationships

14.—(1) The court may make an order under section 140B of the 1974 Act in connection with a credit agreement made before the commencement of section 20 of this Act but only—
  (a) on an application of the kind mentioned in paragraph (a) of subsection (2) of section 140B made at a time after the end of the transitional period; or
  (b) at the instance of the debtor or a surety in any proceedings of the kind mentioned in paragraph (b) or (c) of that subsection which were commenced at such a time.
(2) But the court shall not make such an order in connection with such an agreement so made if the agreement—
  (a) became a completed agreement before the commencement of section 20; or
  (b) becomes a completed agreement during the transitional period.
(3) Expressions used in sections 140A to 140C of the 1974 Act have the same meaning in this paragraph as they have in those sections.
(4) In this paragraph "the transitional period" means the period of one year beginning with the day of the commencement of section 20.
(5) An order under section 69 of this Act may extend, or further extend, the transitional period.
15.—(1) The repeal by this Act of sections 137 to 140 of the 1974 Act shall not affect the court's power to reopen an existing agreement under those sections as set out in this paragraph.
(2) The court's power to reopen an existing agreement which—
  (a) became a completed agreement before the commencement of section 22(3) of this Act, or
  (b) becomes a completed agreement during the transitional period,
  is not affected at all.
(3) The court may also reopen an existing agreement—
  (a) on an application of the. kind mentioned in paragraph (a) of subsection (1) of section 139 made at a time before the end of the transitional period; or
  (b) at the instance of the debtor or a surety in any proceedings of the kind mentioned in paragraph (b) or (c) of that subsection which were commenced at such a time.
(4) Nothing in section 16A or 16B of the 1974 Act shall affect the application of sections 137 to 140 (whether by virtue of this paragraph or otherwise).
(5) The repeal or revocation by this Act of the following provisions has no effect in relation to existing agreements so far as they may be reopened as set out in this paragraph—

    (a) section 16(7) of the 1974 Act;

    (b) in section 143(b) of that Act, the words ", 139(1)(a)";

    (c) section 171(7) of that Act;

    (d) in subsection (1) of section 181 of that Act, the words "139(5) and (7),";

    (e) in subsection (2) of that section, the words "or 139(5) or (7)";

    (f) in section 61(6) of the Bankruptcy (Scotland) Act 1985 (c. 66), the words from the beginning to "but";

    (g) in section 343(6) of the Insolvency Act 1986 (c. 45), the words from the beginning to "But";

    (h) Article 316(6) of the Insolvency (Northern Ireland) Order 1989 (S.I. 1989/2405 (N.I. 19)).

(6) Expressions used in sections 137 to 140 of the 1974 Act have the same meaning in this paragraph as they have in those sections.

(7) In this paragraph—

        "existing agreement" means a credit agreement made before the commencement of section 22(3) of this Act;

        "the transitional period" means the period of one year beginning with the day of the commencement of section 22(3).

(8) An order under section 69 of this Act may extend, or further extend, the transitional period.

16.—(1) It is immaterial for the purposes of section 140C(4)(a) to (c) of the 1974 Act when (as the case may be) a credit agreement or a linked transaction was made or a security was provided.

(2) In relation to an order made under section 140B of the 1974 Act during the transitional period in connection with a credit agreement—

    (a) references in subsection (1) of that section to any related agreement shall not include references to a related agreement to which this sub-paragraph applies;

    (b) the reference to a security in paragraph (d) of that subsection shall not include a reference to a security to which this sub-paragraph applies;

and the order shall not under paragraph (g) of that subsection direct accounts to be taken, or (in Scotland) an accounting to be made, between any persons in relation to a related agreement to which this sub-paragraph applies.

(3) Sub-paragraph (2) applies to a related agreement or a security if—

    (a) it was made or provided before the commencement of section 21 of this Act; and

    (b) it ceased to have any operation before the order under section 140B is made.

(4) In relation to an order made under section 140B after the end of the transitional period in connection with a credit agreement—

    (a) references in subsection (1) of that section to any related agreement shall not include references to a related agreement to which this sub-paragraph applies;

    (b) the reference to a security in paragraph (d) of that subsection shall not include a reference to a security to which this sub-paragraph applies;

and the order shall not under paragraph (g) of that subsection direct accounts to be taken, or (in Scotland) an accounting to be made, between any persons in relation to a related agreement to which this sub-paragraph applies.

(5) Sub-paragraph (4) applies to a related agreement or a security if—

    (a) it was made or provided before the commencement of section 21; and

    (b) it ceased to have any operation before the end of the transitional period.

(6) Expressions used in sections 140A to 140C of the 1974 Act have the same meanings in this paragraph as they have in those sections.

(7) In this paragraph "the transitional period" means the period of one year beginning with the day of the commencement of section 21.

(8) An order under section 69 of this Act may extend, or further extend, the transitional period.

17.—Section 1 of this Act shall have no effect for the purposes of section 140C(1) of the 1974 Act in relation to agreements made before the commencement of section 1.

Applications for licences and fitness to hold a licence etc.

18.—(1) Section 6A of the 1974 Act shall not apply in relation to applications made before the commencement of section 27 of this Act.

(2) Section 6(2A) of the 1974 Act shall not apply in relation to applications so made.

(3) The repeal by this Act of the words "and must be accompanied by the specified fee" in section 6(2) of the 1974 Act has no effect in relation to applications so made.

19.—(1) The OFT shall prepare and publish the guidance required by section 25A of the 1974 Act as soon as practicable after the commencement of section 30 of this Act.

(2) The requirements of subsection (4) of section 25A may be satisfied in relation to the preparation of that guidance by steps taken wholly or partly before the commencement of section 30.

Further powers of OFT to regulate conduct of licensees etc.

20.—The cases in which the OFT may impose requirements under section 33A of the 1974 Act include cases where the matter with which the OFT is dissatisfied arose before the commencement of section 38 of this Act.

21.—The cases in which the OFT may impose requirements under section 33B of the 1974 Act include cases where the matters giving rise to the OFT's dissatisfaction arose before the commencement of section 39 of this Act.

22.—(1) The OFT shall prepare and publish the guidance required by section 33E of the 1974 Act as soon as practicable after the commencement of section 42 of this Act.

(2) The requirements of subsection (4) of section 33E may be satisfied in relation to the preparation of that guidance by steps taken wholly or partly before the commencement of section 42.

Powers and duties in relation to information

23.—(1) Section 44 of this Act has no effect in relation to applications made before the commencement of that section.

(2) Paragraph 12(6) of Schedule A1 to the 1974 Act does not apply in relation to applications so made.

24.—A person is not required by section 36A of the 1974 Act to do anything in relation to an application made by him before the commencement of section 45 of this Act.

Civil penalties

25.—(1) The OFT shall prepare and publish the statement of policy required by section 39C of the 1974 Act as soon as practicable after the commencement of section 54 of this Act.

(2) The requirements of subsection (5) of section 39C may be satisfied in relation to the preparation of that statement of policy by steps taken wholly or partly before the commencement of section 54.

Appeals

26.—(1) A person who—

    (a) immediately before the commencement of section 55 of this Act is a member of a panel established under regulation 24 of the appeals regulations, and

    (b) at the time of his appointment to that panel fell within paragraph (2)(a) of that regulation,

shall be treated as having been appointed to the panel of chairmen on the day of the commencement of section 55.

(2) A person who—

    (a) immediately before the commencement of section 55 is a member of a panel established under regulation 24 of the appeals regulations, and

    (b) is not to be treated as having been appointed to the panel of chairmen in accordance with sub-paragraph (1),

shall be treated as having been appointed to the lay panel on the day of the commencement of section 55.

(3) A person who is to be treated as having been appointed to the panel of chairmen or to the lay panel in accordance with this paragraph shall, subject to paragraph 4(2) and (3) of Schedule A1 to the 1974 Act, hold office as a member of the panel in question—

    (a) for the remainder of the period for which he was appointed under regulation 24 of the appeals regulations; and

    (b) on the terms on which he was so appointed (except as to the renewal of his appointment).

(4) In this paragraph—

        "appeals regulations" means the Consumer Credit Licensing (Appeals) Regulations 1998 (S.I. 1998/1203);

        "lay panel" and "panel of chairmen" have the same meanings as in Schedule A1 to the 1974 Act.

27.—(1) Neither—

    (a) subsections (1) and (2) of section 56 of this Act, nor

    (b) the repeal by this Act of subsections (2) to (5) of section 41 of the 1974 Act,

has effect in relation to determinations of the OFT made before the commencement of section 56.

(2) This Act, so far as it repeals section 11 of the Tribunals and Inquiries Act 1992 (c. 53), has no effect in relation to such determinations so made.

(3) The repeal by this Act of paragraph 27(2) of Schedule 25 to the Enterprise Act 2002 (c. 40) has no effect in relation to such determinations so made.

28.—Neither subsection (1) nor (4)(a) of section 58 of this Act has effect in relation to determinations of the OFT made before the commencement of that section.

Ombudsman scheme

29.—Section 1 of this Act shall have no effect for the purposes of section 226A(4)(a) of the 2000 Act in relation to a complaint which relates to an act or omission occurring before the commencement of section 1.

SCHEDULE 4

SECTION 70

REPEALS

Act or instrument

Extent of repeal

Consumer Credit Act 1974 (c. 39)

In section 2(7), the words "or 150".
In section 6(2), the words "and must be accompanied by the specified fee".
Section 8(2).
In section 15, subsection (1)(c) and the "and" immediately preceding it.
Section 16(7).
Section 22(9) and (10).
Section 23(2).
Section 25(1A).
Section 29(5).
Section 32(5).
Section 36(6).
In section 40(6), the words ", other than a non-commercial agreement,".
In section 41—
(a) subsections (2) to (5); and
(b) in the Table the entry relating to "refusal to give directions in respect of a licensee under section 29(5) or 32(5)".
In section 43, subsection (3)(a) and the "or" immediately after it.
In section 127—
(a) in subsection (1) the words "(subject to subsections (3) and (4))"; and
(b) subsections (3) to (5).
Sections 137 to 140.
In section 143(b), the words ", 139(1)(a)".
In section 147—
(a) subsection (1); and
(b) in subsection (2) the words "(as applied by subsection (1))".
Section 150.
In section 162—
(a) in subsection (1)(b)(i), the words "books or";
(b) in subsection (1)(b), the words "and take copies of, or of any entry in, the books or documents";
(c) in subsections (1)(d) and (e), (2) and (3) the word "books"; and
(d) subsection (7).
Section 171(7).
In section 181—
(a) in subsection (1) the words "43(3)(a)," and the words "139(5) and (7),"; and
(b) in subsection (2) the words "43(3)(a)," and the words "or 139(5) or (7)".
In section 185(3), the words "or 127(3)".
In section 189(1)—

(a) the definition of "costs";
(b) in the definition of "licence" the words from "(including" onwards; and
(c) the definition of "personal credit agreement".
In Schedule 2, in Part 1, the entry relating to "personal credit agreement".

Bankruptcy (Scotland) Act 1985 (c. 66)

In section 61(6), the words from the beginning to "but".

Insolvency Act 1986 (c. 45)

In section 343(6), the words from the beginning to "But".

Insolvency (Northern Ireland) Order 1989 (S.I. 1989/2405 (N.I. 19))

Article 316(6).

Tribunals and Inquiries Act 1992 (c. 53)

In section 11—
(a) subsection (6);
(b) in subsection (7)(a), the words from "or on an appeal" to "Scotland" in the third place where it occurs; and
(c) in subsection (8), the words from "and in relation to" to "Northern Ireland" in the third place where it occurs.

Enterprise Act 2002 (c. 40)

In Schedule 25, paragraphs 6(18)(b) and 27(2).

APPENDIX 2

The Consumer Credit (Advertisements) Regulations 2004

STATUTORY INSTRUMENTS

2004 No. 1484
CONSUMER CREDIT
The Consumer Credit (Advertisements) Regulations 2004

Made	*5th June 2004*
Laid before Parliament	*9th June 2004*
Coming into force	*31st October 2004*

The Secretary of State, in exercise of the powers conferred upon her by sections 44, 151(1), 182(2) and 189(1) of the Consumer Credit Act 1974[1], hereby makes the following Regulations:

Citation, commencement and interpretation

1.—(1) These Regulations may be cited as the Consumer Credit (Advertisements) Regulations 2004, and shall come into force on 31st October 2004.

(2) In these Regulations—

"the Act" means the Consumer Credit Act 1974;

"advance payment" does not include a repayment of credit or any insurance premium or any amount entering into the total charge for credit;

"APR" means the annual percentage rate of charge for credit determined in accordance with the Total Charge for Credit Regulations and Schedule 1 to these Regulations;

"authorised deposit taker" means—

(a) a person who has permission under Part 4 of the Financial Services and Markets Act 2000[2] to accept deposits, or

(b) an EEA firm of the kind mentioned in paragraph 5(b) of Schedule 3 to that Act which has permission under paragraph 15 of that Schedule (as a result of qualifying for authorisation under paragraph 12(1)) to accept deposits,

but sub-paragraph (a) does not include a person who is a credit union within the meaning of the Credit Unions Act 1979[3] or the Credit Unions (Northern Ireland) Order 1985[4], or a specially authorised friendly society within the meaning of section 7(1)(f) of the Friendly Societies Act 1974[5];

"cash price" in relation to any goods, services, land or other things means the price or charge at which the goods, services, land or other things may be purchased by, or supplied to, persons for cash, account being taken of any discount generally available from the dealer or supplier in question;

"cash purchaser" means, in relation to any advertisement, a person who, for a money consideration—

(a) acquires goods, land or other things, or

(b) is provided with services,

under a transaction which is not financed by credit;

"credit advertisement" means an advertisement to which Part 4 of the Act applies by virtue of it falling within section 43(1)(a), or which falls within section 151(1) of the Act in so far as section 44 is applied to such an advertisement;

"current account" means an account under which the customer may, by means of cheques or similar orders payable to himself or to any other person or by any other means, obtain or have the use of money held or made available by the person with whom the account is kept and which records alterations in the financial relationship between the said person and the customer;

"dealer" means, in relation to a hire-purchase, credit sale or conditional sale agreement under which he is not the creditor, a person who sells or proposes to sell goods, land or other things to the creditor before they form the subject matter of any such agreement and, in relation to any other agreement, means a supplier or his agent;

"hire advertisement" means an advertisement to which Part 4 of the Act applies by virtue of it falling within section 43(1)(b), or which falls within section 151(1) of the Act in so far as section 44 is applied to such an advertisement;

"hire payment" means any payment to be made by a person in relation to any period in consideration of the bailment to him of goods, other than an advance payment;

"identified dealer" means, in relation to an advertisement—

(a) a dealer who is named in the advertisement or is identified in it by reference to a business connection he has with the advertiser, or

(b) a dealer upon whose premises the advertisement is published;

"premises" includes any place, stall, vehicle, aircraft or hovercraft at which a person is carrying on any business (whether on a permanent or temporary basis);

"relevant date", in relation to an advertisement relating to credit to be provided under a consumer credit agreement, means—

(a) in a case where a date is specified in or determinable under the agreement at the date of its making as that on which the debtor is entitled to require provision of anything the subject of the agreement, the earliest such date, and

(b) in any other case, the date of the making of the agreement;

"supplier" has the meaning assigned to it by section 189(1) of the Act, except that it does not include, in relation to a hire-purchase, credit sale or conditional sale agreement, a creditor to whom goods, land or other things are sold or proposed to be sold by a dealer before becoming the subject matter of such an agreement;

"the total charge for credit" means the total charge for credit determined in accordance with the Total Charge for Credit Regulations and Schedule 1 to these Regulations;

"the Total Charge for Credit Regulations" means the Consumer Credit (Total Charge for Credit) Regulations 1980[6], and

"the typical APR" is an APR at or below which an advertiser reasonably expects, at the date on which an advertisement is published, that credit would be provided under at least 66% of the agreements he will enter into as a result of the advertisement.

(3) The definition of "authorised deposit taker" in paragraph (2) must be read with—

(a) section 22 of the Financial Services and Markets Act 2000;

(b) any relevant order under that section; and

(c) Schedule 2 to that Act.

(4) In these Regulations as they apply to Scotland—

(a) any reference to bailment is a reference to hiring;

(b) any reference to a mortgage or charge on land, or any other security on land, is a reference to a standard security over land within the meaning of the Conveyancing and Feudal Reform (Scotland) Act 1970[7].

(5) In these Regulations, references to repayment of credit are references to repayment of credit with or without any other amount.

(6) In these Regulations, any reference to the name of any person is—

(a) in the case of any person covered by a standard licence, a reference to any name of his specified in the licence; and

(b) in the case of any other person, a reference to any name under which he carries on business.

(7) Where any expression is used in these Regulations and in the Act, for the purposes of these Regulations that expression shall be construed as if, in the Act (except section 8), references to consumer credit agreements and to regulated agreements (being consumer credit agreements) included references to personal credit agreements.

Duty to comply

2. A person who causes a credit advertisement or a hire advertisement to be published shall ensure that the advertisement complies with all applicable requirements of these Regulations.

General requirements

3. Every credit advertisement or hire advertisement shall—

(a) use plain and intelligible language;

(b) be easily legible (or, in the case of any information given orally, clearly audible), and

(c) specify the name of the advertiser.

Content of advertisements

4.—(1) Where a credit advertisement includes any of the amounts referred to in paragraphs 5 to 7 of Schedule 2 to these Regulations, and where a hire advertisement includes any of the amounts referred to in paragraph 4 or 5 of Schedule 3 to these Regulations, the advertisement shall also—

(a) include all the other items of information (other than any item inapplicable to the particular case) listed in the relevant Schedule, and

(b) specify a postal address at which the advertiser may be contacted, except—

    (i) in the case of advertisements published by means of television or radio broadcast;

    (ii) in the case of advertisements in any form on the premises of a dealer or creditor (not being advertisements in writing which customers are intended to take away);

    (iii) in the case of advertisements which include the name and address of a dealer, and

    (iv) in the case of advertisements which include the name and a postal address of a credit-broker.

(2) The items of information listed in Schedule 2 in the case of a credit advertisement, and the items of information listed in Schedule 3 in the case of a hire advertisement, shall be given equal prominence and shall be shown together as a whole.

(3) Any information in any book, catalogue, leaflet or other document which is likely to vary from time to time shall be taken for the purpose of paragraph (2) to be shown together as a whole if—

(a) it is set out together as a whole in a separate document issued with the book, catalogue, leaflet or other document;

(b) the other information in the credit advertisement or hire advertisement, as the case may be, is shown together as a whole in the book, catalogue, leaflet or other document, and

(c) the book, catalogue, leaflet or other document identifies the separate document in which the information likely to vary is set out.

Credit advertisements in dealers' publications covering a calendar or seasonal period

5.—(1) Regulation 4 shall not apply to a credit advertisement contained in, or in a separate document issued with, a publication published by or on behalf of a dealer which relates to goods or services which may be sold or supplied by him in a calendar or seasonal period specified in the publication if the advertisement contains the information specified in paragraph (2) and no other indication that a person is willing to provide credit.

(2) The information referred to in paragraph (1) is—

(a) the name of the creditor, credit-broker or dealer and a postal address of his with or without his occupation or a statement of the general nature of his occupation, and

(b) an indication that individuals may obtain on request details of the terms on which the advertiser is prepared to do business.

Advertisements in dealers' publications relating to credit under a debtor-creditor-supplier agreement

6. Information contained in a credit advertisement relating to credit to be provided under a debtor-creditor-supplier agreement, being an advertisement contained in a publication published by or on behalf of a dealer which relates to goods or services

which may be sold or supplied by him, shall be taken for the purpose of regulation 4(2) to be shown together as a whole if—

(a) the advertisement clearly indicates—
   (i) the cash price alone, or
   (ii) the cash price, any advance payment and the information specified in paragraphs 5 to 7 of Schedule 2, and (except in the case of agreements for credit under which the total amount payable by the debtor is not greater than the cash price of the goods or services the acquisition of which is to be financed by the credit under the agreement) the APR,

in close proximity to every description of, or specific reference to, goods or services to which the information in the publication relates, and

(b) the remaining information in the advertisement is so presented as to be readily comprehensible as a whole by a prospective debtor and an indication is given in close proximity to any of that information that it relates to all or specified descriptions of goods or services, and

(c) except as mentioned in paragraph (a), no information relating to the provision of credit is shown together with the cash price.

Security

7.—(1) Where the subject-matter of a credit advertisement or hire advertisement is a facility for which security is or may be required, the advertisement shall—

(a) state that security is or may be required, and
(b) specify the nature of the security.

(2) Where, in the case of a credit advertisement, the security comprises or may comprise a mortgage or charge on the debtor's home—

(a) except where sub-paragraph (c) applies, the advertisement shall contain a warning in the form—
   "YOUR HOME MAY BE REPOSSESSED IF YOU DO NOT KEEP UP REPAYMENTS ON A MORTGAGE OR ANY OTHER DEBT SECURED ON IT";

(b) where the advertisement indicates that credit is available for the payment of debts due to other creditors, the warning in sub-paragraph (a) shall be preceded by the words—
   "THINK CAREFULLY BEFORE SECURING OTHER DEBTS AGAINST YOUR HOME."

(c) where the credit agreement is or would be an agreement of a kind described in paragraph (3), the advertisement shall contain a warning in the form—
   "CHECK THAT THIS MORTGAGE WILL MEET YOUR NEEDS IF YOU WANT TO MOVE OR SELL YOUR HOME OR YOU WANT YOUR FAMILY TO INHERIT IT. IF YOU ARE IN ANY DOUBT, SEEK INDEPENDENT ADVICE".

(3) The kinds of agreement referred to in paragraph (2)(c) are—

(a) any credit agreement under which no instalment repayments secured by the mortgage on the debtor's home, and no payment of interest on the credit (other than interest charged when all or part of the credit is repaid voluntarily by the debtor), are due or capable of becoming due while the debtor continues to occupy the mortgaged land as his main residence; and

   (b) any credit agreement—

      (i) which is secured by a mortgage which the creditor cannot enforce by taking possession of or selling (or concurring with any other person in selling) the mortgaged land or any part of it while the debtor continues to occupy it as his main residence, and

      (ii) under which, although interest payments may become due, no full or partial repayment of the credit secured by the mortgage is due or capable of becoming due while the debtor continues to occupy the mortgaged land as his main residence.

(4) Where a credit advertisement is for a mortgage or other loan secured on property and repayments are to be made in a currency other than sterling, the advertisement shall contain a warning in the form—

     "CHANGES IN THE EXCHANGE RATE MAY INCREASE THE STERLING EQUIVALENT OF YOUR DEBT".

(5) Where, in the case of a hire advertisement, the security comprises or may comprise a mortgage or charge on the hirer's home, the advertisement shall contain a warning in the form—

     "YOUR HOME MAY BE REPOSSESSED IF YOU DO NOT KEEP UP REPAYMENTS ON A HIRE AGREEMENT SECURED BY A MORTGAGE OR OTHER SECURITY ON YOUR HOME".

(6) The warnings provided for in paragraphs (2) and (4)—

   (a) shall be given greater prominence in a credit advertisement than is given to—

      (i) any rate of charge other than the typical APR, or

      (ii) any indication or incentive of a kind referred to in regulation 8(1)(c) or (d), and

   (b) shall be given no less prominence in a credit advertisement than is given to any of the items listed in Schedule 2 to these Regulations that appear in the advertisement.

(7) The warning provided for in paragraph (5) shall be given no less prominence in a hire advertisement than is given to any of the items listed in Schedule 3 to these Regulations that appear in the advertisement.

(8) Paragraphs (2)—(7) do not apply in the case of an advertisement which—

   (a) is published by means of television or radio broadcast in the course of programming the primary purpose of which is not advertising;

   (b) is published by exhibition of a film (other than exhibition by television broadcast), or

   (c) contains only the name of the advertiser.

APR

8.—(1) A credit advertisement shall specify the typical APR if the advertisement—

   (a) specifies any other rate of charge;

   (b) includes any of the items of information listed in paragraphs 5 to 7 of Schedule 2 to these Regulations;

   (c) indicates in any way, including by means of the name given to a business or of an address used by a business for the purposes of electronic communication, that—

      (i) credit is available to persons who might otherwise consider their access to credit restricted, or

    (ii) any of the terms on which credit is available is more favourable (either in relation to a limited period or generally) than corresponding terms applied in any other case or by any other creditors, or

  (d) includes any incentive to apply for credit or to enter into an agreement under which credit is provided.

(2) A credit advertisement may not indicate the range of APRs charged where credit is provided otherwise than by specifying, with equal prominence, both—

  (a) the APR which the advertiser reasonably expects, at the date on which the advertisement is published, would be the lowest APR at which credit would be provided under not less than 10% of the agreements he will enter into as a result of that advertisement, and

  (b) the APR which the advertiser reasonably expects, at that date, would be the highest APR at which credit would be provided under any of the agreements he will enter into as a result of that advertisement.

(3) An APR shall be denoted in an advertisement as "%APR".

(4) Where an APR is subject to change, it shall be accompanied by the word "variable".

(5) The typical APR shall be—

  (a) accompanied by the word "typical";

  (b) presented together with any of the items listed in Schedule 2 that are included in the advertisement;

  (c) given greater prominence in the advertisement than—

    (i) any other rate of charge;

    (ii) any of the items listed in Schedule 2, and

    (iii) any indication or incentive of a kind referred to in paragraph (1)(c) or (d), and

  (d) in the case of an advertisement in printed or electronic form which includes any of the items listed in Schedule 2, shown in characters at least one and a half times the size of the characters in which those items appear.

(6) In the case of an advertisement relating to a debtor-creditor agreement enabling the debtor to overdraw on a current account under which the creditor is the Bank of England or an authorised deposit taker, there may be substituted for the typical APR a reference to the statement of—

  (a) a rate, expressed to be a rate of interest, being a rate determined as the rate of the total charge for credit calculated on the assumption that only interest is included in the total charge for credit, and

  (b) the nature and amount of any other charge included in the total charge for credit.

Restrictions on certain expressions in credit advertisements

9.—(1) A credit advertisement shall not include—

  (a) the word "overdraft" or any similar expression as describing any agreement for running-account credit except an agreement enabling the debtor to overdraw on a current account;

  (b) the expression "interest free" or any similar expression indicating that a customer is liable to pay no greater amount in respect of a transaction financed by credit than he would be liable to pay as a cash purchaser in relation to the like transaction, except where the total amount payable by the debtor does not exceed the cash price;

  (c) the expression "no deposit" or any similar expression, except where no advance payments are to be made;

    (d) the expression "loan guaranteed" or "pre-approved" or any similar expression, except where the agreement is free of any conditions regarding the credit status of the debtor, or

    (e) the expression "gift", "present" or any similar expression except where there are no conditions which would require the debtor to return the credit or items that are the subject of the claim.

(2) A credit advertisement shall not include in relation to any repayment of credit, and a hire advertisement shall not include in relation to any hire payment, the expression "weekly equivalent" or any expression to the like effect or any expression of any other periodical equivalent, unless weekly payments or the other periodical payments are provided for under the agreement.

Exclusions

10.—(1) These Regulations do not apply to any advertisement which—

    (a) whether expressly or by implication indicates clearly that a person is willing—

       (i) to provide credit, or

       (ii) to enter into an agreement for the bailment of goods,

    for the purposes of another person's business, and

    (b) does not indicate (whether expressly or by implication) that a person is willing to do either of those things otherwise than for the purposes of such a business.

(2) References in paragraph (1) to a business do not include references to a business carried on by the advertiser or any person acting as a credit-broker in relation to the credit or hire facility to which the advertisement relates.

(3) These Regulations do not apply to any advertisement in so far as it is a communication of an invitation or inducement to engage in investment activity within the meaning of section 21 of the Financial Services and Markets Act 2000, other than an exempt generic communication.

(4) An "exempt generic communication" is a communication to which subsection (1) of section 21 of the Financial Services and Markets Act does not apply, as a result of an order under subsection (5) of that section, because it does not identify a person as providing an investment or as carrying on an activity to which the communication relates.

(5) These Regulations do not apply to any advertisement in so far as it is a communication of an invitation or inducement to enter into a regulated mortgage contract within the meaning of article 61 of the Financial Services and Markets Act 2000 (Regulated Activities) Order 2001[8].

Revocation of superseded provisions

11. The Consumer Credit (Advertisements) Regulations 1989[9], Part III of the Consumer Credit (Content of Quotations) and Consumer Credit (Advertisements) (Amendment) Regulations 1999[10] and regulation 2 of the Consumer Credit (Advertisements and Content of Quotations) (Amendment) Regulations 2000[11] are hereby revoked.

Transitional provisions

12.—(1) Subject to paragraph (2), a person shall not be guilty of an offence under section 47(1) or 167 of the Act for contravention of these Regulations in the case of an advertisement that would have complied with the requirements of the Consumer Credit (Advertisements) Regulations 1989 if those Regulations had not been revoked by these Regulations.

(2) Paragraph (1) only applies to advertisements published in a catalogue, diary or work of reference comprising at least 50 printed pages—

  (a) copies of which are first published, or made available for publication in the ordinary course of business, before 31st May 2005, and

  (b) which, in a reasonably prominent position either contains the date of its first publication or specifies a period, being a calendar or seasonal period, throughout which it is intended to have effect.

Gerry Sutcliffe,

Parliamentary Under Secretary of State for Employment Relations, Competition and Consumer Affairs, Department of Trade and Industry

5th June 2004

SCHEDULE 1

Regulation 1(2)
PROVISIONS RELATING TO CALCULATION AND DISCLOSURE OF THE TOTAL CHARGE FOR CREDIT AND ANY APR

Assumptions about running-account credit

1. In the case of an advertisement relating to running-account credit, the following assumptions shall have effect for the purpose of calculating the total charge for credit and any APR, notwithstanding the terms of the transaction advertised and in place of any assumptions in Part 4 of the Total Charge for Credit Regulations that might otherwise apply—

  (a) the amount of the credit to be provided shall be taken to be £1,500, or, in a case where credit is to be provided subject to a credit limit of less than £1,500, an amount equal to that limit;

  (b) it shall be assumed that the credit is provided for a period of one year beginning with the relevant date;

  (c) it shall be assumed that the credit is provided in full on the relevant date;

  (d) where the rate of interest will change at a time provided in the transaction within a period of three years beginning with the relevant date, the rate shall be taken to be the highest rate at any time obtaining under the transaction in that period;

  (e) where the agreement provides credit to finance the purchase of goods, services, land or other things and also provides one or more of—

    (i) cash loans

    (ii) credit to refinance existing indebtedness of the debtor's, whether to the creditor or another person; and

    (iii) credit for any other purpose,

    and either or both different rates of interest and different charges are payable in relation to the credit provided for all or some of these purposes, it shall be assumed that the rate of interest and charges payable in relation to the whole of the credit are those applicable to the provision of credit for the purchase of goods, services land or other things;

  (f) it shall be assumed that the credit is repaid—

    (i) in twelve equal instalments, and

    (ii) at monthly intervals, beginning one month after the relevant date.

Permissible tolerances in disclosure of an APR

2. For the purposes of these Regulations, it shall be sufficient compliance with the requirement to show an APR if there is included in the advertisement—

(a) a rate which exceeds the APR by not more than one, or

(b) a rate which falls short of the APR by not more than 0.1,

or in a case to which paragraph 3 or 4 of this Schedule applies, a rate determined in accordance with those paragraphs or whichever of them applies to that case.

Tolerance where repayments are nearly equal

3. In the case of an agreement under which all repayments but one are equal and that one repayment does not differ from any other repayment by more whole pence than there are repayments of credit, there may be included in an advertisement relating to the agreement a rate found under regulation 7 of the Total Charge for Credit Regulations as if that one repayment were equal to the other repayments to be made under the agreement.

Tolerance where interval between relevant date and first repayment is greater than interval between repayments

4. In the case of an agreement under which—

(a) three or more repayments are to be made at equal intervals, and

(b) the interval between the relevant date and the first repayment is greater than the interval between the repayments,

there may be included in the advertisement relating to the agreement a rate found under regulation 7 of the Total Charge for Credit Regulations as if the interval between the relevant date and the first repayment were shortened so as to be equal to the interval between repayments.

SCHEDULE 2

Regulations 4(1), 7(6), 8(1) and (6)
INFORMATION TO BE CONTAINED IN A CREDIT ADVERTISEMENT

Amount of credit

1. The amount of credit which may be provided under a consumer credit agreement or an indication of one or both of the maximum amount and the minimum amount of credit which may be provided.

Deposit of money in an account

2. A statement of any requirement to place on deposit any sum of money in any account with any person.

Cash price

3. In the case of an advertisement relating to credit to be provided under a debtor-creditor-supplier agreement, where the advertisement specifies goods, services, land or other things having a particular cash price, the acquisition of which from an identified dealer may be financed by the credit, the cash price of such goods, services, land or other things.

Advance payment

4. A statement as to whether an advance payment is required and if so the amount or minimum amount of the payment expressed as a sum of money or a percentage.

Frequency, number and amount of repayments of credit

5.—(1) In the case of an advertisement relating to running-account credit, a statement of the frequency of the repayments of credit under the advertised transaction and of the amount of each repayment stating whether it is a fixed or minimum amount, or a statement indicating the manner in which the amount will be determined.

(2) In the case of other credit advertisements, a statement of the frequency, number and amounts of repayments of credit.

(3) The amount of any repayment under this paragraph may be expressed as a sum of money or as a specified proportion of a specified amount (including the amount outstanding from time to time).

Other payments and charges

6.—(1) Subject to sub-paragraphs (2) and (3) below, a statement indicating the description and amount of any other payments and charges which may be payable under the transaction advertised.

(2) Where the liability of the debtor to make any payment cannot be ascertained at the date the advertisement is published, a statement indicating the description of the payment in question and the circumstances in which the liability to make it will arise.

(3) Sub-paragraphs (1) and (2) above do not apply to any charge payable under the transaction to the creditor or any other person on his behalf upon failure by the debtor or a relative of his to do or refrain from doing anything which he is required to do or refrain from doing, as the case may be.

Total amount payable by the debtor

7.—(1) Subject to sub-paragraph (2) below, in the case of an advertisement relating to fixed-sum credit to be provided under a consumer credit agreement which is repayable at specified intervals or in specified amounts and other than cases under which the sum of the payments within sub-paragraphs (a) to (c) below is not greater than the cash price referred to in paragraph 3, the total amount payable by the debtor, being the total of—

(a) advance payments;

(b) the amount of credit repayable by the debtor, and

(c) the amount of the total charge for credit.

(2) Sub-paragraph (1) above does not apply in the case of an advertisement relating to a consumer credit agreement where the advertisement does not specify goods, services, land or other things having a particular cash price, the acquisition of which may be financed by credit.

SCHEDULE 3

Regulations 4(1) and 7(7)
INFORMATION TO BE CONTAINED IN A HIRE ADVERTISEMENT

Deposit of money in an account

1. A statement of any requirement to place on deposit any sum of money in any account with any person.

Advance payment

2. A statement as to whether an advance payment is required and if so the amount or minimum amount of the payment, expressed as a sum of money or as a percentage.

Duration of hire

3. In a case where goods are to be bailed under an agreement for a fixed period or a maximum or minimum period, a statement indicating that this is the case and the duration of that period.

Frequency and amount of hire payments

4. The frequency and amount of each hire payment stating, if it be the case, that it is a minimum amount and, in the case where the amount of any hire payment will or may be varied, a statement indicating that the amount will or may be varied and the circumstances in which that would occur.

Other payments and charges

5.—(1) Subject to sub-paragraphs (2) and (3) below, a statement indicating the description and amount of any other payments or charges which may be payable under the transaction advertised.

(2) Where the liability of the debtor to make any payment cannot be ascertained at the date the advertisement is published, a statement indicating the description of the payment in question and the circumstances in which liability to make it will arise.

(3) Sub-paragraphs (1) and (2) above do not apply to any charge payable under the transaction to the creditor or any other person on his behalf upon failure by the debtor or a relative of his to do or refrain from doing anything which he is required to do or refrain from doing, as the case may be.

Variable payments and charges

6. Where any payment or charge referred to in paragraph 4 or 5 may be varied under the hire agreement, except to take account only of a change in value added tax (including a change to or from no tax being charged), a statement indicating that this is the case.

EXPLANATORY NOTE

(This note is not part of the Regulations)

These Regulations impose requirements concerning the form and content of advertisements that relate to the provision of credit and the hiring of goods. They replace the Consumer Credit (Advertisements) Regulations 1989 ("the 1989 Regulations"), which are revoked. By virtue of regulation 10, these Regulations do not apply in relation to advertisements for loans or the hire of goods to businesses, to financial promotions or to advertisements for mortgages which are a first charge on the borrower's home.

Whereas the 1989 Regulations provided for simple, intermediate and full credit and hire advertisements, each subject to different requirements regarding the information to be included, these Regulations contain a single list of items of information for inclusion in credit advertisements (in Schedule 2) and a corresponding list for inclusion in hire advertisements (in Schedule 3). Regulation 4 provides that an advertisement containing particular items in the relevant Schedule must include all of the other items listed.

Regulations 5 and 6 re-enact regulations 4 and 5 of the 1989 Regulations.

Regulation 7 provides for warnings previously required only in the case of full and intermediate credit or hire advertisements to appear in the case of any credit or hire advertisement which relates to a facility for which security is required. Paragraph (2)(b) of this regulation, relating to advertisements for credit to discharge debts owed to other creditors, is a new provision.

Regulation 8 sets out new provisions relating to the annual percentage rate of charge for credit ("APR"). Advertisers are required to specify a typical APR in any advertisement that contains particular financial information, makes particular claims or offers incentives. The typical APR is the rate the advertiser expects to charge in at least two-thirds of the transactions he will enter into as a result of the advertisement. In advertisements for running-account credit, such as is provided by way of credit cards, the APR must be calculated on assumptions set out in paragraph 1 of Schedule 1; these differ from the assumptions applied by the 1989 Regulations as regards the amount of credit taken as having been advanced, the interest rate applied and the manner in which credit is repaid.

Regulation 9 extends the restrictions on the use of particular expressions in credit advertisements to include expressions indicating that the provision of credit is not subject to status requirements or that it attracts a gratuitous benefit.

A full regulatory impact assessment of the effect that this instrument will have on the costs to business is available from the Consumer and Competition Policy Directorate of the Department of Trade and Industry, 1 Victoria Street, London SW1H 0ET.

Notes:

[1] 1974 c. 39; section 189(1) is cited for the definition of "regulations".
[2] 2000 c. 8.
[3] 1979 c. 34.
[4] S.R. (N.I.) 1985 No.12.
[5] 1974 c. 46.
[6] S.I. 1980/51, amended by S.I. 1985/1192, 1989/596, 1999/3177.
[7] 1970 c. 35.
[8] S.I. 2001/544; relevant amending instruments are S.I. 2001/1777 and 2001/3544.
[9] S.I. 1989/1125, amended by S.I. 1999/2725 and 1999/3177.
[10] S.I. 1999/2725.
[11] S.I. 2000/1797.

The Consumer Credit (Agreements) (Amendment) Regulations 2004

STATUTORY INSTRUMENTS

2004 No. 1482
CONSUMER CREDIT
The Consumer Credit (Agreements) (Amendment) Regulations 2004

Made	*5th June 2004*
Laid before Parliament	*9th June 2004*
Coming into force	*31st May 2005*

The Secretary of State, in exercise of the powers conferred upon her by sections 60, 61(1)(a), 105(9), 114(1), 182(2) and 189(1) of the Consumer Credit Act 1974[1], hereby makes the following Regulations:

Citation and commencement

1. These Regulations may be cited as the Consumer Credit (Agreements) (Amendment) Regulations 2004 and shall come into force on 31st May 2005.

Amendment of the Consumer Credit (Agreements) Regulations 1983

2. The Consumer Credit (Agreements) Regulations 1983[2] shall be amended as follows.

3.—(1) Regulation 1(2) (interpretation) shall be amended as follows.

(2) Insert at the appropriate place—

" "contract of shortfall insurance" means anything in writing which contains or purports to contain some promise or assurance (however worded or presented) that if a sum payable under a contract of insurance against loss of or damage to goods is less than the amount necessary to defray—

(a) any amount of credit provided to finance the purchase of those goods; and

(b) any other amount included in the total charge for that credit,

to the extent that these remain unpaid at the date of the loss or damage, a sum up to but not exceeding that shortfall will be paid." "

(3) In the definition of "total charge for credit" after the words "Total Charge for Credit Regulations" insert "and Schedule 7 to these Regulations".

4. For regulation 2 (form and content of regulated consumer credit agreements) substitute—

"Form and content of regulated consumer credit agreements

2.—(1) Subject to paragraphs (2) and (9) below, documents embodying regulated consumer credit agreements (other than modifying agreements) shall contain the information set out in Column 2 of Schedule 1 to these Regulations in so far as it relates to the type of agreement referred to in Column 1.

(2) Where any information about financial and related particulars set out in paragraphs 9 to 11 of Schedule 1 to these Regulations cannot be exactly ascertained by the creditor, estimated information based on the assumptions referred to in paragraph 10 of that Schedule, where applicable, and otherwise such assumptions as the creditor may reasonably make in all the circumstances of the case and a statement of the assumptions made shall be included in documents embodying regulated consumer credit agreements.

(3) Subject to paragraph (9) below, documents embodying regulated consumer credit agreements, other than agreements of the description specified in the Schedule to the Consumer Credit (Notices of Cancellation Rights) (Exemptions) Regulations 1983[3] in relation to which there are no charges forming part of the total charge for credit (in this regulation referred to as "exempted agreements"), shall contain statements of the protection and remedies available to debtors under the Act, in the Form numbered in Column 1 of Part 1 of Schedule 2 to these Regulations and set out in Column 3, in so far as they relate to the type of agreement referred to in Column 2.

(4) Subject to paragraphs (5) and (9) below, the information, statements of the protection and remedies, signature and separate boxes which this regulation requires documents embodying regulated consumer credit agreements to contain, shall be set out in the order given by paragraphs (a) to (f) below under, where applicable, the headings specified below—

(a) the nature of the agreement as set out in paragraph 1 of Schedule 1 to these Regulations;

(b) the parties to the agreement as set out in paragraph 2 of Schedule 1 to these Regulations;

(c) under the heading "Key Financial Information", the financial and related particulars set out in paragraphs 6 to 8B and 11 to 17 of Schedule 1 to these Regulations;

(d) under the heading "Other Financial Information", the financial and related particulars set out in paragraphs 3 to 5, 9, 10, 14A and 18 to 19A of Schedule 1 to these regulations;

(e) under the heading "Key Information"—

(i) the information set out in paragraphs 20 to 24 of Schedule 1 to these Regulations; and

(ii) the statements of protection and remedies set out in Schedule 2 to these Regulations; and

(f) the signature box and, where applicable, the separate box required by paragraph (7)(b) below;

and such information, statements of protection and remedies, signature and separate boxes shall be shown together as a whole and shall not be preceded by any information apart from trade names, logos or the reference number of the agreement or interspersed with any other information or wording apart from subtotals of total amounts and cross references to the terms of the agreement.

(5) In the case of documents embodying restricted-use debtor-creditor-supplier agreements for fixed-sum credit to finance a transaction comprising the acquisition of goods, services, land or other things specified in the agreement or identified and agreed on at the time the agreement is made and relating to more than one description of goods, services, land or other things, the cash prices, and the total cash price, referred to in paragraph 4 of Schedule 1 to these Regulations may be shown in a schedule to such document together with each description of the goods, services, land or other things, provided that the total cash price and a reference to the schedule to such document are shown together with the information required by paragraph (4)(d) above.

(6) The APR referred to in paragraphs 15 to 17 of Schedule 1 to these Regulations shall in documents embodying regulated consumer credit agreements, other than exempted agreements—

(a) be denoted as "APR" or "annual percentage rate" or "annual percentage rate of the total charge for credit; and

(b) where it is subject to change, be accompanied by the word "variable".

(7) Documents embodying regulated consumer credit agreements other than exempted agreements shall, subject to paragraph (9) below, contain a signature box in the Form numbered in Column 1 of Part 1 of Schedule 5 to these Regulations and set out in Column 3 in so far as it relates to the type of agreement referred to in Column 2 and shall—

(a) if—

(i) the documents embody a principal agreement and subsidiary agreement to which paragraph (9) below applies; or

(ii) at the time of entering into the agreement the debtor is also purchasing an optional contract of insurance which will be financed by credit advanced under that agreement,

contain a form of consent in the Form set out in Part III of Schedule 5 immediately below the signature box required by this paragraph; and

(b) if the agreement is one to which section 58(1) of the Act applies, is a cancellable agreement or is an agreement under which a person takes any article in pawn and under which the pawn-receipt is not separate from the document embodying the agreement, contain a separate box immediately above, below or adjacent to the signature box in which shall be included the appropriate statements specified in Forms 1 and 4 to 6 of Part 1, and in Part II, of Schedule 2.

(8) Paragraph (9) applies to documents embodying a debtor-creditor-supplier agreement falling within section 12(a) of the Act or a debtor-creditor agreement (in this paragraph and paragraph (9) in either case referred to as "the principal agreement") and also embodying, or containing the option of, a debtor-creditor-supplier agreement falling within section 12(b) of the Act (in this paragraph and paragraph (9) referred to as "the subsidiary agreement") where the subsidiary agreement is to finance a premium under one or more of—

(a) a contract of insurance to provide a sum payable in the event of the death of a debtor or a debtor suffering one or more of the following:—

      (i) accident;

      (ii) sickness; and

      (iii) unemployment,

at any time before the credit under the principal agreement and the subsidiary agreement has been repaid, where the sum payable does not exceed the amount sufficient to defray the sums payable to the creditor in respect of that credit and of the total charge for credit and where the policy monies payable under the contract of insurance are to be used for a repayment under the principal agreement and the subsidiary agreement;

    (b) a contract of shortfall insurance; and

    (c) a contract of insurance in so far as it relates to the guarantee of goods.

(9) Documents to which this paragraph applies may contain instead of the headings specified in paragraph 1 of Schedules 1 or 8 to these Regulations, statements of protection and remedies available to debtors under the Act and signature boxes that would otherwise apply—

    (a) a heading and signature box in so far as they relate to the principal agreement;

    (b) a statement in Form 14 of Part I of Schedule 2 to these Regulations; and

    (c) other statements (other than in Form 16 of Part I of Schedule 2) of the protection and remedies available to debtors under the Act in so far as they relate to the principal agreement.

(10) Documents embodying regulated consumer credit agreements shall embody any security provided in relation to the regulated agreement by the debtor."

5.—(1) Regulation 3 (form and content of regulated consumer hire agreements) shall be amended as follows.

(2) For paragraph 4 substitute—

"(4) Subject to paragraph (5) below the information, statements of the protection and remedies, signature and separate boxes which this regulation requires documents embodying regulated consumer hire agreements to contain, shall be set out in the order given by paragraphs (a) to (e) below under, where applicable, the headings specified below:—

    (a) the nature of the agreement as set out in paragraph 1 of Schedule 3 to these Regulations;

    (b) the parties to the agreement as set out in paragraph 2 of Schedule 3 to these Regulations;

    (c) under the heading "Key Financial Information", the financial and related particulars set out in paragraphs 3 to 8 of Schedule 3 to these Regulations;

    (d) under the heading "Key Information"—

      (i) the information set out in paragraphs 9 to 11 of Schedule 3 to these Regulations; and

      (ii) the statements of protection and remedies set out in Schedule 4 to these Regulations; and

    (e) the signature box and, where applicable, the separate box required by paragraph (6) below,

and such information, statements of protection and remedies, signature and separate boxes shall be shown together as a whole and shall not be preceded by any information apart from trade names, logos or the reference number of the agreement or interspersed with any other information or wording apart from subtotals of total amounts and cross references to the terms of the agreement.".

(3) In paragraph 5 for the words "paragraphs 4 to 8 of Schedule 3" substitute "paragraph (4)(c) above".

6. In regulation 4(b) (pawn-receipts) for the words "numbered 16" substitute "numbered 18".

7. In regulation 5(4) (statutory forms) omit the words "the APR,".

8. For regulation 6(2) (signing of the agreement) substitute—

"(2) The lettering of the terms of the agreement included in the document referred to in section 61(1)(a) of the Act, containing all the prescribed terms of the regulated agreement, and of the information contained in that document for the purpose of conforming to these Regulations shall—

(a) apart from any signature, be easily legible and, where applicable, be of a colour which is readily distinguishable from the background medium upon which the information is displayed; and

(b) apart from that inserted in handwriting, be of equal prominence, except that headings, trade names and names of parties to the agreement may be afforded more prominence whether by capital letters, underlining, larger or bold print or otherwise.".

9.—(1) Regulation 7 (modifying agreements which are, or are treated as, regulated agreements) shall be amended as follows.

(2) For paragraph (3) substitute—

"(3) Where any information about financial and related particulars set out in paragraphs 8 to 10 of Part 1 of Schedule 8 to these Regulations cannot be exactly ascertained by the creditor, estimated information based on the assumptions referred to in paragraph 9 of that Schedule, where applicable, and otherwise such assumptions as the creditor may reasonably make in all the circumstances of the case and a statement of the assumptions made shall be included in documents embodying modifying agreements varying or supplementing earlier credit agreements.".

(3) For paragraph (4) substitute—

"(4) Subject to paragraph (5) below and regulation 2(9), the information, statements of the protection and remedies, signature and separate boxes which under these Regulations must be contained in documents embodying modifying agreements varying or supplementing earlier credit agreements in relation to the credit being provided under the modifying agreement, shall be set out in the order given by paragraphs (a) to (f) below under, where applicable, the headings specified below—

(a) the nature of the agreement as set out in paragraph 1 of Part 1 of Schedule 8 to these Regulations;

(b) parties to the agreement as set out in paragraph 2 of Part 1 of Schedule 8 to these Regulations;

(c) under the heading "Key Financial Information", the financial and related particulars set out in paragraphs 5 to 7B and 10 to 17 of Part 1 of Schedule 8 to these Regulations;

(d) under the heading "Other Financial Information", the financial and related particulars set out in paragraphs 3, 4, 8, 9, 13A and 18–19A of Part 1 of Schedule 8 to these Regulations;

        (e) under the heading "Key Information"—

            (i) the information set out in paragraphs 20 to 23 of Part 1 of Schedule 8 to these Regulations; and

            (ii) the statements of protection and remedies set out in Schedule 2 to these Regulations; and

        (f) the signature box and, where applicable, separate box required by regulation 2(7)(b),

and such information, statements of protection and remedies, signature and separate boxes shall be shown together as a whole and shall not be preceded by any information apart from trade names, logos or the reference number of the agreement or interspersed with any other information or wording apart from subtotals of total amounts and cross references to the terms of the agreement.".

(4) In paragraph (5) for the words "remaining financial and related particulars" to the end of the paragraph substitute "the information required by paragraph (4)(d) above.".

(5) For paragraph (6)(b) substitute—

    "(b) where it is subject to change, be accompanied by the word "variable".".

(6) For paragraph 11 substitute—

    "(11) The information, statements of the protection and remedies, signature and separate boxes which under these Regulations must be contained in documents embodying modifying agreements varying or supplementing earlier hire agreements in relation to the goods to be bailed or hired under the modifying agreement, shall be set out in the order given by paragraphs (a) to (e) below under, where applicable, the headings specified below—

        (a) the nature of the agreement as set out in paragraph 1 of Part II of Schedule 8 to these Regulations;

        (b) the parties to the agreement as set out in paragraph 2 of Part II of Schedule 8 to these Regulations;

        (c) under the heading "Key Financial Information", the financial and related particulars set out in paragraphs 3 to 8 of Part II of Schedule 8 to these Regulations;

        (d) under the heading "Key Information"—

            (i) the information set out in paragraphs 9 to 11 of Part II of Schedule 8 to these Regulations; and

            (ii) the information set out in Schedule 4 to these Regulations; and

        (e) the signature box and, where applicable, separate box required by regulation 3(6).

and such information, statements of protection and remedies, signature and separate boxes shall be shown together as a whole and shall not be preceded by any information apart from trade names, logos or the reference number of the agreement or interspersed with any other information or wording apart from subtotals of total amounts and cross references to the terms of the agreement.".

10.—(1) Schedule 1 (information to be contained in documents embodying regulated consumer credit agreements other than modifying agreements) shall be amended as follows.

(2) For paragraph 1 substitute—

1. All types. "(1) Subject to paragraph (2) below, a heading in one of the following forms of words—

    (a) "Hire-Purchase Agreement regulated by the Consumer Credit Act 1974";

    (b) "Conditional Sale Agreement regulated by the Consumer Credit Act 1974";

    (c) "Fixed-Sum Loan Agreement regulated by the Consumer Credit Act 1974"; or

    (d) "Credit Card Agreement regulated by the Consumer Credit Act 1974",

as the case may require.

(2) If none of the headings in 1(a) to (d) above are applicable a heading in the following form of words—"Credit Agreement regulated by the Consumer Credit Act 1974".

(3) Where the document and a pawn-receipt are combined, the words ", and Pawn Receipt," shall be inserted in the heading after the word "Agreement".

(4) Where the document embodies an agreement of which at least one part is a credit agreement not regulated by the Act, the word "partly" shall be inserted before "regulated" unless the regulated and unregulated parts of the agreement are clearly separate.

(5) Where the credit is being secured on land the words "secured on" followed by the address of the land shall be inserted at the end of the heading.
".

(3) After paragraph 8 insert—

Term of the agreement

8A. Agreements of fixed duration for running-account credit.	The duration of the agreement.
8B. Agreements for fixed-sum credit.	The duration or minimum duration of the agreement.".

(4) For paragraph 9 substitute—

9. "Agreements for fixed-sum credit except agreements—

    (a) which do not specify either the intervals between repayments or the amounts of repayments or both the intervals and the amounts;

    (b) under which the total amount payable by the debtor to discharge his indebtedness in respect of the amount of credit provided may vary according to any formula specified in the

(1) The total charge for credit, with a list of its constituent parts.

(2) The rate of interest on the credit to be provided under the agreement or, where more than one such rate applies, all the rates in all cases quoted on a per annum basis with details of when each rate applies.

(3) A statement explaining how and when interest charges are calculated and applied under the agreement.".

agreement having effect by reference to movements in the level of any index or to any other factor;

(c) which provide for a variation of, or permit the creditor to vary, (whether or not by reference to any index) the amount or rate of any item included in the total charge for credit after the relevant date; or

(d) under which the total amount payable by the debtor is not greater than the total cash price referred to in paragraph 4.

(5) For paragraph 10 substitute—

10. "Agreements for—

(a) running-account credit; and

(b) fixed-sum credit falling within the exceptions in paragraph 9(a) to (c).

(1) The total charge for credit with a list of its constituent parts and in the case of running-account credit, the total charge for credit shall be calculated on the same assumptions as are set out in paragraph 1 of Schedule 7 for the purpose of calculating the APR in place of the assumptions in Part 4 of the Total Charge for Credit Regulations that might otherwise apply.

(2) The rate of interest on the credit to be provided under the agreement or, where more than one such rate applies, all the rates in all cases quoted on a per annum basis with details of when each rate applies.

(3) A statement whether any interest rate to be shown under (2) above is fixed or variable.

(4) A statement explaining how and when interest charges are calculated and applied under the agreement.

".

(6) After paragraph 14 insert—

14A. "All types where different interest rates or different charges or both are or will be at any time during the term of the agreement payable in respect of—

(a) credit provided under the agreement for different purposes; or

(b) under each of the different parts of the agreement,

whether or not the agreement is a multiple agreement.

A statement of the order or proportions in which any amount paid by the debtor which is not sufficient to discharge the total debt then due under the agreement will be applied or appropriated by the creditor towards the discharge of the sums due—

(a) in respect of the amounts of credit provided for different purposes, or

(b) different parts of the agreement,

as the case may be.".

(7) For paragraph 22 substitute—

Charges

22. All types.   "(1) A list of any charges payable under the agreement to the creditor upon failure by the debtor or a relative of his to do or refrain from doing anything which he is required to do or refrain from doing, as the case may be.

(2) A statement indicating any term of the agreement which provides for charges—

(a) not required to be shown under (1) above; or

(b) not included in the total charge for credit.
"

(8) After paragraph 22 insert—

Cancellation rights

23. Agreements which are not cancellable agreements.   A statement that the agreement is not cancellable.

Amount payable on early settlement

24. Agreements for fixed-sum credit for a term of more than one month.   "(1) Examples based on the amount of credit to be provided under the agreement or the nominal amount of either £1000 or £100, showing the amount that would be payable if the debtor exercised the right under section 94 of the Act to discharge his indebtedness on the date when—

(a) a quarter of the term of the agreement elapses;

(b) half of the term elapses; and

(c) three quarters of the term elapses.

or on the first repayment date after each of those dates.

(2) A statement explaining that, in calculating the amounts shown, no account has been taken of any variation which might occur under the agreement, and that the amounts are accordingly only illustrative.".

11. For Schedule 2 (forms of statement and remedies available under the Consumer Credit Act 1974 to debtors under regulated consumer credit agreements) substitute—

"SCHEDULE 2

Regulation 2(3)

PART I

Forms of Statement of Protection and Remedies Available under the Consumer Credit Act 1974 to Debtors under Regulated Consumer Credit Agreements

FORM NO (1)	TYPE OF AGREEMENT (2)	FORM OF STATEMENT (3)
1	Agreement to which section 58(1) of the Act applies.	YOUR RIGHTS Under the Consumer Credit Act 1974, you should have been given a copy of this agreement at least seven days ago so you could consider whether you wanted to go ahead. If the creditor did not give you a copy of this agreement he can only enforce it with a court order.
2	All types.	MISSING PAYMENTS Missing payments could have severe consequences and make obtaining credit more difficult.
3	All agreements which are secured on land.	YOUR HOME MAY BE REPOSSESSED Your home may be repossessed if you do not keep up repayments on a mortgage or other debt secured on it. Your home may be repossessed if you do not keep up repayments on a mortgage or other debt secured on it.
4	Cancellable agreements to which section 68(b) of the Act applies.	YOUR RIGHT TO CANCEL You can cancel this agreement within FOURTEEN days (starting the day after you signed it) by giving WRITTEN notice to*. If you intend to cancel, you should not use any goods you have under the agreement and you should keep them safe. You can wait for them to be collected and you do not need to hand them over until you receive a written request for them. [However you may return the goods yourself.]**[You are warned that it would be dangerous and could be in contravention of Health and Safety legislation for you to attempt to disconnect and return the goods yourself.]**

Notes:
*Creditor or agent to insert the name and address of person to whom the notice may be given or an indication of the person to whom a notice may be given with clear reference to the place in the document embodying the agreement where his name and address appear.
** Creditor or agent to include the words in the first set of square brackets unless the words in the second set of square brackets are applicable, i.e. in a case where the subject matter of the agreement is a liquefied petroleum gas vessel of greater than 150 litres water capacity.

| 5 | Cancellable agreements not included in paragraphs 3 or 6. | YOUR RIGHT TO CANCEL |

Once you have signed this agreement, you will have a short time in which you can cancel [it]*[that part of this agreement which is regulated by the Consumer Credit Act 1974]*. The creditor will send you exact details of how and when you can do this.

Notes:
*Creditor to omit passage in square brackets which does not apply to the agreement.

| 6 | Modifying agreements treated under section 82(5) of the Act as cancellable agreements. | YOUR RIGHT TO CANCEL |

This agreement modifies an earlier agreement. Once you have signed this agreement your right to cancel [that part of]* the earlier agreement [which was regulated by the Consumer Credit Act 1974]* will be widened to cover the [regulated]* agreement as modified. The cancellation period itself will be unchanged. Details of how to cancel are given in your copy of this agreement.

Notes:
*Creditor to omit passages in square brackets except in the case of an agreement of which at least one part is a credit agreement not regulated by the Act.

| 7 | Hire purchase and conditional sale agreements relating to goods, not included in paragraph 8. | TERMINATION: YOUR RIGHTS |

You have a right to end this agreement. To do so, you should write to the person you make your payments to. They will then be entitled to the return of the goods and to [the cost of installing the goods plus half the rest of the total amount payable under this agreement, that is] [half the total amount payable under this agreement, that is] *£x **. If you have already paid at least this amount plus any overdue instalments and have taken

(1) FORM NO	(2) TYPE OF AGREEMENT	(3) FORM OF STATEMENT
		reasonable care of the goods, you will not have to pay any more. Notes: *Creditor to insert the appropriate passage in square brackets where the amount calculated in accordance with the provisions of section 100 of the Act applies. If the agreement provides for a sum below the minimum prescribed in the Act, both passages in square brackets are to be omitted. **Creditor to insert the amount calculated in accordance with the provisions of section 100 of the Act or such lesser sum as the agreement may provide.
8	Agreements modifying hire-purchase and conditional sale agreements relating to goods.	TERMINATION: YOUR RIGHTS You have a right to end this agreement. To do so, write to the person you make your payments to. They will then be entitled to the return of the goods and to [the cost of installing the goods plus half the total amount yet to be paid under the earlier agreement as modified by this agreement, that is] [half the total amount payable under the earlier agreement as modified by this agreement, that is]* £x**. If you have already paid at least this amount, plus any overdue instalments and have taken reasonable care of the goods, you will not have to pay any more. Notes: *Creditor to insert the appropriate passage in square brackets where the amount calculated in accordance with the provisions of section 100 of the Act applies. If the modified agreement provides for a sum below the minimum prescribed in the Act, both passages in square brackets are to be omitted. **Creditor to insert the amount calculated in accordance with the provisions of section 100 of the Act or such lesser sum as the agreement may provide.
9	Conditional sale agreements relating to land, not included in paragraph 10.	TERMINATION: YOUR RIGHTS Until the title to the land has passed to you, you have a right to end this agreement. To do so write to the person you make your

payments to. They will then be entitled to the return of the land and to [half the total amount payable under this agreement, that is]* **£x.**** If, at the time you end this agreement, you have already paid at least this amount plus any overdue instalments and you have taken reasonable care of the land, you will not have to pay any more.

Notes:

*Creditor to insert the passage in square brackets where the amount calculated in accordance with the provisions of section 100 of the Act applies. If the agreement provides for a sum below the minimum prescribed in the Act, the passage in square brackets is to be omitted.

**Creditor to insert the amount calculated in accordance with the provisions of section 100 of the Act or such lesser sum as the agreement may provide.

10 Agreements modifying conditional sale agreements relating to land.

TERMINATION: YOUR RIGHTS

Until the title to the land has passed to you, you have a right to end this agreement. To do so write to the person you make your payments to. They will then be entitled to the return of the land and to [half the total amount payable under your earlier agreement as modified by this agreement, that is]* £x**. If you have already paid at least this amount plus any overdue instalments and taken reasonable care of the land, you will not have to pay any more.

Notes:

*Creditor to insert the passage in square brackets where the amount calculated in accordance with the provisions of section 100 of the Act applies. If the modified agreement provides for a sum below the minimum prescribed in the Act, the passage in square brackets is to be omitted.

**Creditor to insert the amount calculated in accordance with the provisions of section 100 of the Act or such lesser sum as the modified agreement may provide.

11 Hire-purchase and conditional sale agreements relating to goods, not included in paragraph 12.

REPOSSESSION: YOUR RIGHTS

If you do not keep your side of this agreement but you have paid at least [the cost of installing the goods plus one third of the rest of the total amount payable under this agreement, that is] [one third of the total amount payable under this agreement, that is]*£x** the creditor may not take back the

FORM NO	TYPE OF AGREEMENT	FORM OF STATEMENT
(1)	(2)	(3)

goods against your wishes unless he gets a court order. (In Scotland he may need to get a court order at any time.) If he does take the goods without your consent or a court order, you have the right to get back any money that you have paid under this agreement.

Notes:
*Creditor to insert the appropriate passage in square brackets.
**Creditor to insert the amount calculated in accordance with the provisions of section 90 of the Act.

| 12 | Agreements modifying hire-purchase and conditional sale agreements relating to goods. | REPOSSESSION: YOUR RIGHTS |

If you do not keep to your side of this agreement [but you have paid at least £x*]** the creditor may not take back the goods against your wishes unless he gets a court order. (In Scotland he may need to get a court order at any time.) If he does take the goods without your consent or a court order, you have the right to get back all the money you have paid under this agreement.

Notes:
*Creditor to insert the amount calculated in accordance with the provisions of section 90 of the Act.
**Creditor to omit both passages in square brackets in the case of a modifying agreement where the goods are protected at the time the modifying agreement is made.

| 13 | Agreements, to which section 114 of the Act applies, under which a person takes any article in pawn. | IMPORTANT – READ THIS CAREFULLY TO FIND OUT ABOUT YOUR RIGHTS |

The Consumer Credit Act 1974 lays down certain requirements for your protection which should have been complied with when this agreement was made. If they were not, the creditor cannot enforce this agreement without getting a court order.

The Act also gives you a number of rights. In particular you should read the NOTICE TO DEBTOR [in this agreement]* [in your pawn receipt].**

If you would like to know more about your rights under the Act, contact either your local Trading Standards Department or your nearest Citizens' Advice Bureau.

Notes:

*Phrase in square brackets to be included by creditor in agreements where any document embodying the agreement is not separate from the pawn-receipt. Creditor to omit "in your pawn receipt".

** Phrase in square brackets to be included by creditor in agreements where a separate pawn-receipt is given to the debtor. Creditor to omit "in this agreement".

14   Debtor-creditor-supplier agreements falling within section 12(b) and (c) of the Act, and multiple agreements not falling within paragraph 15 of which at least one part is a debtor-creditor-supplier agreement falling within section 12(b) or (c) of the Act.

IMPORTANT – READ THIS CAREFULLY TO FIND OUT ABOUT YOUR RIGHTS

The Consumer Credit Act 1974 lays down certain requirements for your protection which should have been complied with when this agreement was made. If they were not, the creditor cannot enforce this agreement without getting a court order.

The Act also gives you a number of rights:
1) You can settle this agreement at any time by giving notice in writing and paying off the amount you owe under the agreement [which may be reduced by a rebate]* [Examples indicating the amount you have to pay appear in the agreement.]**
2) If you received unsatisfactory goods or services paid for under this agreement[, apart from any bought with a cash loan,]*** you may have a right to sue the supplier, the creditor or both.
3) If the contract is not fulfilled, perhaps because the supplier has gone out of business, you may still be able to sue the creditor.

If you would like to know more about your rights under the Act, contact either your local Trading Standards Department or your nearest Citizens' Advice Bureau.

Notes:

*Creditor to insert phrase in square brackets in any agreement where rebate would be payable on early settlement under the agreement or the Consumer Credit (Early Settlement) Regulations 2004.

** Creditor to insert phrase in second pair of square brackets in any agreement for fixed-sum credit for a term of more than one month.

***Creditor to insert phrase in square brackets in any multiple agreement, of

FORM NO (1)	TYPE OF AGREEMENT (2)	FORM OF STATEMENT (3)
		which, at least one part is a debtor-creditor-supplier agreement falling within section 12(b) or (c) of the Act and at least one part is a debtor-creditor agreement falling within section 13(c) of the Act.
15	Multiple agreements of which at least one part is a credit agreement not regulated by the Act.	IMPORTANT – READ THIS CAREFULLY TO FIND OUT ABOUT YOUR RIGHTS That part of this agreement which deals with [. . . .;.]* is a regulated agreement under the Consumer Credit Act 1974. As a result certain requirements for your protection should have been complied with when it was made. If they were not, the creditor cannot enforce this agreement without a court order. The Act also gives you a number of rights. You can settle the regulated agreement at any time by giving notice in writing and paying off the amount you owe under this agreement [which may be reduced by a rebate]** [Examples indicating the amount you have to pay appear in the agreement.]*** If you would like to know more about your rights under the Act, contact either your local Trading Standards Department or your nearest Citizens' Advice Bureau. Notes: *Creditor to insert description of regulated agreement example, "the cash advance facility". **Creditor to insert phrase in square brackets in any agreement where rebate would be payable on early settlement under the agreement or the Consumer Credit (Early Settlement) Regulations 2004. *** Creditor to insert phrase in second pair of square brackets in any agreement for fixed-sum credit for a term of more than one month.
16	All types not included in paragraphs 13,14 and 15.	IMPORTANT – READ THIS CAREFULLY TO FIND OUT ABOUT YOUR RIGHTS The Consumer Credit Act 1974 lays down certain requirements for your protection which should have been complied with when this agreement was made. If they were not, the creditor cannot enforce this agreement without getting a court order.

The Act also gives you a number of rights. You can settle this agreement at any time by giving notice in writing and paying off the amount you owe under the agreement [which may be reduced by a rebate]*. [Examples indicating the amount you might have to pay appear in the agreement.]**

If you would like to know more about your rights under the Act, contact either your local Trading Standards Department or your nearest Citizens' Advice Bureau.

Notes:

*Creditor to insert phrase in square brackets in any agreement where rebate would be payable on early settlement under the agreement or the Consumer Credit (Early Settlement) Regulations 2004.

**Creditor to insert phrase in second pair of square brackets in any agreement for fixed-sum credit for a term of more than one month.

17   Credit-token agreements which make debtors liable for loss to the creditor resulting from the misuse of credit-tokens by other persons.

THEFT, LOSS OR MISUSE OF CREDIT-TOKEN*

If your credit-token* is lost, stolen or misused by someone without your permission, you may have to pay up to £x** of any loss to the creditor. If it is misused with your permission you will probably be liable for ALL losses. You will not be liable to the creditor for losses which take place after you have told the creditor about the theft, etc [as long as you confirm this in writing within seven days]. ***[However, the credit-token* can also be used under an agreement to which this protection does not apply. As a result, there may be circumstances under which you may have to pay for all the losses to the creditor.]****

Notes:

*Creditor may insert specific designation or trade name of credit-token for example, credit card instead of "credit-token".

**Creditor to insert the extent of the liability laid down in section 84(1) of the Act or the credit limit if lower or such lower figure as he may decide.

***Creditor to omit phrase in square brackets if written confirmation is not required under the credit-token agreement.

****Creditor to omit passage in square brackets if inapplicable.

PART II

Regulation 4

Notice to be contained in Documents Embodying a Combined Consumer Credit Agreement and Pawn-Receipt

FORM NO (1)	TYPE OF AGREEMENT (2)	FORM OF STATEMENT (3)
18	Agreements, to which section 114 of the Act applies, under which a person takes any article in pawn and where any document embodying the agreement is not separate from the pawn-receipt.	NOTICE TO THE DEBTOR IMPORTANT – YOU SHOULD READ THIS CAREFULLY

Right to Redeem Articles
    If you hand in this agreement (which is also your pawn-receipt) and pay the amount you owe, you may redeem the article(s) in pawn at any time within 6 months of the date of this agreement or any longer time agreed with the creditor ("the redemption period").
IF YOU DO NOT REDEEM THE ARTICLE(S) ON OR BEFORE * YOU MAY LOSE YOUR RIGHT TO REDEEM IT (THEM).
    Loss of Receipt
    If you lose your receipt you may provide either a statutory declaration or, if the credit (or credit limit) is not more than £x** and the creditor agrees, a signed statement instead. The creditor may provide the form to be used and may charge for doing so.
    Unredeemed Articles
    An article not redeemed within the redemption period becomes the creditor's property if the credit (or credit limit) is not more than £x**** and the redemption period is 6 months. In any other case it may be sold by the creditor, but it continues to be redeemable until it is sold. Interest is payable until the actual date of redemption. Where the credit (or credit limit) is more than £x**** the creditor must give you 14 days notice of his intention to sell. When an article has been sold you will receive information about the sale. If the proceeds (less expenses) are more that the amount that would have been payable to redeem the article on the date of the sale you will be entitled to receive the extra amount. If the proceeds are less than the amount you will owe the creditor the shortfall.

> Your goods will not be insured by the creditor while they are in pawn. *****
>
> Notes:
> *Creditor to insert the date at the end of the redemption period.
> **Creditor to insert the amount specified in section 118(1)(b) of the Act.
> ***Creditor to insert the amount specified in section 120(1)(a) of the Act.
> ****Creditor to insert the amount specified in the Consumer Credit (Realisation of Pawn) Regulations 1983
> ***** Creditor to omit this paragraph if inapplicable."

12.—(1) Schedule 3 (information to be contained in documents embodying regulated consumer hire agreements other than modifying agreements) shall be amended as follows.

(2) For paragraph 1 substitute—

Nature of agreement

1. All types.	"(1) A heading in the following form of words – "Hire Agreement regulated by the Consumer Credit Act 1974".
	(2) Where the agreement to hire is being secured on land the words "secured on" and the address of the land shall be inserted at the end of the heading.".

(3) For paragraph 10 substitute—

Charges

10. All types.	"(1) A list of any charges payable under the agreement to the owner upon failure by the hirer or a relative of his to do or refrain from doing anything which he is required to do or refrain from doing, as the case may be.
	(2) A statement indicating any term of the agreement which provides for charges not required to be shown under (1) above."

(4) After paragraph 10 insert—

Cancellation rights

11. Agreements that are not cancellable agreements.	A statement that the agreement is not cancellable."."

13. For Schedule 4 (forms of statement of protection and remedies available under the Consumer Credit Act 1974 to hirers under regulated consumer hire agreements) substitute—

"SCHEDULE 4

Regulation 3(3)

Forms of Statement of Protection and Remedies Available under the Consumer Credit Act 1974 to Hirers Under Regulated Consumer Hire Agreements

FORM (1)	TYPE OF AGREEMENT (2)	FORM OF STATEMENT (3)
1	Agreement to which section 58(1) of the Act applies.	YOUR RIGHTS Under the Consumer Credit Act 1974, you should have been given a copy of this agreement at least seven days ago so you could consider whether to go ahead. If the owner did not give you a copy this agreement can only be enforced with a court order.
2	All types.	MISSING PAYMENTS Missing payments could have severe consequences and may make obtaining credit more difficult.
3	All agreements which are secured on property.	YOUR HOME MAY BE REPOSSESSED Your home may be repossessed if you do not keep up repayments on a hire agreement secured by a mortgage or other security on your home.
4	All cancellable agreements not included in paragraph 5.	YOUR RIGHT TO CANCEL Once you have signed this agreement you have a short time in which you can cancel it. Details of how to cancel it will be sent to you by the owner.
5	Modifying agreements treated under section 82(5) of the Act as cancellable agreements.	YOUR RIGHT TO CANCEL This agreement modifies an earlier agreement. Once you have signed it, your right to cancel the earlier agreement will cover this modified agreement. The cancellation period itself is unchanged. Details of how you can cancel can be found in the copy of this agreement.
6	Agreements to which the hirer is entitled to terminate by notice under section 101(1) of the Act and which provides for the bailment or hiring of goods for at least 18 months after the making of the agreement.	IMPORTANT – READ THIS CAREFULLY TO FIND OUT ABOUT YOUR RIGHTS The Consumer Credit Act 1974 lays down certain requirements for your protection which should have been complied with when this agreement was made. If they were not,

the owner cannot enforce this agreement without getting a court order.

The Act also gives you a number of rights. You can end this agreement by writing to the person you make your payments to and giving at least* notice. In order to do this the agreement must have been allowed to run for at least 18 months [from the date of the original agreement]** though this may include the period of notice. You will have to make all payments and pay any amounts you owe until the date the agreement comes to an end.

If you would like to know more about your rights under the Act, contact either your local Trading Standards Department or your nearest Citizens' Advice Bureau.

Notes:
*Owner to insert minimum period of notice as determined by section 101.
**Owner to omit passage in square brackets except where this notice appears in a modifying agreement.

7	Agreements not included in paragraph 6.	IMPORTANT – READ THIS CAREFULLY TO FIND OUT ABOUT YOUR RIGHTS

The Consumer Credit Act 1974 covers this agreement and lays down certain requirements for your protection which should have been complied with when this agreement was made. If they were not, the owner cannot enforce this agreement against you without getting a court order.

If you would like to know more about your rights under the Act, contact either your local Trading Standards Department or your nearest Citizens' Advice Bureau.".

14. After Part II of Schedule 5 (forms of signature box) insert—

"PART III

Regulation 2(7)

Agreements Under Which a Separate Form of Consent is Required

1 (1)	TYPE OF AGREEMENT (2)	FORM OF CONSENT (3)
	Agreements under which a separate form of consent is required.	I wish to purchase [............................] * / ** I understand that I am purchasing the product(s) ticked above on credit provided by you and that the terms relating to the

credit for the products can be found [ ]*** in this agreement.
Your signature(s):

Notes:
* Creditor to list the products being offered to the debtor for purchase.
** Debtor to indicate which products they wish to purchase by putting a tick next to the name(s) of the product(s).
*** Creditor to insert the cross-references to the terms of the agreement containing the terms relating to the credit for the products being purchased.".

15. In Schedule 7 (provisions relating to the disclosure of the APR) for paragraph 1 substitute—

"Assumptions about running-account credit

1. In the case of an agreement for running-account credit, the following assumptions shall have effect for the purpose of calculating the APR in place of the assumptions in Part 4 of the Total Charge for Credit Regulations that might otherwise apply—

(1) in any case where there will be a credit limit but that limit is not known at the date of making the agreement the amount of the credit to be provided shall be taken to be £1,500 or, in a case where the credit limit will be less than £1,500, an amount equal to that limit;

(2) it shall be assumed that the credit is provided for a period of one year beginning with the relevant date;

(3) it shall be assumed that the credit is provided in full on the relevant date;

(4) where the rate of interest will change at a time provided in the agreement within a period of three years beginning with the date of the making of the agreement, the rate shall be taken to be the highest rate at any time obtaining under the agreement in that period;

(5) where the agreement provides credit to finance the purchase of goods, services, land or other things and also provides one or more of—

   (a) cash loans;

   (b) credit to refinance existing indebtedness of the debtor's, whether to the creditor or another person; and

   (c) credit for any other purpose,

   and either or both different rates of interest and different charges are payable in relation to the credit provided for all or some of these purposes, it shall be assumed that the rate of interest and charges payable in relation to the whole of the credit are those applicable to the provision of credit for the purchase of goods, services, land or other things;

(6) it shall be assumed that the credit is repaid—

   (a) in twelve equal instalments, and

   (b) at monthly intervals, beginning one month after the relevant date.

Permissible tolerances in disclosure of the APR

1A. For the purposes of these Regulations, it shall be sufficient compliance with the requirement to show the APR if there is included in the document—

(1) a rate which exceed the APR by not more than one; or

(2) a rate which falls short of the APR by not more than 0.1; or

(3) in a case to which either of paragraphs 2 or 3 below applies, a rate determined in accordance with the paragraph or such of them as apply to that case.".

16.—(1) Schedule 8, part 1 (information to be contained in documents embodying regulated modifying agreements varying or supplementing earlier credit agreements) is amended as follows.

(2) For paragraph 1 substitute—

1　All types　　"(1) A heading in one of the following forms of words—

    (a) "Agreement modifying a Hire-Purchase Agreement and regulated by the Consumer Credit Act 1974";

    (b) "Agreement Modifying a Conditional Sale Agreement and regulated by the Consumer Credit Act 1974";

    (c) "Agreement modifying a Fixed-Sum Loan Agreement and regulated by the Consumer Credit Act 1974";

    (d) "Agreement modifying a Credit Card Agreement and regulated by the Consumer Credit Act 1974"; or

    (e) "Agreement modifying a Credit Agreement and regulated by the Consumer Credit Act 1974"

as the case may require.

(2) Where the document and a pawn-receipt are combined, the words ", and Pawn-Receipt," shall be inserted in the heading after the word "Agreement" in the second place that it occurs.

(3) Where the document embodies an agreement of which at least one part is a credit agreement not regulated by the Act, the word "partly" shall be inserted before "regulated" unless the regulated and unregulated parts of the agreement are clearly separate.

(4) Where the loan is being secured on land the words "secured on" and the address of the land shall be inserted at the end of the heading.
".

(3) In paragraph 5—

(a) For subparagraph (b) of column 1 substitute—

"(b) modifying agreements where the earlier agreement is an agreement excluded from the scope of the Consumer Credit (Early settlement) Regulations 2004 by regulation 2(2) of these Regulations.".

(b) for subparagraph (3) of column 2 substitute—

"(3) The total amount of the charges on the credit not yet accrued referred to in sub-paragraph (2) above shall be the amount of a notional rebate calculated in accordance with the Consumer Credit (Early Settlement) Regulations 2004 as if early settlement had taken place and as if the settlement date were the relevant date disregarding any deferment of the settlement date under regulation 6 of those Regulations.".

(4) For paragraph 6 substitute—

6 Modifying agreements both under which the amount of credit to be provided under an earlier agreement for fixed-sum credit is varied or supplemented and where the earlier agreement is an agreement excluded from the scope of the Consumer Credit (Early Settlement) Regulations 2004 by regulation 2(2) of those Regulations.

"The total amount of the credit to be provided under the modified agreement calculated as follows, namely the total of—

(a) the balance of the credit outstanding under the earlier agreement at the relevant date;

(b) any charges thereon (included in the total charge for credit in relation to the credit to be provided under the earlier agreement) due and unpaid at the relevant date;

(c) the amount of any additional credit to be provided under the modifying agreement, with a list of its constituent parts.".

(5) After paragraph 7 insert—

Term of the agreement

7A Modifying agreements under which the duration of an earlier agreement for running account credit of fixed duration is varied.

The duration of the modified agreement.

7B Modifying agreements under which the duration of an earlier agreement for fixed-sum credit is varied.

The duration or minimum duration of the modified agreement.".

(6) For paragraph (8) substitute—

8 "Modifying agreements under which any charge included in the total charge for credit in relation to an earlier agreement for fixed-sum credit is varied or supplemented, except modifying agreements—

(a) which do not specify either the intervals between repayments under the modified agreement or the amounts of repayments or both the intervals and the amounts;

(b) under which the total amount payable by the debtor under the modified agreement to discharge his indebtedness in respect of the amount of credit

(1) The total charge for credit in relation to the credit to be provided under the modified agreement, with a list of its constituent parts.

(2) The varied or supplemented rates of any interest on the credit to be provided under the modified agreement quoted on a per annum basis, or a statement that the rates of interest under the earlier agreement are unchanged.

(3) A statement explaining how and when interest charges are calculated and applied under the modified agreement.".

provided may vary according to any formula specified in such agreement having effect by reference to movements in the level of any index or to any other factor;

(c) which provide for a variation of, or permit the creditor to vary, (whether or not by reference to any index) the amount or rate of any item included in the total charge for credit in relation to the modified agreement after the relevant date; or

(d) under which the total amount payable by the debtor under the modified agreement is not greater than the total cash price under that agreement.

(7) For paragraph 9 substitute—

8 "Modifying agreements under which any charge included in the total charge for credit in relation to an earlier agreement for fixed-sum credit is varied or supplemented, except modifying agreements—

(a) which do not specify either the intervals between repayments under the modified agreement or the amounts of repayments or both the intervals and the amounts;

(b) under which the total amount payable by the debtor under the modified agreement to discharge his indebtedness in respect of the amount of credit provided may vary according to any formula specified in such agreement having effect by reference to movements in the level of

(1) The total charge for credit in relation to the credit to be provided under the modified agreement, with a list of its constituent parts.

(2) The varied or supplemented rates of any interest on the credit to be provided under the modified agreement quoted on a per annum basis, or a statement that the rates of interest under the earlier agreement are unchanged.

(3) A statement explaining how and when interest charges are calculated and applied under the modified agreement.".

any index or to any other factor;

(c) which provide for a variation of, or permit the creditor to vary, (whether or not by reference to any index) the amount or rate of any item included in the total charge for credit in relation to the modified agreement after the relevant date; or

(d) under which the total amount payable by the debtor under the modified agreement is not greater than the total cash price under that agreement.

(8) After paragraph 13 insert—

13A. "Modifying agreements under which—

(a) an earlier agreement is varied or supplemented so that different interest rates or different charges forming part of the total charge for credit or both are payable in respect of—

(i) credit provided under the agreement for different purposes; or

(ii) different parts of the agreement,

whether or not the agreement is a multiple agreement; or

(b) an earlier agreement is varied by varying the order or proportions in which any amount paid by the debtor which is not sufficient to discharge the total debt then due under the agreement will be applied or appropriated by the creditor towards the discharge of the sums due—

(i) in respect of the amounts of credit provided for different purposes, or

A statement of the order or proportions in which any amount paid by the debtor which is not sufficient to discharge the total debt then due under the agreement will be applied or appropriated by the creditor towards the discharge of the sums due—

(a) in respect of the amounts of credit provided for different purposes, or

(b) under each of the different parts of the agreement,

as the case may be."

> (ii) under each of the different parts of the agreement,

as the case may require.

(9) For paragraph 22 substitute—

Charges

22 Modifying agreements under which any provision for charges under an earlier agreement are varied, including a variation to or from there being no such charges.

"(1) A list of any charges payable under the modified agreement to the creditor upon failure by the debtor or a relative of his to do or refrain from doing anything which he is required to do or refrain from doing, as the case may be, or a statement indicating that no such charges are payable as the case may be.

(2) A statement indicating any term of the modified agreement which provides for charges

(a) not required to be shown under (1) above; or

(b) included in the total charge for credit."

(10) After paragraph 22 insert—

Charges

22 Modifying agreements under which any provision for charges under an earlier agreement are varied, including a variation to or from there being no such charges.

"(1) A list of any charges payable under the modified agreement to the creditor upon failure by the debtor or a relative of his to do or refrain from doing anything which he is required to do or refrain from doing, as the case may be, or a statement indicating that no such charges are payable as the case may be.

(2) A statement indicating any term of the modified agreement which provides for charges

(a) not required to be shown under (1) above; or(b) included in the total charge for credit."

17.—(1) Schedule 8, Part 2 (information to be contained in documents embodying regulated modifying agreements varying or supplementing earlier hire agreements) is amended as follows.

(2) For paragraph 1 substitute—

1   All types   "(1) A heading in the following form of words – "Agreement modifying a Hire Agreement and regulated by the Consumer Credit Act 1974".

     (2) Where the credit is being secured on land the words "secured on" followed by the address of the land shall be inserted at the end of the heading.".

(3) In column 2 of paragraph 10 for the words "An indication of any" substitute "A list of all".

(4) After paragraph 10 insert—

Cancellation rights

11 Modifying agreements that are not treated as cancellable agreements under section 82(5) of the Act.	A statement that the modifying agreement is not cancellable.".

Transitional provision

18.—(1) This regulation applies to documents embodying regulated agreements, and modifying agreements treated under section 82(3) of the Consumer Credit Act 1974[4] as regulated agreements, which have

    (a) been presented, sent or made available to debtors or hirers for signature but have not become executed agreements before the coming into force of these Regulations ("transitional agreements"); and

    (b) become executed agreements not later than 3 months after the coming into force of these Regulations.

(2) The Consumer Credit (Agreements) Regulations 1983 as they have effect immediately before the coming into force of these Regulations shall continue to apply in relation to transitional agreements.

(3) Accordingly the amendments and repeals made by these Regulations shall not apply in respect of transitional agreements and for the purposes of section 61(1) of the Consumer Credit Act 1974 such agreements shall be properly executed if they conform to the Consumer Credit (Agreements) Regulations 1983[5] as they have effect immediately before the coming into force of these Regulations and otherwise comply with that subsection.

Gerry Sutcliffe,

Parliamentary Under Secretary of State for Employment Relations, Competition and Consumer Affairs, Department of Trade and Industry

5th June 2004

EXPLANATORY NOTE

(This note is not part of the Regulations)

These Regulations amend the Consumer Credit (Agreements) Regulations 1983 ("the 1983 Regulations") with effect from the 31st May 2005 subject to a transitional provision in regulation 18. The principal amendments made by the Regulations are as follows—

(1) they substitute a new paragraph (4) in each of regulations 2, 3 and 7 of the 1983 Regulations. The new paragraphs (4) set out the order in which the prescribed content of documents embodying a regulated consumer credit agreement, a regulated consumer hire agreement and a modifying agreement treated as a regulated agreement under section 82(3) of the Act is to be given and the place of the signature and separate boxes required under the Regulations;

(2) they amend regulation 2(7) by providing for an additional form of consent to be signed by a debtor in specified circumstances where the debtor is purchasing certain insurance products on credit;

(3) they substitute regulation 2(8) and (9) for regulation 2(7A) of the 1983 Regulations which provides that documents embodying certain consumer credit agreements (the principal agreements) and embodying, or containing the option of, certain agreements (the subsidiary agreements) relating to contracts of insurance against accident, sickness, unemployment or death or any contract relating to a guarantee of goods may contain with one minor exception only the information, statements and signature boxes relating to the principal agreement. The new provision extends the meaning of "subsidiary agreements" to cover contracts of shortfall insurance as now defined in regulation 1(2);

(4) they strengthen the legibility and prominence requirements in regulation 6(2) of the 1983 Regulations;

(5) they amend Schedule 7 to the 1983 Regulations by providing for the use of particular assumptions in calculating the APR and the Total Charge for Credit to be stated in running-account credit agreements;

(6) they amend Schedules 1, 3 and 8 by requiring certain additional information to be included in an agreement; and

(7) they amend Schedules 2 and 4 by simplifying the language used.

A full regulatory impact assessment of the effect that this instrument will have on costs to business is available from the Consumer and Competition Policy Directorate of the Department of Trade and Industry, 1 Victoria Street, London SW1H 0ET.

Notes:

[1] 1974 c. 39.; section 189(1) is cited for the definitions of "prescribed", and "regulations".

[2] S.I. 1983/1553, amended by S.I. 1984/1600, 1985/666, 1988/2047, 1999/3177 and 2001/3649.

[3] 1983/1558.

[4] 1974 c. 39.

[5] S.I. 1983/1553, amended by S.I. 1984/1600, 1985/666, 1988/2047, 1999/3177 and 2001/3649.

APPENDIX 4

The Consumer Credit (Disclosure of Information) Regulations 2004

STATUTORY INSTRUMENTS

2004 No. 1481
CONSUMER CREDIT
The Consumer Credit (Disclosure of Information) Regulations 2004

Made	*5th June 2004*
Laid before Parliament	*9th June 2004*
Coming into force	*31st May 2005*

The Secretary of State, in exercise of the powers conferred upon her by sections 55(1), 182(2) and 189(1) of the Consumer Credit Act 1974[1], makes the following Regulations:—

Citation, commencement and interpretation

1.—(1) These Regulations may be cited as the Consumer Credit (Disclosure of Information) Regulations 2004 and shall come into force on 31st May 2005.

(2) In these Regulations—

"the Agreements Regulations" mean the Consumer Credit (Agreements) Regulations 1983[2];

"distance contract" means any regulated agreement made under an organised distance sales or service-provision scheme run by the creditor or owner or by an intermediary of the creditor or owner who, in any such case, for the purpose of that agreement makes exclusive use of one or more means of distance communication up to and including the time at which the agreement is made and for this purpose any means of communication is a means of distance communication if, without the simultaneous physical presence of the creditor or owner or any intermediary of the creditor or owner and of the debtor or hirer, it may be used for the distance marketing of a regulated agreement between the parties to that agreement;

"durable medium" means any instrument which enables the debtor or hirer to store information addressed personally to him in a way accessible for future reference for a period of time adequate for the purposes of the information and which allows the unchanged reproduction of the information stored.

Agreements to which these Regulations apply

2. These Regulations apply in respect of all regulated agreements except—
   (a) agreements to which section 58 of the Consumer Credit Act 1974 (opportunity for withdrawal from prospective land mortgage) applies; and
   (b) distance contracts.

Information to be disclosed to a debtor or hirer before a regulated agreement is made

3.—(1) Before a regulated agreement ("the relevant agreement") is made, the creditor or owner must disclose to the debtor or hirer in the manner set out in regulation 4 the information and statements of protection and remedies that are required to be given—
   (a) in the case of a regulated consumer credit agreement, under regulation 2 of the Agreements Regulations;
   (b) in the case of a regulated consumer hire agreement, under regulation 3 of the Agreements Regulations;
   (c) in the case of a modifying agreement which is, or is treated as, a regulated consumer credit agreement, under regulations 2(3) and 7(2) of the Agreements Regulations;
   (d) in the case of a modifying agreement which is or is treated as a regulated consumer hirer agreement, under regulations 3(3) and 7(9) of the Agreements Regulations.

(2) The information and statements of protection required to be disclosed under paragraph (1) shall be the information and statements that will be included in the document embodying the relevant agreement save that, where any of the information is not known at the time of disclosure, the creditor or owner shall disclose estimated information based on such assumptions as he may reasonably make in all the circumstances of the case.

Manner of disclosure

4. The information and statements of protection and remedies required to be disclosed under regulation 3 must be—
   (a) easily legible and, where applicable, of a colour which is readily distinguishable from the background medium upon which they are displayed;
   (b) not interspersed with any other information or wording apart from subtotals of total amounts and cross references to the terms of the agreement;
   (c) of equal prominence except that headings may be afforded more prominence whether by capital letters, underlining, larger or bold print or otherwise; and
   (d) contained in a document which:
       (i) is separate from the document embodying the relevant agreement (within the meaning of regulation 3) and any other document referred to in the document embodying that agreement;
       (ii) is headed with the words "Pre-contract Information";
       (iii) does not contain any other information or wording apart from the heading referred to in sub-paragraph (ii);
       (iv) is on paper or on another durable medium which is available and accessible to the debtor or hirer; and

   (v) is of a nature that enables the debtor or hirer to remove it from the place where it is disclosed to him.

Gerry Sutcliffe,

Parliamentary Under Secretary of State for Employment Relations, Competition and Consumer affairs, Department of Trade and Industry

5th June 2004

EXPLANATORY NOTE

(This note is not part of the Regulations)

These Regulations specify information which must be disclosed to a debtor or hirer before a regulated agreement within the meaning of the Consumer Credit Act 1974 is made and prescribe the manner in which the information must be disclosed. The Regulations do not apply in respect of agreements to which section 58 of the Act applies nor in respect of distance contracts (as defined in regulation 1(2)).

A full regulatory impact assessment of the effect that this instrument will have on the costs to business is available from the Consumer and Competition Policy Directorate of the Department of Trade and Industry, 1 Victoria Street, London SW1H 0ET.

Notes:

[1] 1974 c. 39; section 189(1) is cited for the definitions of "prescribed" "and "regulated."
[2] SI 1983/1553, amended by SI 1984/1600, 1985/666, 1988/2047, 1999/3177, 2001/3649 and 2004/1482.

APPENDIX 5

The Consumer Credit (Early Settlement) Regulations 2004

STATUTORY INSTRUMENTS

2004 No. 1483
CONSUMER CREDIT
The Consumer Credit (Early Settlement) Regulations 2004

Made	*5th June 2004*
Laid before Parliament	*9th June 2004*
Coming into force	*31st May 2005*

The Secretary of State, in exercise of the powers conferred upon her by sections 95, 97(1), 182(2) and 189(1) of the Consumer Credit Act 1974[1], hereby makes the following Regulations:

Citation, commencement and interpretation

1.—(1) These Regulations may be cited as the Consumer Credit (Early Settlement) Regulations 2004, and shall come into force on 31st May 2005.

(2) In these Regulations—

"the Act" means the Consumer Credit Act 1974;

"the APR" means the annual percentage rate of charge for credit determined in accordance with the Total Charge for Credit Regulations, subject to regulation 3(2) below;

"early settlement" shall be construed in accordance with regulation 2(1) below;

"rebate" means a rebate of charges for credit included in the total charge for credit;

"the relevant date" shall be determined in accordance with the Total Charge for Credit Regulations;

"the settlement date", means the settlement date provided for in regulation 5 and, where applicable, regulation 6;

"the total charge for credit" shall be determined in accordance with the Total Charge for Credit Regulations, subject to regulations 3(2) and 7 below; and

"the Total Charge for Credit Regulations" means the Consumer Credit (Total Charge for Credit) Regulations 1980[2].

(3) The length of any period for the purposes of calculations under these Regulations shall be determined in accordance with regulation 11 of the Total Charge for Credit Regulations, other than paragraph (5)(a) of that regulation.

(4) In these Regulations, references to repayment of credit are references to repayment of credit with any amount included in the total charge for credit payable at the same time.

Entitlement to rebate

2.—(1) Subject to the following provisions of this regulation, the creditor shall allow to the debtor under a regulated consumer credit agreement a rebate at least equal to that calculated in accordance with the following provisions of these Regulations whenever early settlement takes place, that is to say whenever, under section 94 of the Act, on refinancing, on breach of the agreement or for any other reason, the indebtedness of the debtor is discharged or becomes payable before the time fixed by the agreement, or any sum becomes payable by him before the time so fixed.

(2) Paragraph (1) does not apply in the case of agreements of the following descriptions—

    (a) agreements under which no payments of items included in the total charge for credit are required to be made in respect of the period of time commencing on the settlement date;

    (b) agreements for running-account credit;

    (c) land mortgages under which no instalment repayments secured by the mortgage on the debtor's home, and no payment of interest on the credit (other than interest charged when all or part of the credit is repaid voluntarily by the debtor), are due or capable of becoming due while the debtor continues to occupy the mortgaged land as his main residence.

(3) Paragraph (1) does not apply where a hire-purchase or conditional sale agreement is terminated by the debtor under section 99 of the Act.

(4) Where a sum less than the total remaining indebtedness of the debtor is required to be paid before the time fixed by the agreement, no consequential payment of any subsequent instalment required to be paid under the agreement, or under a modifying agreement not relating to the provision of additional credit or an increase in the total charge for credit, shall entitle the debtor to a rebate.

Items included in the calculation of rebate

3.—(1) Subject to paragraph (2), the rebate shall be calculated by reference to all sums paid or payable by the debtor or a relative of his under or in connection with the agreement (whether to the creditor or any other person) and included in the total charge for credit.

(2) There may be excluded from the calculation of the rebate—

    (a) taxes, duties, fees and charges payable under or by virtue of any statute or payable to the Secretary of State or any other Minister or government department (including for this purpose a Northern Ireland department or a government department in any country outside the United Kingdom) or to a local authority or similar body outside the United Kingdom;

    (b) sums paid or payable under linked transactions, except sums paid before the settlement date in respect of cash, goods or services to be supplied under the transaction wholly or partly after that date;

    (c) sums payable under linked transactions excluded under regulations made under section 96(3) of the Act from the operation of section 96(1);

(d) any fee or commission paid by the debtor or a relative of his under a credit brokerage contract relating to the agreement, other than a fee or commission financed by the agreement.

Calculation of the amount of rebate

4.—(1) The amount of the rebate is the difference between the total amount of the repayments of credit that would fall due for payment after the settlement date if early settlement did not take place and the amount given by the following formula—

$$\sum_{i=1}^{m} A_i(1 + r)^{a_i} \text{ minus } \sum_{j=1}^{n} B_j(1 + r)^{b_j}$$

where:

A_i = the amount of the *ith* advance of credit,

B_j = the amount of the *jth* repayment of credit,

r = the periodic rate equivalent of the APR/100,

m = the number of advances of credit made before the settlement date,

n = the number of repayments of credit made before the settlement date,

a_i = the time between the *ith* advance of credit and the settlement date, expressed in periods,

b_j = the time between the *jth* repayment of credit and the settlement date, expressed in periods, and

Σ represents the sum of all the terms indicated.

(2) In calculating the rebate, where the creditor so elects, any repayment of credit made at a time or a rate other than that provided for in the agreement shall be taken to have been made at the time or rate provided for.

(3) The examples set out in the Schedule to these Regulations have effect for the purpose of illustrating the calculation provided for in paragraph (1); in the case of conflict between any example and any other provision of these Regulations, that other provision shall prevail.

Settlement date

5. The settlement date for calculation of the rebate shall be taken to be—

(a) where the debtor has given notice under section 94 of the Act with a view to discharging his indebtedness under the agreement, the date falling 28 days after the date on which the notice was received by the creditor, or any later date specified as the date of early settlement in the notice, if the debtor pays the amount in question (less any rebate allowable under these Regulations) not later than that date;

(b) the date specified as the date for payment of any sum by the debtor involving early settlement in any notice served under section 76(1) of the Act, any default notice or any notice served under section 98(1), if the debtor pays the amount in question (less any rebate allowable under these Regulations) not later than that date;

(c) in any other case, the date on which the debtor pays any sum involving early settlement.

Deferment of settlement date

6. Where the agreement provides for the credit to be repaid over, or at the end of, a period which is more than a year after the relevant date, the settlement date for calculation of the rebate may be deferred by—

(a) one month, or

(b) where the length of a month's deferment would be more or less than 30 days and the creditor so elects, 30 days.

Variation of rates and amounts

7. Where, under a power contained in the agreement, the rate or amount of any item included in the total charge for credit, the amount of any instalment of repayment of credit or the time fixed by the agreement for the debtor's indebtedness to be discharged is or can be varied, the rate or amount, as the case may be, of any item to be included in the total charge for credit or the amount of any instalment of repayment of credit or the time fixed by the agreement for the debtor's indebtedness to be discharged for the purpose of calculation of the rebate shall be taken to be, in respect of any period of time commencing on or after the settlement date, the rate or amount or time subsisting at that date.

Revocation of Regulations

8. Subject to regulation 10, the Consumer Credit (Rebate on Early Settlement) Regulations 1983[3] are revoked.

Amendment of Regulations

9.—(1) Subject to regulation 10, the Consumer Credit (Settlement Information) Regulations 1983[4] are amended as follows.

(2) In regulation 3 (which determines the settlement date to be taken for the purposes of the Regulations)—

(a) paragraph (1) (which applies in the case of an agreement for credit to be repaid in instalments) is omitted, and

(b) in paragraph (2) (which applies in all other cases), the words "Where paragraph (1) does not apply" are omitted.

(3) In regulation 4 (which prescribes the number of working days within which a creditor is required to respond to a request for a statement indicating the amount required to discharge a debt), for "12" there is substituted "7".

(4) In paragraph 7(a) of the Schedule (which provides for the statement to indicate, where any rebate is due, that the rebate has been calculated having regard to Regulations), for "the Consumer Credit (Rebate on Early Settlement) Regulations 1983" there is substituted "the Consumer Credit (Early Settlement) Regulations 2004".

Savings

10.—(1) The Regulations referred to in regulation 8 continue to apply, in place of regulations 1–7 of these Regulations, and the amendments in regulation 9 do not apply, in the case of a regulated consumer credit agreement entered into before the date on which these Regulations come into force—

(a) until 31st May 2007, if the agreement is for a term of 10 years or less;

(b) until 31st May 2010, if the agreement is for a term of more than 10 years.

(2) For the purposes of paragraph (1), the term of an agreement is the term originally provided for, or, in the case where the term was varied before the date on which these Regulations are made, the term provided for on that date.

Gerry Sutcliffe,

Parliamentary Under Secretary of State for Employment Relations, Competition and Consumer Affairs, Department of Trade and Industry

5th June 2004

SCHEDULE

Regulation 4(3)

EXAMPLES ILLUSTRATING USE OF FORMULA FOR CALCULATING REBATE

Example 1—medium term, medium value loan

A loan of £5,000 is repayable by 48 monthly instalments of £134.57, starting one month after the relevant date. The monthly repayments include interest and all other charges included in the total charge for credit. Thus the total amount repayable = £134.57 × 48 = £6,459.36. The total charge for credit = £6,459.36 − £5,000 = £1,459.36.

The creditor receives notice from the debtor requesting early settlement immediately after payment of the 12th instalment (i.e. after one year).

Assuming that no charges are excluded from the calculation of the rebate under regulation 3(2), the APR on the loan required for the calculation of the rebate is 14% per annum.

The creditor opts to calculate the rebate using periods of one month, giving a period rate equivalent of the APR $= (1.14^{(1/12)} - 1) \times 100 = 1.0979\%$ per month. Hence, for the purposes of the formula in regulation 4(1)—

$A_1 = 5,000$
$B_1 = 134.57 = B_2 = \text{.......} = B_{48}$
$r = 1.0979/100 = 0.010979$
$m = 1$
$n = 12$
$a_1 = 12$ (working in periods of 1 month)
$b_1 = 11$
$b_2 = 10$
$b_3 = 9$
$\vdots$
$b_{11} = 1$
$b_{12} = 0$

Then the loan outstanding immediately after payment of the 12th instalment as calculated by the formula in regulation 4(1) is—

$$5,000 \times (1.010979)^{12} - (134.57 \times 1.010979^{11} +$$
$$134.57 \times 1.010979^{10} + \dots + 134.57 \times 1.010979^1 + 134.57 \times 1.010979^0)$$
$$= 5,700.01 - (151.74 + 150.10 + 148.47 + 146.85 + 145.26 +$$
$$143.68 + 142.12 + 140.58 + 139.05 + 137.54 + 136.05 + 134.57)$$
$$= 5,700.01 - 1,716.01 = £3,984.00.$$

231

If regulation 5(a) applies (making the settlement date 28 days after the debtor's notice is received) no further payments will be due; thus the amount outstanding at the settlement date is—

$$£3,984.00 \times 1.010979^{(28/30)} = £4,024.81.$$

(this assumes that there are 30 days between the date for the 12th instalment and the 13th instalment; for months of 31 days, the amount outstanding would be

$$£3,984.00 \times 1.010979^{(28/31)} = £4,023.49.)$$

If the creditor elects to defer the settlement date by a further month under regulation 6, this makes the date for calculating the rebate the 28th day after the payment date for the 13th instalment.

For the calculation using the formula in regulation 4(1)—

$n = 13$
$a_1 = 13$ (working in periods of 1 month)
$b_1 = 12$
$b_2 = 11$
$b_3 = 10$
$b_{12} = 1$
$b_{13} = 0$

Then the loan outstanding to be repaid immediately after payment of the 13th instalment as calculated by the formula in regulation 4(1) is—

$$5,000 \times (1.010979)^{13} - (134.57 \times 1.010979^{12} + 134.57 \times 1.0109791^{1} + \ldots + 134.57 \times 1.0109791 + 134.57 \times 1.010979^{0})$$

$$= 5,762.59 - (153.41 + 151.74 + 150.10 + 148.47 + 146.85 + 145.26 + 143.68 + 142.12 + 140.58 = 139.05 + 137.54 + 136.05 + 134.57)$$

$$= 5,762.59 - 1,869.42 = £3,893.17.$$

The formula gives an amount outstanding after payment of the 13th instalment of £3,893.17. The amount outstanding at the settlement date is $£3,893.17 \times 1.010979^{(28/30)} = £3,933.05$ (assuming that the period between the 13th and 14th instalment dates is 30 days).

The debtor will also have to pay the instalment due between the date of request for early settlement and the settlement date assumed for calculating the rebate (i.e. the 13th repayment of £134.57).

Hence the total amount to be paid at the settlement date (which is 58 days after the date of request for early settlement) is £4,067.62.

For this example, the rebate would be £776.90; this is calculated by deducting the early settlement figure of £3,933.05 from the total payments outstanding after the date assumed for calculating the rebate, which is £4,709.95 (= 35 × £134.57).

N.B. If the period between the 13th and 14th instalments were 31 days, the amount outstanding would be $£3,893.17 \times 1.010979^{(28/31)} = £3,931.76$ and the total amount still to be repaid would be £4,066.33. Other adjustments may be appropriate where the lender opted to choose the period of deferment as 30 days. In this case the settlement date for calculating the rebate would be 58 days after the date on which notice was received).

Example 2—longer term, high value loan

A loan of £10,000 is repayable by 180 monthly instalments of £139.51 starting one month after the relevant date. The monthly repayments include interest and all other charges included in the total charge for credit.

Thus total amount repayable = £139.51 × 180 = £25,111.80. The total charge for credit = £25,111.80—£10,000 = £15,111.80.

The creditor receives notice from the borrower requesting early settlement immediately after payment of the 72nd instalment (i.e. after six years).

Assuming that no charges are excluded from the calculation of the rebate under regulation 3(2), the APR on the loan required for the calculation of the rebate is 16% per annum.

The creditor opts to calculate the rebate using periods of one month, giving a period rate equivalent of the APR = $(1.16^{(1/12)}-1) \times 100 = 1.2445\%$ per month. The creditor also opts to defer the settlement date for 30 days under regulation 6, so that the settlement date for the purposes of calculating the rebate is the 28th day after the payment date of the 73rd instalment. Hence, for the purposes of the formula in regulation 4(1)—

$A_1 = 10,000$

$B_1 = 139.51 = B_2 = \ldots = B_{180}$

$r = 1.2445/100 = 0.012445$

$m = 1$

$n = 73$

$a_1 = 73$ (working in periods of 1 month)

$b_1 = 72$

$b_2 = 71$

$b_3 = 70$

$\vdots$

$b_{71} = 1$

$b_{72} = 0$

Then the loan outstanding to be repaid immediately after payment of the 73rd instalment as calculated by the formula in regulation 4(1) is—

$$10,000 \times (1.012445)^{73} - (139.51 \times 1.012445^{72} + 139.51 \times 1.012445^{71} + \ldots + 139.51 \times 1.012445^{1} + 139.51 \times 1.012445_{0})$$

$$= 24,363.72 - (339.90 + 335.72 + \ldots + 141.25 + 139.51)$$

$$= 24,666.93 - 16,441.81 = £8,225.12$$

The amount outstanding at the settlement date is then—

$$£8,225.12 \times 1.012445^{(28/30)} = £8,320.62$$

(assuming that the period between the 72nd and 73rd instalments is 30 days or the creditor has opted for an additional deferment period of 30 days). The debtor will also have to pay the instalment due between the date of request for early repayment and the settlement date assumed for calculating the rebate (i.e. the 73rd repayment of £139.51).

Hence the total amount to be paid at the settlement date (which is 28 days after the date of request for early repayment) is £8,460.13.

N.B. If the period between the 72nd and 73rd instalments were not 30 days, the amount outstanding would be slightly different.)

For this example, the rebate is £6,606.95; this is calculated by deducting the early settlement figure of £8,320.62 from the total payments outstanding after the date assumed for calculating the rebate which is £14,927.57 (= 107 × £139.51).

EXPLANATORY NOTE

(This note is not part of the Regulations)

These Regulations entitle the debtor under a regulated consumer credit agreement to a rebate where all or part of the amount payable to the creditor is paid before the date on which it is due. The Regulations replace the Consumer Credit (Rebate on Early Settlement) Regulations 1983 ("the 1983 Regulations"), subject to a saving in respect of agreements entered into before the commencement date.

Regulations 4–6 differ from equivalent provisions in the 1983 Regulations. Regulation 4 incorporates an actuarial formula to be used in calculating the amount of the rebate, in place of different formulae provided for in the 1983 Regulations in relation to different cases. The Schedule contains examples which illustrate the application of the new formula. Regulation 5 determines the settlement date to be used in calculating the rebate. It differs from the corresponding provision of the 1983 Regulations in that the relevant date under that provision was generally determined by reference to the date of the next instalment due under the agreement. Regulation 6 provides for the settlement date to be deferred by a month (or, at the option of the creditor, 30 days) in the case of agreements for a term of more than a year. The 1983 Regulations provided for a deferment of two months in the case of an agreement for a term of up to five years, and a deferment of one month in the case of an agreement for a term of more than five years.

These Regulations also amend the Consumer Credit (Settlement Information) Regulations 1983, which relate to the right of a debtor to a statement indicating the amount payable in order to settle a debt under a regulated consumer credit agreement. The settlement date assumed for the purpose of calculating this amount in a case where the credit is repayable in instalments becomes the date 28 days after the debtor's request for a statement is received (as in cases where repayment is not in instalments), rather than the date of the first instalment due after 28 days have elapsed. The period within which the creditor must respond to a request for a statement is reduced from 12 to 7 days. There is also a consequential amendment related to the coming into force of the new provisions for calculating the rebate due on early settlement.

A full regulatory impact assessment of the effect that this instrument will have on the costs to business is available from the Consumer and Competition Policy Directorate of the Department of Trade and Industry, 1 Victoria Street, London SW1H 0ET.

Notes:

[1] 1974 c. 39; section 189(1) is cited for the definitions of "prescribed" and "regulations".
[2] S.I. 1980/51, amended by S.I. 1985/1192, 1989/596, 1999/3177.
[3] S.I. 1983/1562, amended by S.I. 1989/596.
[4] S.I. 1983/1564.

APPENDIX 6

The Consumer Credit Act 1974 (Electronic Communications) Order 2004

STATUTORY INSTRUMENTS

2004 No. 3236
CONSUMER CREDIT
The Consumer Credit Act 1974 (Electronic Communications) Order 2004

Made	*6th December 2004*
Laid before Parliament	*9th December 2004*
Coming into force	*31st December 2004*

The Secretary of State considering that the authorisation of the use of electronic communications by the following Order for any purpose is such that the extent (if any) to which records of things done for that purpose will be available will be no less satisfactory in cases where use is made of electronic communications than in other cases, in exercise of the powers conferred upon her by sections 8 and 9 of the Electronic Communications Act 2000[1] hereby makes the following Order:

Citation, commencement and interpretation

1.—(1) This Order may be cited as the Consumer Credit Act 1974 (Electronic Communications) Order 2004 and shall come into force on 31st December 2004.

(2) In this Order, the "Act" means the Consumer Credit Act 1974[2].

Amendments to the Act

2.—(1) The Act shall be amended as follows:

(2) In section 61 (signing of the agreement), in paragraph (b) of subsection (2) (unexecuted agreement to be sent to debtor or hirer by post for signature), for "by post" substitute "by an appropriate method".

(3) In section 63(3) (duty to supply copy of executed agreement), for "by post" substitute "by an appropriate method".

(4) In section 64 (duty to give notice of cancellation rights), for "by post", in each place where it occurs, substitute "by an appropriate method".

(5) For section 69(7) substitute—

"(7) Whether or not it is actually received by him, a notice of cancellation sent to a person shall be deemed to be served on him—

(a) in the case of a notice sent by post, at the time of posting, and

(b) in the case of a notice transmitted in the form of an electronic communication in accordance with section 176A(1), at the time of the transmission.".

(6) In section 176 (service of documents), in subsection (2) (permitted methods of service), for "by post" substitute "by an appropriate method".

(7) After section 176 insert—

"176A Electronic transmission of documents

(1) A document is transmitted in accordance with this subsection if—

(a) the person to whom it is transmitted agrees that it may be delivered to him by being transmitted to a particular electronic address in a particular electronic form,

(b) it is transmitted to that address in that form, and

(c) the form in which the document is transmitted is such that any information in the document which is addressed to the person to whom the document is transmitted is capable of being stored for future reference for an appropriate period in a way which allows the information to be reproduced without change.

(2) A document transmitted in accordance with subsection (1) shall, unless the contrary is proved, be treated for the purposes of this Act, except section 69, as having been delivered on the working day immediately following the day on which it is transmitted.

(3) In this section, "electronic address" includes any number or address used for the purposes of receiving electronic communications.".

(8) In section 189 (definitions), in subsection (1), insert the following at the appropriate places—

" "appropriate method" means—

(a) post, or

(b) transmission in the form of an electronic communication in accordance with section 176A(1);" ".

"electronic communication" means an electronic communication within the meaning of the Electronic Communications Act 2000 (c.7)" ".

(9) In that subsection, in the definitions of the expressions "give" and "serve on" for "by post" substitute "by an appropriate method".

Amendments to the Consumer Credit (Termination of Licences) Regulations 1976

3.—(1) The Consumer Credit (Termination of Licences) Regulations 1976[3] shall be amended as follows:

(2) In regulation 7, for "by post", in each place where it occurs, substitute "by an appropriate method".

Amendments to the Consumer Credit (Agreements) Regulations 1983

4.—(1) The Consumer Credit (Agreements) Regulations 1983[4] shall be amended as follows:

(2) In regulation 6 (signing of agreement)—

(a) In subsection (2) for "colour of the paper" substitute "background medium upon which the information is displayed"; and

(b) After subsection 4 insert—

"(5) Where an agreement is intended to be concluded by the use of an electronic communication nothing in this Regulation shall prohibit the inclusion in the signature box of information about the process or means of providing, communicating or verifying the signature to be made by the debtor or hirer.".

(3) In Column 2 of paragraph 2 of Schedule 1 (information to be contained in documents embodying regulated consumer credit agreements other than modifying agreements), for "and a postal address" in each place where it occurs substitute ", postal address and, where appropriate, any other address".

(4) In Column 3 of Form 3 of Part 1 of Schedule 2 (forms of statement of protection and remedies available under the Consumer Credit Act 1974 to debtors under regulated consumer credit agreements)—

(a) for "by post" substitute "[by post]^2"; and

(b) at the end insert—

"2 Creditor to replace words in square brackets with a description of the form of electronic communication agreed with the debtor in accordance with section 176A of the Act where the agreement is intended to be concluded by the use of an electronic communication.".

(5) In Column 2 of paragraph 2 of Schedule 3 (information to be contained in documents embodying regulated consumer hire agreements other than modifying agreements), for "and a postal address" in each place where it occurs substitute ", postal address and, where appropriate, any other address".

(6) In Column 3 of Form 2 of Schedule 4 (forms of statement of protection and remedies available under the Consumer Credit Act 1974 to hirers under regulated consumer hire agreements)—

(a) for "by post" substitute "[by post]^1; and

(b) at the end insert—

"Note

1 Owner to replace words in square brackets with a description of the form of electronic communication agreed with the hirer in accordance with section 176A of the Act where the agreement is intended to be concluded by the use of an electronic communication.".

(7) In Column 2 of paragraph 2 of Part I of Schedule 8, for "and a postal address", in each place where it occurs, substitute ", postal address and, where appropriate, any other address".

(8) In Column 2 of paragraph 2 of Part II of Schedule 8, for "and a postal address", in each place where it occurs, substitute ", postal address and, where appropriate, any other address".

Consumer Credit (Guarantees and Indemnities) Regulations 1983

5.—(1) The Consumer Credit (Guarantees and Indemnities) regulations 1983[5] shall be amended as follows:

(2) In regulation 3(1)(a) delete the words "the first page of ".

(3) In regulation 4(1) for "colour of the paper" substitute "background medium upon which the information is displayed".

(4) After subsection 4 insert—

"(5) Where a security instrument is intended to be concluded by the use of an electronic communication nothing in this Regulation shall prohibit the inclusion in the signature box of information about the process or means of providing, communicating or verifying the signature to be made by or on behalf of the surety.".

(5) In Part II of the Schedule (information to be contained in security instruments), for "and a postal address", in each place where it occurs, substitute ", postal address and, where appropriate, any other address".

Amendments to the Consumer Credit (Cancellation Notices and Copies of Documents) Regulations 1983

6.—(1) The Consumer Credit (Cancellation Notices and Copies of Documents) Regulations 1983[6] shall be amended as follows:

(2) In regulation 2 (legibility of notices and copy documents and wording of prescribed Forms)—

(a) in paragraph (1) for "colour of the paper" substitute "background medium upon which the information is displayed"; and

(b) in paragraph (2) for "by post" substitute "by an appropriate method"; and

(c) in paragraph (6) for "by post" substitute "by an appropriate method".

(3) In regulation 4(a) (copies of unexecuted agreements given under section 58(1) of the Act) for "shown prominently on the first page of" substitute "shown prominently on".

(4) In regulation 5 (copies of cancellable unexecuted and executed agreements) —

(a) in paragraph (2) for "by post" substitute "by an appropriate method"; and

(b) after paragraph (2) insert—

"(2A) Nothing in this Regulation shall prohibit the inclusion in the cancellable unexecuted or executed agreement of information about the process or means of providing, communicating or verifying the cancellation by the use of an electronic communication.".

(5) In regulation 6 (notices of cancellation rights sent by post under section 64(1)(b) or (2) of the Act) for "by post" substitute "by an appropriate method".

(6) After regulation 6 insert—

"**6A.** Regulation 6(b) shall not apply to a notice which is transmitted in the form of an electronic communication in accordance with section 176A of the Act.

6B. Nothing in this Regulation shall prohibit the inclusion in a notice of information about the process or means of providing, communicating or verifying the cancellation by the use of an electronic communication.".

(7) In the Schedule—

(a) in the heading to Part III (forms of notice of cancellation rights to be included in copies of cancellable executed agreements sent by post to the debtor or hirer under section 63(2) or (4) of the Act) for "by post" substitute "by an appropriate method";

(b) in Part IV (cancellation form to be included in copy cancellable executed agreements sent by post to the debtor or hirer under section 63(2) or (4) of the Act)—

(i) in the heading for "by post" substitute "by an appropriate method"; and

(ii) in Column 2 of form 16 for "by post" substitute "by an appropriate method"; and

(c) In the heading to Part VI (forms of notice of cancellation rights to be sent by post to the debtor or hirer under section 64(1)(b) or (2) of the Act) for the words "by post" substitute "by an appropriate method".

Amendments to the Consumer Credit (Repayment of Credit on Cancellation) Regulations 1983

7.—(1) The Consumer Credit (Repayment of Credit on Cancellation) Regulations 1983[7] shall be amended as follows:

(2) In Schedule 1 (form of request for repayment of credit under a cancelled regulated consumer credit agreement repayable by instalments)—
   (a) in paragraph 2 for "postal address" substitute "postal address and, where appropriate, any other address"; and
   (b) in paragraph 3 for "postal address" substitute "postal address and, where appropriate, any other address".

(3) In Schedule 2 (form of request for repayment of credit following withdrawal of party from a prospective regulated consumer credit agreement payable by instalments)—
   (a) in paragraph 2 for "postal address" substitute "postal address and, where appropriate, any other address"; and
   (b) in paragraph 3 for "postal address" substitute "postal address and, where appropriate, any other address".

Amendments to the Consumer Credit (Settlement Information) Regulations 1983

8.—(1) The Consumer Credit (Settlement Information) Regulations[8] shall be amended as follows:

(2) In paragraph 2 of the Schedule (information to be contained in a statement given by a creditor of the amount of the payment required to discharge the debtor's indebtedness under a regulated consumer credit agreement together with particulars showing how the amount is arrived at), for "and a postal address", in each place where it occurs, substitute ", postal address and, where appropriate, any other address".

Amendments to the Consumer Credit (Conduct of Business) (Pawn Records) Regulations 1983

9.—(1) The Consumer Credit (Conduct of Business) (Pawn Records) Regulations 1983[9] shall be amended as follows:

(2) In paragraph 1(c) of the Schedule (information to be contained in entries in the books or other records to be kept by a person who takes any article in pawn under a regulated consumer credit agreement) after the words "postal address" insert "and, where appropriate, other address".

Amendments to the Consumer Credit (Pawn Receipts) Regulations 1983

10.—(1) The Consumer Credit (Pawn Receipts) Regulations 1983[10] shall be amended as follows:

(2) In regulation 2—
   (a) in subparagraph (a) for "colour of the paper" substitute "background medium upon which the information is displayed"; and
   (b) in subparagraph (c)—
      (i) delete the words "front of the" in each place where it occurs; and
      (ii) after the words "postal address" in each place where it occurs insert "and, where appropriate, other address".

Amendments to the Consumer Credit (Realisation of Pawn) Regulations 1983

11.—(1) The Consumer Credit (Realisation of Pawn) Regulations 1983[11] shall be amended as follows:

(2) In Schedule 1 (particulars to be indicated in addition to the asking price in a notice of the intention to sell an article taken in pawn under a regulated consumer credit agreement)—

  (a) In paragraph 1, for "and a postal address" substitute ", postal address and, where appropriate, other address".

  (b) In paragraph 2, for "and a postal address" substitute ", postal address and, where appropriate, other address".

(3) In Schedule 2 (Information to be given as to the sale of an article taken in pawn under a regulated agreement, its proceeds and expenses)—

  (a) In paragraph 1, for "and a postal address" substitute ", postal address and, where appropriate, other address".

  (b) In paragraph 2, for "and a postal address" substitute ", postal address and, where appropriate, other address".

Amendment to the Consumer Credit (Running Account Credit Information) Regulations 1983

12.—(1) The Consumer Credit (Running Account Credit Information) Regulations 1983[12] shall be amended as follows:

(2) In regulation 2(2) (form and contents of statements) for "colour of the paper" substitute "background medium upon which the information is displayed".

Jacqui Smith,

Minister of State for Industry and the Regions and Deputy Minister for Women and Equality Department of Trade and Industry

6th December 2004

EXPLANATORY NOTE

(This note is not part of the Order)

This Order inserts or modifies provisions of the Consumer Credit Act 1974 (c 39) and secondary legislation made under that Act for the purpose of enabling and facilitating the use of electronic communications for concluding regulated agreements and when sending notices and other documents.

Article 2(8) makes provision to facilitate the use by a person of electronic communications for the service of statutory notices and documents. Article 2(7) to (8) amends section 176 of the Act (service of documents) to clarify that a requirement under the Act to serve a document on a person may be discharged by sending that document to an electronic address and in electronic form agreed by that person. Article 2(9) to (10) insert new definitions of "appropriate method" and "electronic communication" in section 189 (definitions) of the Act for this purpose.

Article 2(2) to (6) make amendments to relevant parts of the Act that deal with the service, giving or sending of documents so as to include transmission in the form of an electronic communication.

Article 3 amends the Consumer Credit (Termination of Licences) Regulations 1976 to enable service of a notice in the form of an electronic communication.

Article 4 amends the Consumer Credit (Agreements) Regulations 1983 to enable agreements to be concluded electronically and to enable the creditor or owner to include in the signature box information about the process or means of providing, communicating or verifying the signature made by the debtor or hirer.

Article 5 amends the Consumer Credit (Guarantees and Indemnities) Regulations 1983 to enable security instruments to be in the form of an electronic communication and to enable the creditor or owner to include in the security instrument information about the process or means of providing, communicating or verifying the signature made or on behalf of the surety.

Article 6 amends the Consumer Credit (Cancellation Notices and Copies of Documents) Regulations 1983 to enable copies of agreements and cancellation notices to be in the form of an electronic communication. It also enables the creditor or owner to include in the cancellation notice information about the process or means of providing, communicating or verifying such cancellation in the form of an electronic communication.

Article 7 amends the Consumer Credit (Repayment of Credit on Cancellation) Regulations 1983 to enable requests for repayment of credit to include where appropriate an electronic address.

Article 8 amends the Consumer Credit (Settlement Information) Regulations 1983 to allow for an electronic address to be contained in a statement given to the debtor showing the amount required to discharge their indebtedness.

Article 9 amends the Consumer Credit (Conduct of Business) (Pawn Records) Regulations 1983 to allow for an electronic address to be contained in entries in books and records of a person who takes an item in pawn.

Article 10 amends the Consumer Credit (Pawn Receipts) Regulations 1983 to enable pawn receipts to be in the form of an electronic communication.

Article 11 amends the Consumer Credit (Realisation of Pawn) Regulations 1983 to allow for an electronic address to be given, where appropriate, in a notice of an intention to sell an item held in pawn.

Article 12 amends the Consumer Credit (Running Account Information) Regulations 1983 to enable statements to be sent in the form of an electronic communication.

A full regulatory impact assessment of the effect that this instrument will have on costs to business is available from the Consumer and Competition Policy Directorate of the Department of Trade and Industry, 1 Victoria Street, London SW1H 0ET.

Notes:

[1] 2000 c.7.
[2] 1974 c.39.
[3] S.I. 1976/1002, amended by S.I. 1981/614.
[4] S.I. 1983/1553, to which there are amendments not relevant to these Regulations.
[5] S.I. 1983/1556
[6] S.I. 1983/1557; relevant amending instruments are S.I. 1984/1108 and S.I. 1988/2047.
[7] S.I. 1983/1559
[8] S.I. 1983/1564

[9]   S.I. 1983/1565
[10] S.I. 1983/1566
[11] S.I. 1983/1568
[12] S.I. 1983/1570

The Consumer Credit (Enforcement, Default and Termination Notices) (Amendment) Regulations 2004

STATUTORY INSTRUMENTS

2004 No. 3237
CONSUMER CREDIT
The Consumer Credit (Enforcement, Default and Termination Notices) (Amendment) Regulations 2004

Made	*6th December 2004*
Laid before Parliament	*9th December 2004*
Coming into force	*31st December 2004*

The Secretary of State, in exercise of the powers conferred upon her by sections 76(3), 88(1), 98(3) and 189(1) of the Consumer Credit Act 1974[1] hereby makes the following Regulations:

Citation and commencement

1. These Regulations may be cited as the Consumer Credit (Enforcement, Default and Termination Notices) (Amendment) Regulations 2004 and shall come into force on the 31st December 2004.

Amendment of the Consumer Credit (Enforcement, Default and Termination) Regulations 1983

2. The Consumer Credit (Enforcement, Default and Termination) Regulations 1983[2] shall be amended as follows:

3. After regulation 2(4) insert—

"(4A) Any notice to be given under a provision of these Regulations shall be in writing and given to the debtor or hirer in paper form.".

Jacqui Smith,

Minister of State for Industry and the Regions and Deputy Minister for Women and Equality Department of Trade and Industry

9th December 2004

EXPLANATORY NOTE

(This note is not part of the Regulations)

These Regulations amend the Consumer Credit (Enforcement, Default and Termination Notices) Regulations 1983 to ensure that all notices sent under the Regulations are sent in paper format.

A full regulatory impact assessment of the effect that this instrument will have on costs to business is available from the Consumer and Competition Policy Directorate of the Department of Trade and Industry, 1 Victoria Street, London SW1H 0ET.

Notes:

[1] 1974 c.39; section 189(1) is cited for the definition of "prescribed" and "regulations".
[2] S.I. 1983/1561; to which there are amendments not relevant to these Regulations.

APPENDIX 8

The Financial Services (Distance Marketing) Regulations 2004

STATUTORY INSTRUMENTS

2004 No. 2095
FINANCIAL SERVICES AND MARKETS
The Financial Services (Distance Marketing) Regulations 2004

Made	*4th August 2004*
Laid before Parliament	*5th August 2004*
Coming into force	*31st October 2004*

The Treasury, being a government department designated[1] for the purposes of section 2(2) of the European Communities Act 1972[2] in relation to matters concerning the distance marketing of consumer financial services, in the exercise of the powers conferred on them by that section, hereby make the following Regulations:

Citation, commencement and extent

1. These Regulations may be cited as the Financial Services (Distance Marketing) Regulations 2004 and come into force on 31st October 2004.

Interpretation

2.—(1) In these Regulations—
"the 1974 Act" means the Consumer Credit Act 1974[3];
"the 2000 Act" means the Financial Services and Markets Act 2000[4];
"the Authority" means the Financial Services Authority;
"appointed representative" has the same meaning as in section 39(2) of the 2000 Act (exemption of appointed representatives);
"authorised person" has the same meaning as in section 31(2) of the 2000 Act (authorised persons);
"breach" means a contravention by a supplier of a prohibition in, or a failure by a supplier to comply with a requirement of, these Regulations;
"business" includes a trade or profession;
"consumer" means any individual who, in contracts to which these Regulations apply, is acting for purposes which are outside any business he may carry on;

"court" in relation to England and Wales and Northern Ireland means a county court or the High Court, and in relation to Scotland means the Sheriff Court or the Court of Session;

"credit" includes a cash loan and any other form of financial accommodation, and for this purpose "cash" includes money in any form;

"designated professional body" has the same meaning as in section 326(2) of the 2000 Act (designation of professional bodies);

"the Directive" means Directive 2002/65/EC of the European Parliament and of the Council of 23 September 2002 concerning the distance marketing of consumer financial services and amending Council Directive 90/619/EEC and Directives 97/7/EC and 98/27/EC[5];

"distance contract" means any contract concerning one or more financial services concluded between a supplier and a consumer under an organised distance sales or service-provision scheme run by the supplier or by an intermediary, who, for the purpose of that contract, makes exclusive use of one or more means of distance communication up to and including the time at which the contract is concluded;

"durable medium" means any instrument which enables a consumer to store information addressed personally to him in a way accessible for future reference for a period of time adequate for the purposes of the information and which allows the unchanged reproduction of the information stored;

"EEA supplier" means a supplier who is a national of an EEA State, or a company or firm (within the meaning of Article 48 of the Treaty establishing the European Community) formed in accordance with the law of an EEA State;

"EEA State" means a State which is a contracting party to the Agreement on the European Economic Area signed at Oporto on 2nd May 1992, as adjusted by the Protocol signed at Brussels on 17th March 1993;

"exempt regulated activity" has the same meaning as in section 325(2) of the 2000 Act;

"financial service" means any service of a banking, credit, insurance, personal pension, investment or payment nature;

"means of distance communication" means any means which, without the simultaneous physical presence of the supplier and the consumer, may be used for the marketing of a service between those parties;

"the OFT" means the Office of Fair Trading;

"regulated activity" has the same meaning as in section 22 of the 2000 Act (the classes of activity and categories of investment);

"Regulated Activities Order" means the Financial Services and Markets Act 2000 (Regulated Activities) Order 2001[6];

"rule" means a rule—

    (a) made by the Authority under the 2000 Act, or

    (b) made by a designated professional body, and approved by the Authority, under section 332 of the 2000 Act,

as the context requires;

"supplier" means any person who, acting in his commercial or professional capacity, is the contractual provider of services.

(2) In these Regulations, subject to paragraph (1), any expression used in these Regulations which is also used in the Directive has the same meaning as in the Directive.

Scope of these Regulations

3.—(1) Regulations 7 to 14 apply, subject to regulations 4 and 5, in relation to distance contracts made on or after 31st October 2004.

(2) Regulation 15 applies in relation to financial services supplied on or after 31st October 2004 under an organised distance sales or service-provision scheme run by the supplier or by an intermediary, who, for the purpose of that supply, makes exclusive use of one or more means of distance communication up to and including the time at which the financial services are supplied.

4.—(1) Where an EEA State, other than the United Kingdom, has transposed the Directive or has obligations in its domestic law corresponding to those provided for in the Directive—

(a) regulations 7 to 14 do not apply in relation to any contract made between an EEA supplier contracting from an establishment in that EEA State and a consumer in the United Kingdom, and

(b) regulation 15 does not apply to any supply of financial services by an EEA supplier from an establishment in that EEA State to a consumer in the United Kingdom,

if the provisions by which that State has transposed the Directive, or the obligations in the domestic law of that State corresponding to those provided for in the Directive, as the case may be, apply to that contract or that supply.

(2) Subject to paragraph (5) and regulation 6(3) and (4)—

(a) regulations 7 to 11 do not apply in relation to any contract made by a supplier who is an authorised person, the making or performance of which constitutes or is part of a regulated activity carried on by him;

(b) regulation 15 does not apply to any supply of financial services by a supplier who is an authorised person, where that supply constitutes or is part of a regulated activity carried on by him.

(3) Subject to regulation 6(3) and (4)—

(a) regulations 7 and 8 do not apply in relation to any contract made by a supplier who is an appointed representative, the making or performance of which constitutes or is part of a regulated activity (other than an exempt regulated activity) carried on by him;

(b) regulation 15 does not apply to any supply of financial services by a supplier who is an appointed representative, where that supply constitutes or is part of a regulated activity (other than an exempt regulated activity) carried on by him.

(4) Subject to regulation 6(3) and (4)—

(a) regulations 7 and 8 do not apply in relation to any contract where—

(i) the supplier is bound, or is controlled or managed by one or more persons who are bound, by rules of a designated professional body which are equivalent to those regulations, and

(ii) the making or performance of that contract constitutes or is part of an exempt regulated activity carried on by the supplier;

(b) regulation 15 does not apply to any supply of financial services where—

(i) the supplier is bound, or is controlled or managed by one or more persons who are bound, by rules of a designated professional body which are equivalent to that regulation, and

      (ii) that supply constitutes or is part of an exempt regulated activity carried on by the supplier.

(5) Paragraph (2) does not apply in relation to any contract or supply of financial services made by a supplier who is the operator, trustee or depositary of a scheme which is a recognised scheme by virtue of section 264 of the 2000 Act (schemes constituted in other EEA States), where the making or performance of the contract or the supply of the financial services constitutes or is part of a regulated activity for which he has permission in that capacity.

(6) In paragraph (5)—

"the operator", "trustee" and "depositary" each has the same meaning as in section 237(2) of the 2000 Act (other definitions); and

"permission" has the same meaning as in section 266 of that Act (disapplication of rules).

5.—(1) Where a consumer and a supplier enter an initial service agreement and—

(a) successive operations of the same nature, or

(b) a series of separate operations of the same nature,

are subsequently performed between them over time and within the framework of that agreement, then, if any of regulations 7 to 14 apply, they apply only to the initial service agreement.

(2) Where a consumer and a supplier do not enter an initial service agreement and—

(a) successive operations of the same nature, or

(b) a series of separate operations of the same nature,

are performed between them over time, then, if regulations 7 and 8 apply, they apply only—

     (i) when the first operation is performed, and

    (ii) to any operation which is performed more than one year after the previous operation.

(3) For the purposes of this regulation, "initial service agreement" includes, for example, an agreement for the provision of—

(a) a bank account;

(b) a credit card; or

(c) portfolio management services.

(4) For the purposes of this regulation, "operations" includes, for example—

(a) deposits to or withdrawals from a bank account;

(b) payments by a credit card;

(c) transactions carried out within the framework of an initial service agreement for portfolio management services; and

(d) subscriptions to new units of the same collective investment fund,

but does not include adding new elements to an existing initial service agreement, for example adding the possibility of using an electronic payment instrument together with an existing bank account.

Financial services marketed by an intermediary

6.—(1) This regulation applies where a financial service is marketed by an intermediary.

(2) These Regulations have effect as if—

(a) each reference to a supplier in the definition of "breach" in regulation 2(1) were a reference to a supplier or an intermediary;

   (b) the reference to the supplier in the definition of "means of distance communication" in regulation 2(1), each reference to the supplier in regulations 7, 8(1) and (2), 10 and 11(3)(b), and the first reference to the supplier in regulation 8(4), were a reference to the intermediary;

   (c) the reference to the supplier in regulation 8(3) were a reference to the supplier or the intermediary;

   (d) for regulation 11(2) there were substituted—

      "(2) Paragraph (1) does not apply to a distance contract if the intermediary has not complied with regulation 8(1) (and the supplier has not done what the intermediary was required to do by regulation 8(1)), unless—

        (a) the circumstances fall within regulation 8(1)(b); and

        (b) either—

           (i) the intermediary has complied with regulation 7(1) and (2) or, if applicable, regulation 7(4)(b), and with regulation 7(5), or

          (ii) the supplier has done what the intermediary was required to do by regulation 7(1) and (2) or, if applicable, regulation 7(4)(b), and by regulation 7(5).";

   (e) the reference to a supplier in regulation 22(1) were a reference to an intermediary; and

   (f) each reference to the supplier in paragraphs 2, 4, 5 and 19 of Schedule 1 were a reference to the supplier and the intermediary.

(3) Notwithstanding paragraphs (2) to (4) of regulation 4, regulations 7 and 8 apply in relation to the intermediary unless—

   (a) the intermediary is an authorised person and the marketing of the financial service constitutes or is part of a regulated activity carried on by him;

   (b) the intermediary is an appointed representative and the marketing of the financial service constitutes or is part of a regulated activity (other than an exempt regulated activity) carried on by him; or

   (c) the intermediary is not an authorised person, but—

      (i) he is bound, or is controlled or managed by one or more persons who are bound, by rules of a designated professional body which are equivalent to regulations 7 and 8, and

      (ii) the marketing of the financial service constitutes or is part of an exempt regulated activity carried on by him.

(4) Notwithstanding paragraphs (2) to (4) of regulation 4, regulation 15 applies to the intermediary unless—

   (a) the intermediary is an authorised person and is acting in the course of a regulated activity carried on by him;

   (b) the intermediary is an appointed representative and is acting in the course of a regulated activity (other than an exempt regulated activity) carried on by him; or

   (c) the intermediary is not an authorised person, but—

      (i) he is bound, or is controlled or managed by one or more persons who are bound, by rules of a designated professional body which are equivalent to regulation 15, and

      (ii) he is acting in the course an exempt regulated activity carried on by him.

Information required prior to the conclusion of the contract

7.—(1) Subject to paragraph (4), in good time prior to the consumer being bound by any distance contract, the supplier shall provide to the consumer the information specified in Schedule 1.

(2) The supplier shall provide the information specified in Schedule 1 in a clear and comprehensible manner appropriate to the means of distance communication used, with due regard in particular to the principles of good faith in commercial transactions and the principles governing the protection of those who are unable to give their consent such as minors.

(3) Subject to paragraph (4), the supplier shall make clear his commercial purpose when providing the information specified in Schedule 1.

(4) In the case of a voice telephone communication—

    (a) the supplier shall make clear his identity and the commercial purpose of any call initiated by him at the beginning of any conversation with the consumer; and

    (b) if the consumer explicitly consents, only the information specified in Schedule 2 need be given.

(5) The supplier shall ensure that the information he provides to the consumer pursuant to this regulation, regarding the contractual obligations which would arise if the distance contract were concluded, accurately reflects the contractual obligations which would arise under the law presumed to be applicable to that contract.

Written and additional information

8.—(1) The supplier under a distance contract shall communicate to the consumer on paper, or in another durable medium which is available and accessible to the consumer, all the contractual terms and conditions and the information specified in Schedule 1, either—

    (a) in good time prior to the consumer being bound by that distance contract; or

    (b) immediately after the conclusion of the contract, where the contract has been concluded at the consumer's request using a means of distance communication which does not enable provision in accordance with sub-paragraph (a) of the contractual terms and conditions and the information specified in Schedule 1.

(2) The supplier shall communicate the contractual terms and conditions to the consumer on paper, if the consumer so requests at any time during their contractual relationship.

(3) Paragraph (2) does not apply if the supplier has already communicated the contractual terms and conditions to the consumer on paper during that contractual relationship, and those terms and conditions have not changed since they were so communicated.

(4) The supplier shall change the means of distance communication with the consumer if the consumer so requests at any time during his contractual relationship with the supplier, unless that is incompatible with the distance contract or the nature of the financial service provided to the consumer.

Right to cancel

9.—(1) Subject to regulation 11, if within the cancellation period set out in regulation 10 notice of cancellation is properly given by the consumer to the supplier, the notice of cancellation shall operate to cancel the distance contract.

(2) Cancelling the contract has the effect of terminating the contract at the time at which the notice of cancellation is given.

(3) For the purposes of these Regulations, a notice of cancellation is a notification given—

(a) orally (where the supplier has informed the consumer that notice of cancellation may be given orally),

(b) in writing, or

(c) in another durable medium available and accessible to the supplier,

which, however expressed, indicates the intention of the consumer to cancel the contract by that notification.

(4) Notice of cancellation given under this regulation by a consumer to a supplier is to be treated as having been properly given if the consumer—

(a) gives it orally to the supplier (where the supplier has informed the consumer that notice of cancellation may be given orally);

(b) leaves it at the address of the supplier last known to the consumer and addressed to the supplier by name (in which case it is to be taken to have been given on the day on which it was left);

(c) sends it by post to the address of the supplier last known to the consumer and addressed to the supplier by name (in which case it is to be taken to have been given on the day on which it was posted);

(d) sends it by facsimile to the business facsimile number of the supplier last known to the consumer (in which case it is to be taken to have been given on the day on which it was sent);

(e) sends it by electronic mail to the business electronic mail address of the supplier last known to the consumer (in which case it is to be taken to have been given on the day on which it is sent); or

(f) by other electronic means—

(i) sends it to an internet address or web-site which the supplier has notified the consumer may be used for the purpose, or

(ii) indicates it on such a web-site in accordance with instructions which are on the web-site or which the supplier has provided to the consumer,

(in which case it is to be taken to have been given on the day on which it is sent to that address or web-site or indicated on that web-site).

(5) The references in paragraph (4)(b) and (c) to the address of the supplier shall, in the case of a supplier which is a body corporate, be treated as including a reference to the address of the secretary or clerk of that body.

(6) The references in paragraph (4)(b) and (c) to the address of the supplier shall, in the case of a supplier which is a partnership, be treated as including a reference to the address of a partner or a person having control or management of the partnership business.

(7) In this regulation—

(a) every reference to the supplier includes a reference to any other person previously notified by or on behalf of the supplier to the consumer as a person to whom notice of cancellation may be given;

(b) the references to giving notice of cancellation orally include giving such notice by voice telephone communication, where the supplier has informed the consumer that notice of cancellation may be given in that way; and

(c) "electronic mail" has the same meaning as in regulation 2(1) of the Privacy and Electronic Communications (EC Directive) Regulations 2003 (interpretation)[7].

Cancellation period

10.—(1) For the purposes of regulation 9, the cancellation period begins on the day on which the distance contract is concluded ("conclusion day") and ends as provided for in paragraphs (2) to (5).

(2) Where the supplier complies with regulation 8(1) on or before conclusion day, the cancellation period ends on the expiry of fourteen calendar days beginning with the day after conclusion day.

(3) Where the supplier does not comply with regulation 8(1) on or before conclusion day, but subsequently communicates to the consumer on paper, or in another durable medium which is available and accessible to the consumer, all the contractual terms and conditions and the information required under regulation 8(1), the cancellation period ends on the expiry of fourteen calendar days beginning with the day after the day on which the consumer receives the last of those terms and conditions and that information.

(4) In the case of a distance contract relating to life insurance, for the references to conclusion day in paragraphs (2) and (3) there are substituted references to the day on which the consumer is informed that the distance contract has been concluded.

(5) In the case of a distance contract relating to life insurance or a personal pension, for the references to fourteen calendar days in paragraphs (2) and (3) there are substituted references to thirty calendar days.

Exceptions to the right to cancel

11.—(1) Subject to paragraphs (2) and (3), regulation 9 does not confer on a consumer a right to cancel a distance contract which is—

(a) a contract for a financial service where the price of that service depends on fluctuations in the financial market outside the supplier's control, which may occur during the cancellation period, such as services related to—
  (i) foreign exchange,
  (ii) money market instruments,
  (iii) transferable securities,
  (iv) units in collective investment undertakings,
  (v) financial-futures contracts, including equivalent cash-settled instruments,
  (vi) forward interest-rate agreements,
  (vii) interest-rate, currency and equity swaps,
  (viii) options to acquire or dispose of any instruments referred to in sub-paragraphs (i) to (vii), including cash-settled instruments and options on currency and on interest rates;

(b) a contract whose performance has been fully completed by both parties at the consumer's express request before the consumer gives notice of cancellation;

(c) a contract which—
  (i) is a connected contract of insurance within the meaning of article 72B(1) of the Regulated Activities Order (activities carried on by a provider of relevant goods or services)[8],

      (ii) covers travel risks within the meaning of article 72B(1)(d)(ii) of that Order, and

      (iii) has a total duration of less than one month;

  (d) a contract under which a supplier provides credit to a consumer and the consumer's obligation to repay is secured by a legal mortgage on land;

  (e) a credit agreement cancelled under regulation 15(1) of the Consumer Protection (Distance Selling) Regulations 2000 (automatic cancellation of a related credit agreement)[9];

  (f) a credit agreement cancelled under section 6A of the Timeshare Act 1992 (automatic cancellation of timeshare credit agreement)[10]; or

  (g) a restricted-use credit agreement (within the meaning of the 1974 Act) to finance the purchase of land or an existing building, or an agreement for a bridging loan in connection with the purchase of land or an existing building.

(2) Paragraph (1) does not apply to a distance contract if the supplier has not complied with regulation 8(1), unless—

  (a) the circumstances fall within regulation 8(1)(b); and

  (b) the supplier has complied with regulation 7(1) and (2) or, if applicable, regulation 7(4)(b), and with regulation 7(5).

(3) Where—

  (a) the conditions in sub-paragraphs (a) and (b) of paragraph (2) are satisfied in relation to a distance contract falling within paragraph (1),

  (b) the supplier has not complied with regulation 8(1), and

  (c) the consumer has not, by the end of the sixth day after the day on which the distance contract is concluded, received all the contractual terms and conditions and the information required under regulation 8(1),

the consumer may cancel the contract under regulation 9 during the period beginning on the seventh day after the day on which the distance contract is concluded and ending when he receives the last of the contractual terms and conditions and the information required under regulation 8(1).

Automatic cancellation of an attached distance contract

12.—(1) For the purposes of this regulation, where there is a distance contract for the provision of a financial service by a supplier to a consumer ("the main contract") and there is a further distance contract ("the secondary contract") for the provision to that consumer of a further financial service by—

  (a) the same supplier, or

  (b) a third party, the further financial service being provided pursuant to an agreement between the third party and the supplier under the main contract,

then the secondary contract (referred to in these Regulations as an "attached contract") is attached to the main contract if any of the conditions in paragraph (2) are satisfied.

(2) The conditions referred to in paragraph (1) are—

  (a) the secondary contract is entered into in compliance with a term of the main contract;

  (b) the main contract is, or is to be, financed by the secondary contract;

  (c) the main contract is a debtor-creditor-supplier agreement within the meaning of the 1974 Act, and the secondary contract is, or is to be, financed by the main contract;

    (d) the secondary contract is entered into by the consumer to induce the supplier to enter into the main contract;

    (e) performance of the secondary contract requires performance of the main contract.

(3) Where a main contract is cancelled by a notice of cancellation given under regulation 9—

    (a) the cancellation of the main contract also operates to cancel, at the time at which the main contract is cancelled, any attached contract which is not a contract or agreement of a type listed in regulation 11(1); and

    (b) the supplier under the main contract shall, if he is not the supplier under the attached contract, forthwith on receipt of the notice of cancellation inform the supplier under the attached contract.

(4) Paragraph (3)(a) does not apply to an attached contract if, at or before the time at which the notice of cancellation in respect of the main contract is given, the consumer has given and not withdrawn a notice to the supplier under the main contract that cancellation of the main contract is not to operate to cancel that attached contract.

(5) Where a main contract made by an authorised person, the making or performance of which constitutes or is part of a regulated activity carried on by him, is cancelled under rules made by the Authority corresponding to regulation 9—

    (a) the cancellation of the main contract also operates to cancel, at the time at which the main contract is cancelled, any attached contract which is not a contract or agreement of a type listed in regulation 11(1); and

    (b) the supplier under the main contract shall, if he is not the supplier under the attached contract, inform the supplier under the attached contract forthwith on receiving notification of the consumer's intention to cancel the main contract by that notification.

(6) Paragraph (5)(a) does not apply to an attached contract if, at or before the time at which the consumer gives notification of his intention to cancel the main contract by that notification, the consumer has given and not withdrawn a notice to the supplier under the main contract that cancellation of the main contract is not to operate to cancel that attached contract.

Payment for services provided before cancellation

13.—(1) This regulation applies where a cancellation event occurs in relation to a distance contract.

(2) In this regulation, "cancellation event" means the cancellation of a distance contract under regulation 9 or 12.

(3) The supplier shall refund any sum paid by or on behalf of the consumer under or in relation to the contract to the person by whom it was paid, less any charge made in accordance with paragraph (6), as soon as possible and in any event within a period not exceeding 30 calendar days beginning with—

    (a) the day on which the cancellation event occurred; or

    (b) if the supplier proves that this is later—

        (i) in the case of a contract cancelled under regulation 9, the day on which the supplier in fact received the notice of cancellation, or

        (ii) in the case of an attached contract under which the supplier is not the supplier under the main contract, the day on which, pursuant to regulation

12(3)(b) or (5)(b), he was in fact informed by the supplier under the main contract of the cancellation of the main contract.

(4) The reference in paragraph (3) to any sum paid on behalf of the consumer includes any sum paid by any other person ("the creditor"), who is not the supplier, under an agreement between the consumer and the creditor by which the creditor provides the consumer with credit of any amount.

(5) Where any security has been provided in relation to the contract, the security (so far as it has been provided) shall, on cancellation under regulation 9 or 12, be treated as never having had effect; and any property lodged solely for the purposes of the security as so provided shall be returned forthwith by the person with whom it is lodged.

(6) Subject to paragraphs (7), (8) and (9), the supplier may make a charge for any service actually provided by the supplier in accordance with the contract.

(7) The charge shall not exceed an amount which is in proportion to the extent of the service provided to the consumer prior to the time at which the cancellation event occurred (including the service of arranging to provide the financial service) in comparison with the full coverage of the contract, and in any event shall not be such that it could be construed as a penalty.

(8) The supplier may not make any charge unless he can prove on the balance of probabilities that the consumer was informed about the amount payable in accordance with—
   (a) regulation 7(1) and paragraph 13 of Schedule 1,
   (b) regulation 7(4) and paragraph 5 of Schedule 2, or
   (c) rules corresponding to those provisions,
   as the case may be.

(9) The supplier may not make any charge if, without the consumer's prior request, he commenced performance of the contract prior to the expiry of the relevant cancellation period.

(10) In paragraph (9), the relevant cancellation period is the cancellation period which—
   (a) in the case of a main contract, is applicable to that contract, or
   (b) in the case of an attached contract, would be applicable to that contract if that contract were a main contract,
   under regulation 10, or under rules corresponding to that regulation, as the case may be.

(11) The consumer shall, as soon as possible and in any event within a period not exceeding 30 calendar days beginning with the day on which the cancellation event occurred—
   (a) refund any sum paid by or on behalf of the supplier under or in relation to that contract to the person by whom it was paid; and
   (b) either restore to the supplier any property of which he has acquired possession under that contract, or deliver or send that property to any person to whom, under regulation 9, a notice of cancellation could have been given in respect of that contract.

(12) Breach of a duty imposed by paragraph (11) on a consumer is actionable as a breach of statutory duty.

Payment by card

14.—(1) Subject to paragraph (2), where—

    (a) a payment card has been issued to an individual who, when entering the contract for the provision of that card, was acting for purposes which were outside any business he may carry on ("the card-holder"), and

    (b) fraudulent use is made of that card to make a payment under or in connection with a distance contract to which these Regulations apply, by another person who is neither acting, nor to be treated as acting, as the card-holder's agent,

the card-holder may request cancellation of that payment, and is entitled to be recredited with the sum paid, or to have it returned, by the card issuer.

(2) Where paragraph (1) applies and, in any proceedings, the card-holder alleges that any use made of the payment card was not authorised by him, it is for the card issuer to prove that the use was so authorised.

(3) Paragraph (1) does not apply if the contract for the provision of the payment card is an agreement to which section 83(1) of the 1974 Act (liability for misuse of credit facilities) applies.

(4) After subsection (3B) of section 84 of the 1974 Act (misuse of credit-tokens)[11] insert—

    "(3C) Subsections (1) and (2) shall not apply to any use, in connection with a distance contract within the meaning of the Financial Services (Distance Marketing) Regulations 2004, of a card which is a credit-token.".

(5) For the purposes of this regulation—

    "card issuer" means the owner of the card;

    "payment card" includes a credit card, a charge card, a debit card and a store card.

Unsolicited services

15.—(1) A person ("the recipient") who receives unsolicited financial services for purposes other than those of his business from another person who supplies those services in the course of his business, shall not thereby become subject to any obligation (to make payment, or otherwise).

(2) Where, in the course of any business—

    (a) unsolicited financial services are supplied for purposes other than those of the recipient's business, and

    (b) a person includes with the supply of those services a demand for payment, or an assertion of a present or prospective right to payment in respect of those services,

that person is guilty of an offence and liable, on summary conviction, to a fine not exceeding level 4 on the standard scale.

(3) A person who, not having reasonable cause to believe that there is a right to payment, in the course of any business and with a view to obtaining payment for what he knows are unsolicited financial services supplied as mentioned in paragraph (2)—

    (a) threatens to bring any legal proceedings,

    (b) places or causes to be placed the name of any person on a list of defaulters or debtors or threatens to do so, or

    (c) invokes or causes to be invoked any other collection procedure or threatens to do so,

is guilty of an offence and liable, on summary conviction, to a fine not exceeding level 5 on the standard scale.

(4) In this regulation, "unsolicited" means, in relation to financial services supplied to any person, that they are supplied without any prior request made by or on behalf of that person.

(5) For the purposes of this regulation, a person who sends to a recipient an invoice or similar document which—

    (a) states the amount of a payment, and

    (b) does not comply with the requirements, applicable to invoices and similar documents, of regulations made under section 3A of the Unsolicited Goods and Services Act 1971 (contents and form of notes of agreement, invoices and similar documents)[12] or, as the case may be, article 6 of the Unsolicited Goods and Services (Northern Ireland) Order 1976 (contents and form of notes of agreement, invoices and similar documents)[13],

is to be regarded as asserting a right to the payment.

(6) Section 3A of the Unsolicited Goods and Services Act 1971 applies for the purposes of this regulation in its application to England, Wales and Scotland as it applies for the purposes of that Act.

(7) Article 6 of the Unsolicited Goods and Services (Northern Ireland) Order 1976 applies for the purposes of this regulation in its application to Northern Ireland as it applies for the purposes of that Order.

(8) This regulation is without prejudice to any right a supplier may have at any time, by contract or otherwise, to renew a distance contract with a consumer without any request made by or on behalf of that consumer prior to the renewal of that contract.

Prevention of contracting-out

16.—(1) A term contained in any contract is void if, and to the extent that, it is inconsistent with the application of a provision of these Regulations to a distance contract or the application of regulation 15 to a supply of unsolicited financial services.

(2) Where a provision of these Regulations specifies a duty or liability of the consumer in certain circumstances, a term contained in a contract is inconsistent with that provision if it purports to impose, directly or indirectly, an additional or greater duty or liability on him in those circumstances.

(3) These Regulations apply notwithstanding any contract term which applies or purports to apply the law of a State which is not an EEA State if the contract or supply has a close connection with the territory of an EEA State.

Enforcement authorities

17.—(1) For the purposes of regulations 18 to 21—

    (a) in relation to any alleged breach concerning a specified contract, the Authority is the enforcement authority;

    (b) in relation to any alleged breach concerning a contract under which the supplier is a local authority, but which is not a specified contract, the OFT is the enforcement authority;

    (c) in relation to any other alleged breach—

        (i) the OFT, and

        (ii) in Great Britain every local weights and measures authority, and in Northern Ireland the Department of Enterprise, Trade and Investment,

    is an enforcement authority.

(2) For the purposes of paragraph (1) and regulation 22(6), each of the following is a specified contract—

    (a) a contract the making or performance of which constitutes or is part of a regulated activity carried on by the supplier;

    (b) a contract for the provision of a debit card;

    (c) a contract relating to the issuing of electronic money by a supplier to whom the Authority has given a certificate under article 9C of the Regulated Activities Order (persons certified as small issuers etc.)[14];

    (d) a contract the effecting or carrying out of which is excluded from article 10(1) or (2) of the Regulated Activities Order (effecting and carrying out contracts of insurance) by article 12 of that order (breakdown insurance), where the supplier is a person who does not otherwise carry on an activity of the kind specified by article 10 of that order;

    (e) a contract under which a supplier provides credit to a consumer and the obligation of the consumer to repay is secured by a first legal mortgage on land;

    (f) a contract, made before 14th January 2005, for insurance mediation activity other than in respect of a contract of long-term care insurance.

(3) For the purposes of the application of this regulation and regulations 18 to 22 in relation to breaches of, and offences under, regulation 15, "contract"—

    (a) wherever it appears in this regulation other than in the expression "contract of long-term care insurance", and

    (b) in regulation 22(6),

is to be taken to mean "supply of financial services".

(4) For the purposes of this regulation—

    "contract of long-term care insurance" has the same meaning as in the Financial Services and Markets Act 2000 (Regulated Activities) (Amendment) (No. 2) Order 2003[15];

    "insurance mediation activity" means any activity which is not a regulated activity at the time the contract is made but will be a regulated activity of the kind specified by article 21, 25(1) or (2), 39A or 53 of the Regulated Activities Order when the amendments to that order made by the Financial Services and Markets Act 2000 (Regulated Activities) (Amendment) (No. 2) Order 2003 come into force[16];

    "local authority" means—

        (a) in England and Wales, a local authority within the meaning of the Local Government Act 1972[17], the Greater London Authority, the Common Council of the City of London or the Council of the Isles of Scilly,

        (b) in Scotland, a council constituted under section 2 of the Local Government etc. (Scotland) Act 1994[18], and

        (c) in Northern Ireland, a district council within the meaning of the Local Government Act (Northern Ireland) 1972[19].

Consideration of complaints

18.—(1) An enforcement authority shall consider any complaint made to it about a breach unless—

    (a) the complaint appears to that authority to be frivolous or vexatious; or

    (b) that authority is aware that another enforcement authority has notified the OFT that it agrees to consider the complaint.

(2) If an enforcement authority notifies the OFT that it agrees to consider a complaint made to another enforcement authority, the first mentioned authority shall be under a duty to consider the complaint.

Injunctions to secure compliance with these Regulations

19.—(1) Subject to paragraph (2), an enforcement authority may apply for an injunction (including an interim injunction) against any person who appears to that authority to be responsible for a breach.

(2) An enforcement authority, other than the OFT or the Authority, may apply for an injunction only where—

(a) that authority has notified the OFT, at least fourteen days before the date on which the application is to be made, of its intention to apply; or

(b) the OFT consents to the application being made within a shorter period.

(3) On an application made under this regulation, the court may grant an injunction on such terms as it thinks fit to secure compliance with these Regulations.

(4) An enforcement authority which has a duty under regulation 18 to consider a complaint shall give reasons for its decision to apply or not to apply, as the case may be, for an injunction.

(5) In deciding whether or not to apply for an injunction in respect of a breach, an enforcement authority may, if it considers it appropriate to do so, have regard to any undertaking as to compliance with these Regulations given to it or to another enforcement authority by or on behalf of any person.

(6) In the application of this regulation to Scotland, for references to an "injunction" or an "interim injunction" there are substituted references to an "interdict" or an "interim interdict" respectively.

Notification of undertakings and orders to the OFT

20. An enforcement authority, other than the OFT and the Authority, shall notify the OFT of—

(a) any undertaking given to it by or on behalf of any person who appears to it to be responsible for a breach;

(b) the outcome of any application made by it under regulation 19 and the terms of any undertaking given to, or order made by, the court; and

(c) the outcome of any application made by it to enforce a previous order of the court.

Publication, information and advice

21.—(1) The OFT shall arrange for the publication, in such form and manner as it considers appropriate, of details of any undertaking or order notified to it under regulation 20.

(2) Each of the OFT and the Authority shall arrange for the publication in such form and manner as it considers appropriate of—

(a) details of any undertaking as to compliance with these Regulations given to it by or on behalf of any person;

(b) details of any application made by it under regulation 19[a], and of the terms of any undertaking given to, or order made by, the court; and

(c) details of any application made by it to enforce a previous order of the court.

(3) Each of the OFT and the Authority may arrange for the dissemination, in such form and manner as it considers appropriate, of such information and advice concerning the operation of these Regulations as may appear to it to be expedient to give to the public and to all persons likely to be affected by these Regulations.

Offences

22.—(1) A supplier under a distance contract who fails to comply with regulation 7(3) or (4)(a) or regulation 8(2) or (4) is guilty of an offence and liable, on summary conviction, to a fine not exceeding level 3 on the standard scale.

(2) If an offence under paragraph (1), or under regulation 15(2) or (3), committed by a body corporate is shown—

(a) to have been committed with the consent or connivance of any director, manager, secretary or other similar officer of the body corporate, or any person who was purporting to act in any such capacity, or

(b) to be attributable to any neglect on his part,

he as well as the body corporate is guilty of the offence and liable to be proceeded against and punished accordingly.

(3) If the affairs of a body corporate are managed by its members, paragraph (2) applies in relation to the acts and defaults of a member in connection with his functions of management as if he were a director of the body.

(4) If an offence under paragraph (1), or under regulation 15(2) or (3), committed by a partnership is shown—

(a) to have been committed with the consent or connivance of any partner, or any person who was purporting to act as a partner, or

(b) to be attributable to any neglect on his part,

he as well as the partnership is guilty of an offence and liable to be proceeded against and punished accordingly.

(5) If an offence under paragraph (1), or under regulation 15(2) or (3), committed by an unincorporated association (other than a partnership) is shown—

(a) to have been committed with the consent or connivance of an officer of the association or a member of its governing body, or any person who was purporting to act in any such capacity, or

(b) to be attributable to any neglect on his part,

he as well as the association is guilty of an offence and liable to be proceeded against and punished accordingly.

(6) Except in Scotland—

(a) the Authority may institute proceedings for an offence under these Regulations which relates to a specified contract;

(b) the OFT, and—

(i) in Great Britain, every local weights and measures authority,

(ii) in Northern Ireland, the Department of Enterprise, Trade and Investment,

may institute proceedings for any other offence under these Regulations.

Functions of the Authority

23. The functions conferred on the Authority by these Regulations shall be treated as if they were conferred by the 2000 Act.

Amendment of the Unfair Terms in Consumer Contracts Regulations 1999

24.—(1) The Unfair Terms in Consumer Contracts Regulations 1999[20] are amended as follows.

(2) After regulation 3(1) (interpretation), insert—

"(1A) The references—

(a) in regulation 4(1) to a seller or a supplier, and

(b) in regulation 8(1) to a seller or supplier,

include references to a distance supplier and to an intermediary.

(1B) In paragraph (1A) and regulation 5(6)—

"distance supplier" means—

(a) a supplier under a distance contract within the meaning of the Financial Services (Distance Marketing) Regulations 2004, or

(b) a supplier of unsolicited financial services within regulation 15 of those Regulations; and

"intermediary" has the same meaning as in those Regulations.".

(3) After regulation 5(5) (unfair terms), insert—

"(6) Any contractual term providing that a consumer bears the burden of proof in respect of showing whether a distance supplier or an intermediary complied with any or all of the obligations placed upon him resulting from the Directive and any rule or enactment implementing it shall always be regarded as unfair.

(7) In paragraph (6)—

"the Directive" means Directive 2002/65/EC of the European Parliament and of the Council of 23 September 2002 concerning the distance marketing of consumer financial services and amending Council Directive 90/619/EEC and Directives 97/7/EC and 98/27/EC; and

"rule" means a rule made by the Financial Services Authority under the Financial Services and Markets Act 2000 or by a designated professional body within the meaning of section 326(2) of that Act.".

Amendment of the Consumer Protection (Distance Selling) Regulations 2000

25.—(1) The Consumer Protection (Distance Selling) Regulations 2000[21] are amended as follows.

(2) In regulation 3(1) (interpretation)—

(a) before the definition of "breach" insert—

" "the 2000 Act" means the Financial Services and Markets Act 2000;

"appointed representative" has the same meaning as in section 39(2) of the 2000 Act;

"authorised person" has the same meaning as in section 31(2) of the 2000 Act;";

(b) after the definition of "excepted contract" insert—

" "financial service" means any service of a banking, credit, insurance, personal pension, investment or payment nature;";

(c) after the definition of "personal credit agreement" insert—

" "regulated activity" has the same meaning as in section 22 of the 2000 Act;".

(3) In regulation 5(1)(c) (excepted contracts) omit ", a non-exhaustive list of which is contained in Schedule 2".

(4) After regulation 6(3) (contracts to which only part of those Regulations apply) insert—

"(4) Regulations 7 to 14, 17 to 20 and 25 do not apply to any contract which is made, and regulation 24 does not apply to any unsolicited services which are supplied, by an authorised person where the making or performance of that contract or the supply of those services, as the case may be, constitutes or is part of a regulated activity carried on by him.

(5) Regulations 7 to 9, 17 to 20 and 25 do not apply to any contract which is made, and regulation 24 does not apply to any unsolicited services which are supplied, by an appointed representative where the making or performance of that contract or the supply of those services, as the case may be, constitutes or is part of a regulated activity carried on by him.".

(5) Omit Schedule 2 (non-exhaustive list of financial services).

Amendment of the Enterprise Act 2002

26. In Part 1 of Schedule 13 to the Enterprise Act 2002 (listed directives)[22], after paragraph 9 insert—

"9A Directive 2002/65/EC of the European Parliament and of the Council of 23 September 2002 concerning the distance marketing of consumer financial services and amending Council Directive 90/619/EEC and Directives 97/7/EC and 98/27/EC.".

Amendment of the Enterprise Act 2002 (Part 8 Community Infringements Specified UK Laws) Order 2003

27. In the table in the Schedule to the Enterprise Act 2002 (Part 8 Community Infringements Specified UK Laws) Order 2003 (listed directives)[23], after the entry for Directive 2000/31/EC ("Directive on electronic commerce") insert—

Directive 2002/65/EC of the European Parliament and of the Council of 23 September 2002 concerning the distance marketing of consumer financial services and amending Council Directive 90/619/EEC and Directives 97/7/EC and 98/27/EC.	Financial Services (Distance Marketing) Regulations 2004; rules corresponding to any provisions of those Regulations made by the Financial Services Authority or a designated professional body within the meaning of section 326(2) of the Financial Services and Markets Act 2000.".

Amendment of the Enterprise Act 2002 (Part 8 Notice to OFT of Intended Prosecution Specified Enactments, Revocation and Transitional Provision) Order 2003

28. In the table in the Schedule to the Enterprise Act 2002 (Part 8 Notice to OFT of Intended Prosecution Specified Enactments, Revocation and Transitional Provision) Order 2003[24], after the entry for the Fair Trading Act 1973[25] insert—

Financial Services (Distance Marketing) Regulations 2004.	All offences under those Regulations.".

Transitional provisions

29.—(1) In relation to any contract made before 31st May 2005 which is a consumer credit agreement within the meaning of the 1974 Act and a regulated agreement within the meaning of that Act—

(a) regulations 7, 8, 10 and 11 apply subject to the modifications in paragraphs (2) to (5); and

(b) references in these Regulations to regulations 7, 8, 10 and 11 or to provisions contained in them shall be construed accordingly.

(2) In regulation 7—

(a) in paragraphs (1) to (3), before "Schedule 1" at each place where it occurs insert "paragraph 13 of"; and

(b) in paragraph (4)(b), before "Schedule 2" insert "paragraph 5 of".

(3) In regulation 8(1), for "contractual terms and conditions and the information specified in" at each place where it occurs substitute "information specified in paragraph
13 of".

(4) In regulation 10(3), omit—

    (a) "the contractual terms and conditions and"; and

    (b) "those terms and conditions and".

(5) In regulation 11(3), omit "the contractual terms and conditions and" at each place
where it occurs.

John Heppell Joan Ryan

Two of the Lords Commissioners of Her Majesty's Treasury

4th August 2004

SCHEDULE 1

Regulations 7(1) and 8(1)

Information required prior to the conclusion of the contract

1. The identity and the main business of the supplier, the geographical address at which
the supplier is established and any other geographical address relevant to the
consumer's relations with the supplier.

2. Where the supplier has a representative established in the consumer's State of
residence, the identity of that representative and the geographical address relevant to
the consumer's relations with him.

3. Where the consumer's dealings are with any professional other than the supplier, the
identity of that professional, the capacity in which he is acting with respect to the
consumer, and the geographical address relevant to the consumer's relations with
that professional.

4. Where the supplier is registered in a trade or similar public register, the particulars of
the register in which the supplier is entered and his registration number or an equivalent means of identification in that register.

5. Where the supplier's activity is subject to an authorisation scheme, the particulars of
the relevant supervisory authority.

6. A description of the main characteristics of the financial service.

7. The total price to be paid by the consumer to the supplier for the financial service,
including all related fees, charges and expenses, and all taxes paid via the supplier or,
where an exact price cannot be indicated, the basis for the calculation of the price
enabling the consumer to verify it.

8. Where relevant, notice indicating that: (i) the financial service is related to instruments involving special risks related to their specific features or the operations to be
executed or whose price depends on fluctuations in the financial markets outside the
supplier's control; and (ii) historical performances are no indicators for future
performances.

9. Notice of the possibility that other taxes or costs may exist that are not paid via the
supplier or imposed by him.

10. Any limitations of the period for which the information provided is valid.

11. The arrangements for payment and for performance.

12. Any specific additional cost for the consumer of using the means of distance communication, if such additional cost is charged.

13. Whether or not there is a right of cancellation and, where there is a right of cancellation, its duration and the conditions for exercising it, including information on the amount which the consumer may be required to pay in accordance with regulation 13, as well as the consequences of not exercising that right.

14. The minimum duration of the distance contract in the case of financial services to be performed indefinitely or recurrently.

15. Information on any rights the parties may have to terminate the distance contract early or unilaterally by virtue of the terms of the contract, including any penalties imposed by the contract in such cases.

16. Practical instructions for exercising the right to cancel in accordance with regulation 9 indicating, among other things, the address at which the notice of cancellation should be left or to which it should be sent by post, and any facsimile number or electronic mail address to which it should be sent.

17. The EEA State or States whose laws are taken by the supplier as a basis for the establishment of relations with the consumer prior to the conclusion of the distance contract.

18. Any contractual clause on the law applicable to the distance contract or on the competent court.

19. In which language, or languages: (i) the contractual terms and conditions, and the prior information specified in this Schedule, are supplied; and (ii) the supplier, with the agreement of the consumer, undertakes to communicate during the duration of the distance contract.

20. Whether or not there is an out-of-court complaint and redress mechanism for the consumer and, if so, the methods for having access to it.

21. The existence of guarantee funds or other compensation arrangements, except to the extent that they are required by Directive 94/19/EC of the European Parliament and of the Council of 30 May 1994 on deposit guarantee schemes[26] or Directive 97/9/EC of the European Parliament and of the Council of 3 March 1997 on investor compensation schemes[27].

SCHEDULE 2

Regulation 7(4)(b)

Information required in the case of voice telephone communications

1. The identity of the person in contact with the consumer and his link with the supplier.

2. A description of the main characteristics of the financial service.

3. The total price to be paid by the consumer to the supplier for the financial service including all taxes paid via the supplier or, if an exact price cannot be indicated, the basis for the calculation of the price enabling the consumer to verify it.

4. Notice of the possibility that other taxes or costs may exist that are not paid via the supplier or imposed by him.

5. Whether or not there is a right to cancel and, where there is such a right, its duration and the conditions for exercising it, including information on the amount which the consumer may be required to pay in accordance with regulation 13, as well as the consequences of not exercising that right.

6. That other information is available on request and the nature of that information.

EXPLANATORY Note

(This note is not part of the Regulations)

These Regulations give effect in the United Kingdom to Directive 2002/65/EC of the European Parliament and of the Council of 23 September 2002 concerning the distance marketing of consumer financial services and amending Council Directive 90/619/EEC and Directives 97/7/EC and 98/27/EC (O.J. L 271, 9.10.2002, p.16) ("the Directive") so far as it is not given effect by rules made by the Financial Services Authority under the Financial Services and Markets Act 2000 or made by a professional body designated under that Act.

Regulations 3 to 5 identify the transactions to which the substantive provisions of these Regulations apply. Regulation 3 defines these as "distance contracts", as defined in regulation 2(1) (or, for the purposes of regulation 15, comparable supplies of financial services) made on or after the date on which the Regulations come into force. Regulation 4 then disapplies certain provisions from various categories of contract and supply where equivalent provision is made by other regimes: paragraph (1) excludes contracts and supplies made by suppliers established in another State within the European Economic Area where the law of that State regulates the contract or supply in accordance with the Directive; paragraphs (2) to (4), taken with paragraphs (5) and (6), exclude contracts and supplies in relation to which effect is given to the Directive by rules made or approved by the Financial Services Authority under the Financial Services and Markets Act 2000. Regulation 5 gives effect to Article 1(2) of the Directive in the light of Recital (17) in the Directive's preamble, under which the substantive provisions of the Directive only apply to an "initial service agreement" with a financial services supplier or the first in a series of similar operations, and not to every subsequent transaction carried out under that agreement or in that series.

Regulation 6 sets out how the Regulations apply in cases where financial services are marketed through an intermediary, as contemplated by Recital (19) in the preamble to the Directive. Some provisions of the Regulations apply to the intermediary instead of the supplier; others apply to either or both of them; others again still apply only to the supplier.

Regulations 7 and 8 and the Schedules contain the first set of main provisions, requiring suppliers of financial services, where the Regulations apply, to provide consumers with certain information listed in the Schedules. This information generally has to be provided before the consumer is bound by a distance contract for supply of the financial services in question.

Regulations 9 to 13 contain the next set of main provisions, giving consumers a right to cancel most distance contracts for financial services during a set period after commencement of the contract.

Regulation 9 contains the right to cancel, specifying the means by which the right can be exercised and defining the effect of cancellation as termination of the contract at the time at which the notice of cancellation is given. Regulation 10 defines the period during which the cancellation right can be exercised: generally from the time the consumer is bound by the contract until 14 days after that, or until 14 days after the information required by regulation 8 is provided if later, but until 30 days after the later of those dates in the case of a contract for a personal pension and until 30 days after the day on which the consumer is informed that the distance contract has been concluded in the case of a contract for life insurance. Paragraph (1) of regulation 11 lists certain types of contract to which, as permitted by the Directive, the cancellation right does not apply except in the circumstances dealt with in paragraphs (2) and (3) of that regulation.

Regulation 12 provides that, where a distance contract is cancelled under regulation 9, certain other subsidiary distance contracts connected with that contract—defined in paragraph (1) as "attached contracts"—are automatically cancelled too.

Regulation 13 then provides for the consequences of cancellation of distance contracts, whether by notice under regulation 9 or automatically under regulation 12: the supplier must refund any sums received from the consumer under the contract, less a proportionate charge for any services already supplied, and must release and return to the consumer any security taken under the contract; the consumer must repay to the supplier any money paid to the consumer under the contract, and return any property acquired under it.

Regulation 14 provides that, where a plastic card issued to a consumer is used fraudulently by someone else to make a payment in connection with a distance contract (other than where the Consumer Credit Act 1974 (c. 39) covers the matter), the consumer is entitled to cancel the payment and to have all sums paid recredited or returned by the card issuer.

Regulation 15 prevents consumers from being bound by any obligation in respect of financial services supplied to them but for which they have not asked; and makes it a criminal offence to demand or assert a right to payment with any such supply, or to take or threaten enforcement action with a view to obtaining payment for such a supply, without reason to believe payment is legally due.

Regulation 16 is designed to prevent the Regulations being undermined. It renders void any contractual term which is inconsistent with any provision of these Regulations or purports to impose on a consumer additional or greater duties or liabilities than those provided for in the Regulations; and it overrides any contractual term which aims to apply the law of a non-EEA State so as to prevent a contract or supply closely connected with an EEA State from being governed by the provisions of the Directive.

Regulations 17 to 21 and 26 to 28 contain or provide for enforcement mechanisms in relation to the substantive provisions of the Regulations.

Paragraph (1) of regulation 17 specifies for these purposes that the enforcement authority for certain types of distance contract or supply listed in paragraph (2) is the Financial Services Authority, and that the enforcement authorities for other distance contracts and supplies are the Office of Fair Trading with local weights and measures authorities (in Great Britain) or with the Department of Enterprise, Trade and Investment (in Northern Ireland). Regulation 18 requires any such enforcement authority to consider complaints made to it about breaches of the Regulations unless the complaint is frivolous or vexatious or another enforcement authority has agreed to deal with it. Regulation 19 enables enforcement authorities to apply to the courts for injunctions against persons responsible for breaches of the Regulations, and regulations 20 and 21 provide for notification and publication of details about injunctions granted and undertakings given in relation to such breaches.

Regulations 26 and 27 bring the Directive, these Regulations, and relevant rules corresponding to them, within the scope of Part 8 of the Enterprise Act 2002 (c. 40), which contains special powers for the enforcement of certain consumer legislation; regulation 28 brings offences under these Regulations within the scope of section 230 of that Act, so that local weights and measures authorities must notify the OFT of intended prosecutions under these Regulations.

Regulation 22 provides that breaches of certain provisions of the Regulations are criminal offences, provides for personal criminal liability on the part of certain officers or members of corporate and other bodies where they are responsible for the commission by such bodies of offences under the Regulations, and gives the enforcement authorities power to prosecute offences under the Regulations within their respective spheres of responsibility.

Regulation 23 provides that the functions of the FSA under the Regulations are to be treated as functions under the Financial Services and Markets Act 2000 (c. 8) so as to apply for the purposes of these Regulations various general powers and provisions of that Act.

Regulation 24 amends the Unfair Terms in Consumer Contracts Regulations 1999 (S.I. 1999/2083) so as to deem automatically unfair, for the purposes of those Regulations, any contractual term placing on a consumer the burden of proving whether a supplier or intermediary has complied with obligations deriving from the Directive or any provision implementing it.

Regulation 25 makes amendments to the Consumer Protection (Distance Selling) Regulations 2000 (S.I. 2000/2334) consequential upon the provisions of these Regulations.

Regulation 29 contains transitional provisions in connection with the application of these Regulations to regulated consumer credit agreements.

A full regulatory impact assessment of the effect that this instrument will have on the costs of business is available. Copies of it have been placed in the libraries of both Houses of Parliament, and copies are also available from the Savings and Investment Products Team, HM Treasury, 1 Horse Guards Road, London SW1A 2HQ and at www.hm-treasury.gov.uk.

Notes:

[1] S.I. 2004/1283.
[2] 1972 c. 68; by virtue of the amendment of section 1(2) of the European Communities Act 1972 by section 1 of the European Economic Area Act 1993 (c. 51) regulations may be made under section 2(2) of the European Communities Act to implement obligations of the United Kingdom created or arising by or under the Agreement on the European Economic Area signed at Oporto on 2nd May 1992 (Cm 2073) and the Protocol adjusting the Agreement signed at Brussels on 17th March 1993 (Cm 2183).
[3] 1974 c. 39.
[4] 2000 c. 8.
[5] O.J. L 271, 9.10.2002, p. 16; the Directive applies to EEA States which are not Member States of the European Community by virtue of Decision No. 47/2003 of the EEA Joint Committee dated 16th May 2003 (O.J. L 193, 31.7.2003, p. 18).
[6] S.I. 2001/544, as amended by S.I. 2001/3544, S.I. 2002/682, S.I. 2002/1310, S.I. 2002/1776, S.I. 2002/1777, S.I. 2003/1475, S.I. 2003/1476, S.I. 2003/2822 and S.I. 2004/1610.

[7] S.I. 2003/2426.

[8] Article 72B was inserted by article 11 of S.I. 2003/1476, and comes into force on 31st October 2004 for certain purposes and on 14th January 2005 for other purposes: see article 1(3) of S.I. 2003/1476.

[9] S.I. 2000/2334.

[10] 1992 c. 35; section 6A was inserted by regulation 11(3) of S.I. 1997/1081.

[11] Subsection (3B) was inserted into section 84 by regulation 21(5) of S.I. 2000/2334.

[12] 1971 c. 30; section 3A was inserted by section 1 of the Unsolicited Goods and Services (Amendment) Act 1975 (c. 13).

[13] S.I. 1976/57 (N.I. 1), amended by S.I. 2000/2334 and S.R. 2004 No. 23.

[14] Article 9C was inserted by article 4 of S.I. 2002/682.

[15] S.I. 2003/1476, as amended by S.I. 2004/1610.

[16] Articles 4(1), 5(1), 7 and 9(1) of S.I. 2003/1476 amend articles 21 and 25(1), insert article 39A, and amend article 53 of the Regulated Activities Order with effect from 31st October 2004 for certain purposes and from 14th January 2005 for other purposes: see article 1(3).

[17] 1972 c. 70; the definition of "local authority" in section 270 has been repealed in part by section 102(2) of and Schedule 17 to the Local Government Act 1985 (c. 51) and amended by section 1(5) of the Local Government (Wales) Act 1994 (c. 19).

[18] 1994 c. 39.

[19] 1972 c. 9 (N.I.).

[20] S.I. 1999/2083, amended by S.I. 2001/1186 and S.I. 2003/3182.

[21] S.I. 2000/2334.

[22] 2002 c. 40.

[23] S.I. 2003/1374.

[24] S.I. 2003/1376.

[25] 1973 c. 41.

[26] O.J. L 135, 31.5.1994, p. 5.

[27] O.J. L 84, 26.3.1997, p. 22.

[a] Amended by Correction Slip. Page 13, regulation 21(2)(b), "regulation 18" should read "regulation 19".

The Consumer Credit Act 2006

DTI's TIMETABLE FOR IMPLEMENTATION

(May 2006)

The calendar below sets out the DTI's working timetable for implementation of the new Act.

Date	Provision(s) coming into force (relevant section of the 2006 Act given in brackets)
June 2006	Disapplication of section 101 of the 1974 Act (section 63)—smoothes process in relation to disapplying right to terminate hire agreements, when in hirer's interest
,,	Miscellaneous/technical provisions (sections 65–69)
,,	Enabling powers for Statutory Instruments (SIs) to be made later on, and other 'supporting' provisions
1 October 2006	Extension of period for consumers to respond to default notices, from 7 to 14 days (section 14(1))
Late 2006	Change to definition of an individual (section 1)—excludes from regulation new lending to partnerships of more than three people
6 April 2007	Abolition of automatic enforceability (section 15)—gives courts discretion over whether a credit agreement is enforceable (i.e. this is no longer automatic)
,,	Unfair relationships (sections 19–22) for *new* agreements—replaces existing 'extortionate credit' test with a new, broader test based on the principle of unfairness (Note: there will be a one-year transitional period (i.e. until 6 April 2008) before the unfair relationships test applies to *existing* agreements)
,,	Establishment of alternative dispute resolution scheme for consumer credit disputes, to be provided by the Financial Ombudsman Service (sections 59–61, Schedule 2)—adds a new Consumer Credit Jurisdiction to FOS's existing mandate
6 April 2008	Removal of financial limit (section 2)—brings all new consumer credit agreements, regardless of value, into regulation
,,	'High net worth' and business exemptions (sections 3–4)—enables very wealthy individuals to opt out of regulation, and exempts lending for business purposes over £25,000

(continued)

The Consumer Credit Act 2006

Date	Provision(s) coming into force (relevant section of the 2006 Act given in brackets)
6 April 2008	Post-contract transparency requirements (sections 6–14, 16–18)—require lenders to provide consumers with regular information about the state of their credit accounts, e.g. statements about fixed-sum credit agreements, notices of arrears and notices of default sums incurred (Note: includes section 13, requiring that interest charged on default sums may only be simple, not compound interest)
,,	Reform of consumer credit licensing regime and enhancement of Office of Fair Trading powers (sections 23, 26–54, 62, 64)
,,	Establishment of Consumer Credit Appeals Tribunal (sections 55–58, Schedule 1)—replaces the existing system of appeals to the Secretary of State
1 October 2008	New categories of business—debt administration and credit information services (sections 24–25)

Index

References are to paragraph numbers